Revitalizing Residential Settings

Problems and Potential in Education, Health, Rehabilitation, and Social Service

Martin Wolins

Yochanan Wozner

Revitalizing Residential Settings

Jossey-Bass Publishers

San Francisco • Washington • London • 1982

REVITALIZING RESIDENTIAL SETTINGS
Problems and Potential in Education, Health, Rehabilitation, and Social Service
by Martin Wolins and Yochanan Wozner

Copyright © 1982 by: Jossey-Bass Inc., Publishers
433 California Street
San Francisco, California 94104
&
Jossey-Bass Limited
28 Banner Street
London EC1Y 8QE

Library of Congress Cataloging in Publication Data

Wolins, Martin.
      Revitalizing residential settings.

      Bibliography: p. 275
      Includes index.
      1. Institutional care. 2. Public institutions—
Social aspects. I. Wozner, Yochanan. II. Title.
HV59.W64   362'.0925   81-20804
ISBN 0-87589-517-4   AACR2

Manufactured in the United States of America

JACKET DESIGN BY WILLI BAUM

FIRST EDITION

Code 8207

The Jossey-Bass
Social and Behavioral Science Series

Preface

Powerful and relatively secluded environments exist in most societies. Used for healing the sick, confining and rehabilitating the deviant, developing and reaffirming the elite, socializing the young, and more or less humanely housing the enfeebled aged, these settings bear a variety of labels. Residential programs, their names, and society's attitudes toward them have evolved in the Western world over more than two millenniums. Today's community hospital, residential treatment center, prison, and military academy are conceptual descendants of previous institutional arrangements. They have been affected, though often unknowingly and indirectly, by the Roman valetudinarium, the Jewish residential yeshiva, the Christian monastery, the English public school, and the American "moral treatment" hospital. They are also heirs to less noble experiments in residential care that over the years were thought appropriate for a variety of deviant members of society.

This common heritage of total institutional environments for the elite, for the outcast, and for the needy of whatever kind is usually forgotten by the contemporary observer. Also unnoticed are the considerable functional similarities between residential institutions, regardless of the populations they house. In recent years, professionals and public alike have viewed West Point as *substantively* different from San Quentin and the elitist boarding school as a form apart from the residential treatment center. We believe otherwise. An analysis of such settings with regard to various operating concerns shows their considerable similarity and the possibility of one adapting arrangements found effective in another. Thus, for example, a look at modeling and rewards shows the advantages of a selected elite population at West Point and the serious disadvantages of negative selectivity for San Quentin or the residential treatment center. Similarly, both the boarding school and the juvenile hall develop a predisposition to calculated risks, which enhance growth and improve self-image; but the former tends to expand opportunities, while the latter tends to limit them. The utility of a clear unifying theme for any residential setting is illustrated when one compares the effectiveness of modern hospitals for the physically ill and those for the mentally ill.

All residential environments have fundamentally the same concerns. West Point and San Quentin, the elitist boarding school and the residential treatment center alike must confront their isolation and otherness from more open, accessible, and familiar communal institutions. Operating within these constraints, often even converting them into assets, modern residential settings establish goals and assess their attainment, adapt to their external environments, regulate internal functioning, and maintain continuity while functioning as instruments of change. Some are profound and decried failures, others remarkable successes. Most residential programs occupy the middle ground—

tolerated partial outcasts whose societies simultaneously support and castigate them. Subject to segmented description and analysis, the successful settings have had little effect upon their failing counterparts.

Our premise is that a look at the broadest range of residential settings offers valuable insights for improving them all. And our message is directed to those who inhabit such environments or cause others to do so. Caretakers and care recipients alike should be interested in models and rewards, risk and growth, unifying theme and successful operation, and other attributes of residential settings. Particularly, though, we write for the caretakers in various residential environments, who may learn from past and present experience in operating these unusual, people-changing organizations. More specifically, this book is for:

· The *hospital administrator* who wishes to operate something more organically unified than a good hotel with expert physicians, their assistants, and technological gadgetry, and who should know about the uses and meaning of physical design and social influence in a healing environment.

· The *psychiatrist* who realizes that the achievements of each fifty-minute hour are quickly undone by the flow of life in the mental hospital and should appreciate insights into the powerful environment of an inmate culture.

· The *social worker* who is concerned with maintaining a bond between those inside the residential setting and the world outside it, and should learn about the ambivalences of purpose and attitude that complicate this task.

· The *educator* who—having the self-image of a French *éducateur,* an English master, a Russian *vospitatel'*, or a Hebrew *mechanech*—is concerned with the socialization of the whole person and should gain an awareness of the causal connections between population balance and success.

· The *nursing home staff* who, if it aims to operate something more hopeful and stimulating than a terminal warehouse, should realize the importance of allowing the expression of patient competencies.

· The *prison warden, guard, psychiatrist, psychologist,* and *social worker* who want to understand why their institution is failing and will continue to fail as long as it retains failing inmates and discharges successful ones.

· The *commandants* at West Point, Annapolis, the Air Force Academy, and like institutions, who are in charge of powerful environments for fashioning an American elite and should learn why they suffer from periodic lapses of internal clarity and public support.

In addressing these residential care constituencies, we do not mean to imply that they and their programs have not been the objects of continuous public concern. On the contrary, these caretakers and settings have received much attention—most of it negative. Their constructive aspects have received little emphasis. This volume is an attempt to redress the balance in some measure. We begin, in Chapter One, by describing the population currently residing in American establishments of various kinds. People of all ages and all levels of competence are to be found in the various settings. Nevertheless, societies tend to be selective, and representation is quite unequal for various subgroups, indicating some purposive use of this arrangement. Society's objective, it seems, is the maintenance of its social order. How that is achieved, and with what effect on both the care recipient and society, are the topics of Chapters Two through Six.

Specifically, in Chapter Two we address the relationships between attributes of residents and the activity of the setting. We also propose some new terminology to replace the term *institution* now used to designate some, but not all, the settings of interest. This traditional label does not generally connote the image of a military academy or residential yeshiva, public school, or community residence for reclaiming criminals, addicts, or the mentally retarded, and it fails to fit our proposed new aggregation. Thus, in Chapter Two, we introduce the term *internat,* a neutral word used in several European languages, which appropriately connotes the considerable preoccupation with *internal* operations that all residential settings share.

In Chapter Three, we focus on the goals of residential set-

tings, their achievement and evaluation. The difficulties of arriv-
ing at goal consensus and the problems of evaluating outcomes
are discussed. The adaptation of residential programs to their
external societal milieu is considered in Chapter Four. To segregate some people from their communities and subject them to
powerful instruments of change poses problems for both the society and the particular institutional device it uses. The integration of the various elements comprising the setting is the topic
of Chapter Five. Strains and convergences of variously positioned
individuals—inmates and staff, newcomers and veterans—are the
common lot of these somewhat isolated, special mechanisms.
Finally, these organizations, whose function is change, must
also provide continuity. The tasks and difficulties of *conservation* are analyzed in Chapter Six.

In Chapters Seven through Nine we attempt to integrate
the personal predispositions of caretakers and care recipients
with the institutional demands of their settings. We place emphasis on the means of assuring organizational survival and societal acceptance while promoting personal growth of the residents for whom these various facilities were established. Using a
systems approach, we discuss internat structure, interaction, decision making, and sanctions. The last chapter in particular addresses the organizational and behavioral phenomena that characterize successful residential environments. These include,
among others, such issues as the provision of successful models,
the management of risk, the functions of professionals, and the
role of ideology.

An analysis of generic qualities develops from an interest
in specific programs. The single facility, person, and incident are
of interest because they shed light on the genre and, conversely,
the concepts introduced and the models proposed are intended
to apply to hospital and prison, to boarding school and home
for the aged, to medical, correctional, and instructional settings.

Such an undertaking is replete with hazards. Inclusivity is
elusive and comparability is at times dubious. Evidence is often
inadequate or even suspect. Wise and compassionate teachers
and careful, critical readers have helped a great deal. We owe
many insights to those named in our dedication. More signifi-

cantly, their values and actions still stand as beacons in the exploration of residential care. Our more contemporary and more proximate colleagues Stuart Hanson, Mary O'Day, Mordecai Rotenberg, Samuel Shye, and Barbara Weiss have been tough and honest critics and have spared the reader some errors of fact and judgment. Other errors undoubtedly remain. However, we hope that the insights we provide on this complex and emotion-laden subject will kindle the discussion necessary for residential care to achieve its potential. Despite the frequent aspersions cast upon some categories of institutions, it is most unlikely that Western society will abolish all its residential institutions—although some individuals or even groups will be removed from such care. While castigation may serve certain personal and societal needs, improvement of residential care would seem the more prudent course. In this endeavor our book will, we hope, exert some influence.

If any of our hopes for this book materialize, they will justify the support received from the U.S. National Institute of Mental Health (Grant #MH 23793); the University of California, Berkeley, Committee on Research; and the Lois and Samuel Silberman Fund. Our thanks to these sources are particularly merited since they willingly and generously joined us in exploring a topic that has of late been either ignored or deprecated.

January 1982   Martin Wolins
                                                     Berkeley, California

                                                    Yochanan Wozner
                                                      Jerusalem, Israel

Contents

The Authors

Martin Wolins is professor of social welfare at the University of California, Berkeley. He received his D.S.W. degree from Columbia University in 1955. His academic appointments have included professorships at Hebrew University and at Tel Aviv University. He was also the first director of research of the Child Welfare League of America (1954-1958). He has written or edited several books, including *Selecting Foster Parents* (1963), *Group Care: An Israeli Approach* (with M. Gottesmann, 1971), and *Successful Group Care* (1974).

Yochanan Wozner is a senior lecturer in the School of Social Work of Tel Aviv University. He received his B.A. degree in sociology and education from the Hebrew University, Jerusalem, and his M.S.W. and D.S.W. degrees from the University of California, Berkeley. He has served as director of the Israeli Youth Protection Authority and has been involved in residential care in practice, administration, and research. He has published articles in the *Social Service Review, Social Work Research and Abstracts,* and *Residential and Community Child Care Administration,* among others. His current projects include the planning and organizing of an S.O.S. children's village in Israel.

Dedicated to

Hermann Gmeiner, the Austrian Catholic who turned his own wartime prison experience into a benevolent worldwide movement of more than 200 SOS Kinderdörfer

Maxwell Jones, the English psychiatrist whose Belmont Hospital experiment and book *The Therapeutic Community* (1953) were powerful rays of light in the hopeless darkness surrounding the mentally ill at mid-twentieth century

Thomas S. Kirkbride, the American Quaker whose work in mental health and book *On the Construction, Organization, and General Arrangements of Hospitals for the Insane* (1854) were milestones in the care of the mentally ill

Janusz Korczak (Henryk Goldschmidt), the Polish-Jewish pediatrician who became the embodiment of selfless, humane, and effective childcare inside the residential institution and outside it

Siegfried Lehmann, the Israeli educator, founder of the Ben Shemen youth village, a humanist and cultural pluralist, who served as model and inspiration to several generations of innovators in institutional care

Anton S. Makarenko, the Russian Bolshevik who in the midst of revolutionary turmoil built an outstanding children's commune and described it in *The Road to Life*

Johann H. Pestalozzi, the Swiss educator and founder of the famous boarding school at Yverdon, whose method and book *How Gertrude Teaches Her Children* (1801) were example and inspiration to generations of thinkers

Albert Schweitzer, the Alsatian theologian, musician, and mission doctor who in his Lambaréné hospital went beyond the treatment of physical malady, comprehending and deliberately affecting the whole person

Georg K. Stürup, the Danish penologist who expressed his beliefs in his book *Treating the "Untreatable"* and whose work with chronic criminals provides evidence that even this most difficult of institutional populations may be positively affected

. . . and all others who confronted the paradox of total institutions and resolved it for the well-being of their charges. We learned from them that extrafamilial care of people, while often regrettable, can also be creative, humane, and even ennobling.

Revitalizing
Residential Settings

Problems and Potential
in Education, Health,
Rehabilitation,
and Social Service

1

Who Resides in Institutions?

Overview

Most people live with their families or with friends or alone, but a significant minority live in institutions. Various institutions differ so much in both form and population that we do not usually think of them as a single genre. Yet prisons and orphanages, hospitals and boarding schools, West Point and Boys Town have much in common. They are all more or less effective social instruments for maintaining and changing people. They are also the only available alternative to family environments for dependent, disturbed, and troublesome individuals as well as singularly oriented individuals such as monastics, mili-

1

tary officers, or scholars. While the differences among these settings are obvious, their commonalities are many. Perhaps, as Sykes (1958, p. xiii) notes of prisons, the similarities are "due to diffusion of ideas, customs, and laws; perhaps they are a matter of similar social structures arising independently from attempts to solve much the same problems. Most probably it is some combination of both."

A particular commonality shared by institutions is that all are the subject of public concern. Institutions have been very much on the public's mind since Dorothea Dix first lamented the problems of mental asylums and prisons (see Dix, 1845; Marshall, 1937), and the good citizens of Pennsylvania and New York proudly implemented rehabilitation procedures in the Eastern and Auburn penitentiaries, respectively (President's Commission on Law Enforcement, 1972; Rothman, 1980; Sellin, 1972). Many factors have contributed to this sustained interest. One obvious reason for public concern is cost. No matter how they are populated, staffed, or intentioned, institutions are expensive. Institutions also attract public attention because their physical appearance is unlike more traditional, familial architecture. Finally, institutions are socially "other" than the established environment for maintaining and changing people—the family.

Much has been written about institutions of various kinds. The reader may find stringently analytic and warmly romantic narratives of a positive or negative flavor about any type of institution. Such assessments, of course, reflect the judgment of their authors, but in part they are dictated by the temper of the times. Reformatories have been considered good and bad. Children's villages (boys' towns, boys' republics, and so forth) have had their days in the public sunshine. Hospitals for the physically ill were the lot of the indigent at one time and an acceptable place of rest for the elite at another.

Even the U.S. Military Academy at West Point or the English public schools that have reared generations of martial and civil leaders are not always perceived favorably. A congressional committee studied West Point just before the Civil War and found many defects. These ranged from "the low standard

of admission" (*U.S. Commission to Examine* ... , 1881, p. 7)
to food that "was neither nutritious nor wholesome, neither
sufficient nor nicely dressed" (p. 6). (The report was delayed
some twenty years apparently due to the war.) More recent critics address other concerns. Galloway and Johnson (1973), for
example, accuse West Point of turning out elitist officers who
are at the "heart of the separation of the American Army from
the American people" (p. 18). Criticism of English public
schools has been somewhat similar in nature (see Public Schools
Commission, 1968).

   Recently, negative views about institutional programs
have been predominant. Critics stress their monetary and social
costs, their lack of success in changing people, and in some instances, their elitist posture. The recent call for deinstitutionalization, the removal of persons from institutional environments,
is not a new campaign. Deinstitutionalization, by one name or
another, has been periodically urged, even as institutional programs increase, and has been proposed for variously positioned
persons. Criminals and orphans, physically and mentally ill,
abandoned children or the aged, the supremely or insufficiently
endowed have been judged by some as best served by families
and the communal programs in which they partake. At times
even the total abolition of institutional care has been proposed.

   Yet institutional care has persisted, and for certain populations—specifically the aged—it is expanding rapidly. Even
when deinstitutionalization is apparently successful in reducing
the census, as for example in mental illness, its net effect is
sometimes   reinstitutionalization—patients'   movement   from
large central facilities to dispersed, community-based smaller
institutions: "Since 1960, the population in state and county
mental hospitals has decreased from 520,000 to 340,000 while
the population in nursing homes and homes for the aged has increased almost 50 percent, from 510,000 in 1963 to 780,000 in
1967. Part of the change has involved the direct transfer of
many thousands of elderly patients from state hospitals to nursing homes" (Lawton, 1974, p. 60; see also Segal and Aviram,
1978).

   The current number of institutional residents and their

variety are both considerable. This population includes inmates of institutions for the mentally ill, retarded, and aged; young people in private boarding schools and correctional settings; prisoners; soldiers in military barracks and service academies; and patients occupying at any given time the 1.5 million hospital beds in this country (American Hospital Association, 1977).

Census of Institutional Residents

When institutional forms were less varied and their labels less ambiguous, it may have been possible to answer precisely the question, Who is in the institutions? Prisons contained the "bad," lazarettes the "sick," workhouses the "improvident," and monasteries the "spiritually noble." The label of the setting automatically described its inhabitants and the activity appropriate for them. Not only did it designate their competence and problems at entry, but also the goals held for the inhabitants by themselves, by those operating the facility (that is, staff and administration), and by the relevant community. Thus, institutional populations fell into rather distinct groups: the deprived or depraved usually entered under duress, while others, the respected, came to this life by their own choice.

Although this division of institutional populations into the unworthy and the worthy has had, and still has, great social significance, it also severely limits the development of an integrated conceptualization of institutions. Any theory of institutional care must be applicable to the full range of settings, whatever their own attributes or the qualities of their inhabitants. If we define the total population that resides in group settings as institutional, we can easily answer the question as to who may be in them: Anyone. To be sure, modern industrial societies intend institutions to be used for some populations more than for others; infants, for example, are considered to be inappropriately placed in them, and the severely debilitated aged appropriately so. Yet, some of the former and by no means all of the latter are in institutions.

A survey of institutional populations takes us, therefore, over the full range of the human condition and of attempts at its modification. (Some perceptive institutional inhabitants have also noted that a lengthy personal experience in an institution is itself a tour of the human condition. See Bettelheim, 1960; Solzhenitsyn, 1963; Tillion, 1975.) Institutions for the young offer a good sampling. West Point, surely an institution by every criterion, exists, in the opinion of one of its deans, "just for one purpose—to prepare a man to become an officer in the Regular Army" (Ellis and Moore, 1974, p. 3). The head of the department of social sciences at West Point comments, "There is an element of elitism here. That's simply nothing more than an effort to get the very best people here and a reasonable amount of success in doing it" (Ellis and Moore, 1974, p. 20).

What young people of nearly the same ages are prepared for in correctional institutions we are rarely told. Some are confined in detention centers that offer "temporary care in a physically restricting environment . . . pending court disposition"; others in shelters providing "temporary care . . . but in a physically unrestricting environment," or in training schools "serving delinquent juveniles committed directly"; yet others live on ranches, forestry camps, or farms for juveniles "whose behavior does not necessitate the strict confinement of a training school," or in halfway houses and group homes allowing "extensive contact with the community . . . through jobs and schools" (U.S. Department of Justice, Law Enforcement Assistance Administration, 1977, p. 816).

Similarly, institutionalized youth include the residents of boarding schools such as Asheville, for example, which describes its elitist objectives as the setting of "high standards of intellectual, ethical, and physical development . . . for approximately 150 boarding boys and 50 day girls and boys" (Porter Sargent, 1977, p. 1040). Also included are youths in places like St. Paul's School, which in the words of its rector "is more than a four-year coeducational boarding school of the highest academic standards and achievements . . . [it is also] a community" (Porter Sargent, 1977, p. 783).

Our inclusion of West Point and Asheville as examples of institutional environments is a departure from convention. Institutions such as these take care to draw a distinction between themselves and the several thousand boarding settings, often called disciplinary or corrective, which are intended for children and adolescents variously described as "deprived, dependent, neglected, delinquent, maladjusted, emotionally disturbed, or mentally ill" (Pappenfort and Kilpatrick, 1970, vol. 1, p. xxvi). Nor do they see themselves in the same category as many Indian boarding schools, whose functions could be nothing but "intellectual, ethical, and physical development" such as Asheville claims to foster.

As Gil (1974, p. 74) notes, "a striking differentiation between the two types of institutions is the absence of professional and theoretical linkages between them. These facilities are usually not inspected, licensed, and accredited by the same agencies. Their staff members rarely belong to the same professional organizations . . . [or] share common educational and psychological theories."

These distinctions are one source of difficulty for any demographic analysis of institutional populations. Residents of elitist programs are often not counted. There are, for example, no authoritative data on the numbers of children and youth in American boarding schools. Nor are there readily available counts of monastics. (Our data on both are estimates based on listings of their facilities.) Another difficulty is that most available census materials for other institutional populations are dated and should be considered in the light of rapidly changing trends yielding reductions in mental patients and retardates who reside in institutions, but increases in delinquents, aged, and certain categories of physically ill who may be found in them.

These are serious constraints. Yet, even with such limitations, a general discussion of range and of magnitude is feasible. Moreover, available demographic data suggest a number of questions significant to an understanding of the institution phenomenon:

1. Are age, gender, race, and similar variables appropriate for the description of institutional environments?
2. Are institutional populations randomly or particularly selected members of their societies?

3. Are there some socially significant criteria for designating who will be accepted or even compelled into institutional care?
4. Are the absolute numbers of institutional residents large enough to merit public and professional concern?
5. Are trends in institutional populations indicative of larger social phenomena in society as a whole?

An analysis of the institutional population suggests that the inhabitants are many and rather purposively selected reflecting certain societal predispositions. Our census allows us to draw inferences about the role of institutions in American society. Let us first review some data by age group.

Infants and Preschool Children. Although both the incidence and rate of young children in American institutions has been declining steadily, they are still to be found among the population. We estimate the number of young children in American institutions as follows:

Institutions for retarded	7,000
Institutions for dependent, neglected, and disturbed	6,000
Short-stay hospitals	37,000

In addition, small numbers of young children may be found in group care in such settings as prison nurseries. (Estimates based on American Hospital Association, 1977; Beuf, 1979; Conley, 1973; North, Wilkinson, and Oliver, 1977; Pappenfort and Kilpatrick, 1970; U.S. Department of Health, Education and Welfare, National Center for Health Statistics, 1976.)

School-Age Children. School-age children are those between five and twelve years of age; this group is also often referred to as the primary school-age group, children from kindergarten to junior high school. Because societal aversion to institutional care for this age group is neither as universal nor as profound as it is with regard to infants and toddlers, school-age children are found in a larger range of environments. In addition to the settings for the retarded, the dependent or neglected or disturbed, and short-stay hospitals for the physically ill, educational boarding facilities house members of this age group.

The numbers of children in these four types of institutional settings are estimated to be as follows:

Public institutions for mentally retarded children and
    other institutions housing retarded children   45,000
Residential institutions for the dependent,
    neglected, and disturbed   31,000
Short-stay hospitals   35,000
Private boarding schools   20,000
Indian boarding schools   7,500

(Estimates based on American Hospital Association, 1977; Conley, 1973; Pappenfort and Kilpatrick, 1970; Porter Sargent, 1977; U.S. Department of Health, Education and Welfare, National Center for Health Statistics, 1976; U.S. Department of the Interior, 1976; U.S. Department of Justice, Law Enforcement Assistance Administration, 1971.)

Adolescents and Young People. The group of adolescents and young people—those between thirteen and twenty years of age—is heavily represented among the institutional population. Such young people may be found in a large number of settings:

Public institutions for the mentally retarded   53,000
Residential institutions for the dependent,
    neglected, and disturbed   110,000
Prisons and jails   45,000
Short-stay hospitals   90,000
Private boarding schools   180,000
Indian boarding schools   23,000
Federal service academies   15,000
Armed services (including 200,000 people on
    ships   2,000,000

(Estimates based on Carter, Glaser, and Wilkins, 1972; Conley, 1973; Ellis and Moore, 1974; Pappenfort and Kilpatrick, 1970; Porter Sargent, 1977; U.S. Congress, 1975; U.S. Department of the Interior, 1976; U.S. Department of Justice, Law Enforcement Assistance Administration, 1971 and 1977.)

Adults. The category of adults includes all persons between twenty-one and sixty-four. This age-extensive category includes relatively few persons who reside in places conventionally labeled as institutions for other than negative reasons. Although this sector of the population is reported on in generally available statistics, unavailable for this age group is a census of persons who reside in various task-specific environments designed to accomplish a narrow goal agreed on by all participants (for example, smoking abatement, weight reduction, or language training). For this reason the true numbers of institutional residents of this age group cannot be estimated. Thus the following estimates are only a fraction of the total:

Public institutions for the mentally retarded	110,000
Mental hospitals	230,000
Prisons and jails	360,000
Short-stay hospitals	450,000
Veterans Administration facilities	120,000
Institutions for adults seeking to acquire certain skills or seeking self-segregation (as in monasteries)	?

(Estimates based on Conley, 1973; "Prison Growth Continues Record Pace," 1980; U.S. Congress, Senate Committee on Veterans' Affairs, 1977; U.S. Department of Commerce, 1977; U.S. Department of Health, Education and Welfare, National Institute of Mental Health, *Note* 104, 1974; 106, 1974; and 114, 1975.)

Aged. Our final group, the aged, includes those sixty-five or older. Over the past two decades, the institutional population of the aged has skyrocketed, while the resident population in state and county mental hospitals leveled off (at about .5 million in the 1950s and early 1960s) and then declined to less than half that number (see U.S. Department of Health, Education and Welfare, National Institute of Mental Health, *Note* 114, 1975). Further, one suspects that many elderly persons in group facilities are not so reported in the U.S. Bureau of the Census counts of "inmates of institutions" by virtue of confused terminology. Most likely the numbers of the institutionalized elderly are not only understated but also represent a sample biased in the direction of the poor and generally "less eligible" members of society. Among those not counted by conventional surveys are the aged living in resident hotels, privately financed homes, and other establishments for the well-to-do.

The numbers of elderly people who currently reside in institutions include:

Nursing homes of various types	960,000
Short-stay hospitals	150,000
Resident hotels and retirement homes	?

(Estimates based on Manard, Kart, and Van Gils, 1975; U.S. Department of Commerce, Bureau of the Census, 1974.)

Institutional Population: An Analysis

As our estimates show, institutional residence is a possibility for anyone at any age. The number of Americans living in institutions is substantial—in the millions. Furthermore, since institutions by their very nature compel close interaction among all their members, any census ought at least allude to staff as well. The 1 million elderly in nursing homes are attended to by more than 600,000 full-time employees who, it may be argued, are only slightly less "institutionalized" than the residents. Similarly, the approximately 200,000 inmates in state prisons share facilities with 45,000 staff members. And St. Paul's School boasts that it is "a community of 496 boys and girls, 79 teachers and their families and over 100 members of the staff who live with their families either on the school grounds or in Concord [N.H]" (Porter Sargent, 1977, p. 783). We may note in passing that St. Paul's ratio of residents to staff lies between those of the prison and the nursing home.

Let us examine our estimates to see how four demographic characteristics—age, sex, race, and socioeconomic status—relate to the institutionalized population.

Age. Our informed estimate of the institutional population of the U.S. shows that both the numbers of residents and types of settings vary with the age groups. Relatively few children are institutionalized, but relatively many adolescents and a large number of the elderly are. Consider this summary of the estimated population of settings conventionally deemed institutions, arranged by age and rounded to the nearest 10,000:

- 50,000 infants and preschoolers, mostly in short-stay hospitals but also in settings for the retarded, dependent, and mentally ill.
- 140,000 school-age children, most of whom are in programs for the retarded and dependent, and in short-stay hospitals.
- 520,000 adolescents, most of whom are in settings for dependent and delinquent, and in private boarding schools.
- 1,270,000 adults, most of whom are in prisons, mental hospitals, short-stay hospitals, and Veterans Administration residential facilities.
- 1,110,000 aged persons who live in nursing homes or short-stay hospitals. (The 1980 estimate for this group is over 1.5 million.)

In addition to these 3 million people, about 1 million staff members work inside these settings, and about 2 million young people are in facilities provided by the armed services. As we noted earlier, these figures do not include the residents of various settings that are conventionally not considered as institutions.

Our estimate, for example, does not include the inhabitants of monasteries, institutions that are of great significance to our understanding of the institutional phenomenon. Although maintained by various religious groups, they are primarily Roman Catholic. Actual numbers of individuals *residing* in such settings are difficult to obtain. However, the *1980 Catholic Almanac* (Foy, 1979) lists a large number of residential religious institutes for men, including Benedictines (10,000 members), Cistercians (1,500) and Trappists (3,000). However, the residential status of all the nearly 100,000 members listed is not clear. A large listing of second-order (that is, female) monasteries is given but no membership numbers. Our estimate, admittedly somewhat hazardous, is of a total well above 150,000 (including 10,000 to 15,000 seminarians). (See also Secretaria Status . . . , n.d., which provides worldwide data that are not itemized by country.) Horn and Born's (1980) recent, magnificent work, *The Plan of St. Gall,* provides a comprehensive view of the components and organic unity of a Benedictine monastery of the ninth century, a fully *total* institution.

The American distribution of institutional residents is unlike those found in other countries. In the USSR, for example, at the time of Khrushchev there was considerable planning to expand the *shkoly internaty* (state-operated boarding schools) to a capacity of 5 million in the 1970s. While these goals were abolished by Khrushchev's successors, a 1964 report in *Pravda* showed 2.4 million pupils in such settings (see Weeks, 1974, p. 88). In Cuba the Castro regime set aside a whole island (formerly the Isle of Pines, renamed the Isle of Youth) as one large boarding school. And in Israel, a recent report stated that about one fifth of the young people between the ages of thirteen and seventeen live in group facilities (Prime Minister's Committee, 1972).

Sex. We have noted the predominance of adolescents and the aged in our census. The data also show that the former are primarily male and the latter mainly female. With the marked exceptions of nursing homes, which provide care to a disproportionate number of older women who outlive their husbands, and certain psychiatric facilities, the institutional population is largely male. Women comprise only a small portion of the population of institutions for both "problem" and "nonproblem" adults. For example, only 3 percent of the inmates in state correctional facilities are women (U.S. Department of Justice, Law Enforcement Assistance Administration, 1977) and 10 percent of the 1981 class at the Air Force Academy and 7 percent of the 1981 class at West Point are women. Although some facilities (for example, convents, some boarding schools and training schools) are exclusively designed for women, less than one fourth of the total population of institutional residents is female.

The preponderance of males among those institutionalized raises a fundamental question about the nature of institutionalization. If such settings are designed for those who need special care or rehabilitation, do not as many women as men need such services? If women have been discriminated against when they sought to attain special care, then why did not discrimination increase the placement of women in undesirable settings? In other words, why are women underrepresented in both elitist and nonelitist settings?

Physical, social, and psychological capabilities do play an important role in residential confinement, but may be overbalanced by the factor of gender. As Conley (1973, p. 83) observes for retardates, "one striking feature of the institutional population is the preponderance of males over females, in spite of our earlier conclusion that [in the general population] there are as many female retardates as male retardates and that among the severely retarded, females may slightly predominate. The preponderance of males over females was even more pronounced among first admissions." Moreover, Conley reports that the percentage of males varies inversely with the severity of retardation: "In a study of over 23,000 residents in nineteen public institutions located in western states, it was found that 54 percent of the profoundly retarded were males, as compared to 63 percent of the borderline retarded" (p. 83). Short-term hospital use (measured by discharge rates per 1,000 population) is similarly more heavily male than female, except for comparisons of women of childbearing age and their male contemporaries (U.S. Department of Health, Education and Welfare, National Center for Health Statistics, 1976, p. 22).

The temptation to ascribe the gender discrepancies to sexism must, therefore, be viewed with suspicion. Women are likely *not* to be in institutions because they are women, yet they appear to be rarely in them because of their sex (except as part of reproductive functions and longevity).

Race. Like women, blacks are underrepresented in elitist settings. For example, despite considerable effort to recruit blacks, blacks comprised only 5.8 percent of West Point's 1979 class, 4.3 percent of the Air Force Academy's 1981 class, and

4.2 percent of Annapolis' 1981 class. In contrast, blacks represented nearly 50 percent of the prison population (U.S. Department of Justice, Law Enforcement Assistance Administration, 1977, Table 6.49). Furthermore, there is some evidence that blacks are treated more severely than whites throughout the juvenile justice system. For example, when individuals with three serious offenses are sentenced, 55 percent of blacks and 37 percent of whites are sent to correctional facilities (Thornberry, 1973, p. 96).

Admissions of nonwhites to state and county mental hospitals show a similar pattern. In 1972 the admission rate per 100,000 total population was 197.2. The rate for whites was 181.7, that for nonwhites 306.3. If we consider sex and race, we find even greater discrepancies: the rate for white males was 226, and that for nonwhite males 424—nearly a 1:2 ratio. In both racial groups rates are again substantially lower for women than for men (.6:1) (U.S. Department of Health, Education and Welfare, National Institute of Mental Health, *Note* 116, 1975, p. 19).

Socioeconomic Status. Institutions are often considered to be the lot of persons of lower social status. This assumption is part of the institutional paradox since, in a reasonably humane society, these are inevitably costly settings. However, Hollingshead and Redlich (1958) provide some evidence for this common assumption. They report, for example, "that hospitalized neurotic patients are in the minority in all classes, but the lower the class, the higher the percentage who are hospitalized" (p. 261). Similarly, "the state hospital reveals a strong inverse relationship between class position and the percentage of schizophrenics under its care" (p. 287). Further evidence is provided by the fact that in the mid-1970s 63 percent of the U.S. population had completed four years of high school or more, but only 39 percent of the prison inmates and 38 percent of the patients entering public mental hospitals had done so.

An argument may be made that the rates of institutionalization are due to behavioral differences by social status. However, in one rather careful study on court disposition of juveniles by seriousness of their offense it was found that "low SES [socioeconomic status] subjects are less likely to be put on probation and more likely to be institutionalized than high SES subjects" (Thornberry, 1973, p. 97).

Status also affects the probability of admission to elite settings. Some institutions accommodate individuals who are considerably above the average in social status and educational achievement. For example, parents of the 1979 entering class at West Point had incomes above the national average; 89 percent of the fathers and 93 percent of the mothers were high school graduates and almost half of the fathers and a third of the mothers held college degrees. The cadets themselves averaged A— in their high school work and the class's mean score on the Scholastic Aptitude Test fell into the 92nd percentile for all high school seniors. Annapolis and the Air Force Academy boast similar statistics. Elitism at entry is compounded to even higher status at exit. As a midshipman notes: "This place has prestige. Americans admire someone who graduates from the Naval Academy" (U.S. Naval Academy, Annapolis, 1978-1979, p. 58).

Summary. Institutions, then, are discriminatory settings. They admit, by compulsion or intensive recruitment and self-selection, those whom society wants to alter or strongly reinforce. They usually exclude those whom a society opts to ignore. In general, with the exception of the terminally ill, anyone whom society does not care about enough to provide maintenance or change is denied admission. Women are, therefore, right in their charge of sexism if they mean that their underrepresentation in various institutions reflects society's lesser concern for changing (rehabilitating or improving) women. Blacks and American Indians are right in their charge of discrimination, because their rates are high in compelled environments and low in self-selected elitist ones.

In understanding institutions as instruments of change, we should not be misled by the overwhelming evidence that many institutions fail to alter in the *desired* ways those entrusted to their charge. This failure leads to periodic public demands for deinstitutionalization, but it does not detract from the social role of institutions as agents for change. Their task is to function as powerful environments such that "only relatively few individuals are able to resist the effects of the environmental pressure" (Bloom, 1964, p. 212).

2

Objectives
and Functions
of Residential Programs

Overview

Total (or residential institutions, like all social instru-
mentalities, begin with raw materials, contribute activity, and
yield a product. The raw material and the product of these
kinds of institutions are people, and the goal of institutions is
to reclaim the residents by modifying (usually improving) the
mastery with which they conduct themselves and relate to the
environment. While reclaiming is most often aimed at body and
soul, *in extremis* a society may opt to kill the body in order to
salvage the soul, as did Spain during the Inquisition.

Institutions, then, accept persons of certain levels of competence and by means of planned activity try to change these

levels in certain ways. Thus the primary components of institutions are the competencies of the residents and staff and their activities or interactions. Institutions are as they are because of the selected populations they admit, although various constraints of goals, predispositions, and resources affect the relationships between them. For the purposes of our analysis, we will refer to the institution's task as Reclaiming, the individual's competency as Mastery, and the interactions between the institution and the individual as Activity. Let us first consider Mastery.

Mastery

Development and protection of Mastery is ordinarily and universally the function of families. As a family helps its members acquire competencies, it also helps them understand and fulfill society's expectations of individuals. Institutional care is employed when either the objective of such socialization or the individual family member is in some manner unusual. Especially demanding goals (for example, the training of military officers or Olympic athletes or the acculturation of priests and rabbinic scholars) and particularly difficult persons (for example, the ill, retarded, severely misbehaving, and politically precocious) are assigned to institutions. Societies presume that normal families with normal individuals will be able to produce persons whose competencies are adequate to cope with the exigencies of the normal world. Societies operate on the general assumption of familial success in socializing all their members. Evidence to the contrary is usually, but not universally, ignored—possibly because less costly or more effective alternatives are unavailable. (See, for example, the views of Cooper, 1971, or of Strumilin, 1960, a Soviet Academician.)

Mastery, whether it is to be achieved in a family or in an institution, entails development of competencies in the physical, psychological, social, and cultural *fields* and their appropriate application in *modes* of achievement, adaptation, integration, and conservation of the person. (For the derivation of these categories, see the quality of life map proposed by Shye, 1979.) Jointly, fields and modes may be conceived as a personal subsystem grid with sixteen cells defining a person's quality of life. For each cell one may define an ideal type, the specific objectives that a benevolent, helping, developmental environment will set as goals for individuals. The personal subsystems of Mastery and their ideal types are described in Table 1.

All societies have some general Mastery expectations. For almost all categories of persons (except the very old or very incorrigible) the usual objective is expansion of Mastery and social normalization. In humane societies, the ideal is maximum Mastery at lowest possible pain for the individual, although inevitably social cost and Mastery are balanced and some efforts are discontinued because they are considered too costly. An extreme example of a social decision to discontinue socialization is the death penalty. We can probably assert that a society (or an institution) is humane when its definition of Reclaiming includes maximal expansion of Mastery for all its members. However, the ideal type is hardly achievable by family or institution. Moreover, since institutions have in their care some difficult populations, they are often presumed to fail in their Reclaiming and many of them do fail.

Regrettably, the mix of populations and goals in most institutions leads to conceptual and operational confusion in all but the specifically elitist programs. Even in humane societies, some institutions may deplete rather than increase their population's Mastery. For example, inmates serving life sentences, the minimally developed retardates, and the maximally degenerated aged are simply stored as a matter of social convenience. Every institution is, therefore, an instrument that serves the pattern maintenance of society, even though some of its members are by legal or pseudolegal definition unsocializable. Societal needs are served even if the Mastery of institutionalized individuals remains constant or is reduced. Thus, the public evaluation of the institution as a social mechanism is understandably clouded by misconceptions and uncertainty. Misconceptions are caused by the lack of overt and functional distinctions between settings with reclaiming and nonreclaiming objectives. Public

Table 1. Personal Subsystems and Their Ideal Types

Mode \ Field	Personal–Psychological	Physical–Behavioral	Social	Cultural–Valuative
Goals and Achievement	Understands potential and moves steadily toward personal development; takes initiative; can choose among alternatives without conflicting with establishment; can make decisions to advance personal growth; is industrious; completes tasks; is optimistic; attempts to change environment to meet personal needs.	Healthy, well-developed, with good manipulative skills and body control; tries to control physical environment and the instruments needed for control.	Has standing in society; strives continuously to progress up social ladder; a leader, spokesman, adviser to friends; promotes personal advancement through social position.	Wants to belong to cultured, value-conscious society; has taste for arts and for spiritual expression; can internalize cultural values, esteems their external form; acquires additional values through study; expands cultural, religious, and value horizons.
Adaptation	Derives satisfaction from usual sources of leisure and entertainment; finds outlet for some drives in hobbies; knows how to use recreational opportunities for personal needs; adjusts to what environment offers.	Can produce useful things from simple materials; knows utility of various tools and equipment and uses them efficiently; knows how to dress and to use eating utensils properly; is capable of keeping body and surroundings clean; comprehends relationship between physical needs and the use of tools, materials, and physical objects to meet those needs.	Derives personal usefulness from social environments; satisfies personal needs by participating in various social systems; fits readily into new environments; derives advantage and pleasure from simple participation.	Goes to theater, concerts, religious services; gets satisfaction from cultural activities; has broad comprehension of religious practices, good taste and critical ability in the arts; is open to new developments in arts, culture, science.
Integration	Psychologically balanced, without extreme guilt, but able to feel appropriate remorse; can solve personal conflicts; does not become overly frustrated, depressed, or aggressive; does not fear new situations, but is aware of possible danger or difficulty; has strength to take on new learning tasks; is self-confident, responsible, and independent.	Is reasonably healthy, with normal organic function and no chronic illness; is capable of a satisfactory sex life.	Is able to fit into and function in various social settings; understands difference between own various social roles; resolves role conflict by conformity without loss of identity; gladly and successfully carries out socially assigned tasks; feels strong tie to own social environment.	Has healthy moral judgment, behaves in accord with socially accepted values; is at peace with cultural heritage, comfortable with behavior in accord with heritage.
Conservation	Has a positive personality, kindhearted and good-natured; behaves consistently in easy and difficult circumstances; has strong character and opinions; is not easily influenced; has positive self-image; knows own abilities and limitations; can use talents, plan for future, and execute plans.	Has genetic makeup that enables management of environment; does not suffer from any deficiency exaggerated by environment; has physical build that fits environment; is not of abnormal weight or height.	Gets sense of meaning from membership in human society; understands that while member of special environment, he still belongs to larger society; has goals guided by models in larger society, not just those in immediate environment.	Has cultural ties deeply rooted in individual and familial past; has values from heritage of generations, artistic tastes molded by cultural origins; is proud of cultural heritage and tries to perpetuate it.

uncertainty results from lack of evidence that reclaiming objectives are realistic, that is, are achieved or even achievable.

Although we usually think of societies as seeking to increase their members' Mastery, sometimes societies seek to reduce the Mastery of those individuals they consider to pose a social threat. Threatening individuals include criminals, but also such individuals as pastor Martin Niemöller during the Nazi period in Germany, Martin Luther King in the U.S., and physicist Andrei Sakharov in the USSR. All of them challenged the established order and thus were perceived as a threat to the collective safety of their society. And, of course, society felt threatened by the high Mastery of Willie Sutton, the consummate safecracker (Reynolds, 1953), and the expert art forger Van Meegeren (Sparrow, 1963); society sought to reduce their Mastery through incarceration.

All societies institutionalize the Suttons and the Van Meegerens. But societies differ in their treatment of the Niemöllers, Kings, and Sakharovs. Established, open, humanitarian, participatory societies place fewer political demands on their members and subject fewer of them to compulsory institutional care. However, all societies require certain adaptation of their members. Such adaptation becomes particularly painful for both individuals and society when rapid change in periods of natural and social upheavals compels the growth of institutional programs.

Invariably, society attempts to maintain or reestablish its own steady state by correcting nonnormative behavior or by isolating the deviant. While, usually, this corrective is accomplished through increased Mastery, in some circumstances the reclaimed person is one whose Mastery has been reduced along certain dimensions. Whether the primary goal is the personal growth of the inmate or the reduction of risk he poses to society, his Mastery is a component of institutional care made overt in every moment of Activity. All institutional decisions—to accept or reject, to retain or discharge, to treat or neglect—regarding Activity are related to Mastery. Assessment and modification are expressed in various fields of Mastery as selected by a particular environment. Mental hospitals evaluate their inmates primarily as psychological entities; Olympic training camps and tuberculosis sanatoria emphasize physical attributes in their self-description and that of their residents; prisons tend to stress various aspects of social integration; and ideological components are emphasized in monasteries.

The reclaiming duties of an institution are always expressed in such selected Mastery terminology, although they may have societal as well as personal implications. Tuberculosis patients should be healed of their disease and rendered noncontagious. Prisoners should accept their "proper" role in society. An American Indian child in a 1930s boarding school was to learn the white man's culture. All such expectations show the two aspects of Reclaiming: personal change along selected dimensions *and* the social implications of such a change in Mastery.

Attention to Mastery begins with an institution's criteria for admissions. Consider the following discussion of selection criteria for West Point cadets in the nineteenth century: "It is possible that the low standard of admission, and the untrained state of the cadet's mind when entering upon his studies, are serious obstacles to his acquiring the course. It has been proposed to raise the standard of admission. . . . But this would greatly limit the field of selection for cadets, and exclude from the Academy many sons of worthy but poor parents, and some brilliant minds would be lost to the public service. . . . [The Commission is] unwilling to do anything to alter the eminently popular, republican, and equal conditions of admission which open the military career to the ambition and genius of all the sons of the Republic" (*U.S. Commission to Examine . . . ,* 1881, p. 7).

Reclaiming expectations and selection criteria are stated in terms of Mastery, and their achievement is measured in the same terms. Activity is planned to fit the Mastery level of entrants and the desired level of their competencies during their residence and after it. Evaluation of individuals' behavior during institutionalization is also expressed in terms of Mastery, as is the institution's judgment about whether it has succeeded in Reclaiming the individual. Such an assessment and its implications for public support may even be formalized. Thus, a resolution of the California Senate's Rules Committee affirms that the program for former addicts and criminals known as Delancey Street "is deserving of public recognition and the highest commendation for its efforts and successes in returning its residents to the mainstream of society" (Hampden-Turner, 1976, p. 7).

The importance of Mastery in institutional operation points to its role in any understanding of the genre. It also explains why the institutions and even the literature about institutional care are so often population-specific (orphanages, old-age homes, and so on): A one-dimensional focus is the easiest to maintain. However, Activity is the life blood of the institutional arrangement. Here lies the source of impact, the origin of changes in Mastery. To be sure, in some instances, such as in the case of debilitated persons, the institution seeks only to arrest the decline of its population's Mastery (Gubrium, 1975; Tobin and Lieberman, 1976). But even such stabilization of Mastery is to be achieved by Activity.

Activity

Along with Mastery, Activity is the subject of all treatises on institutions. Goffman (1961) on asylums, Makarenko (1955) on education, Polsky (1962) on homes for young delinquents, and Stanton and Schwartz (1954) on mental hospitals all discuss institutions by describing the behavior of their inhabitants —the so-called inmates and staff. However, a careful look at these and other well-known works shows that Activity is more than the behavior of people. Activity includes persons, animals, and objects that, along with their psychosocial valuation, are comprised by the institutional entity. Of course, as Murphy (1974, p. 30) notes in describing a children's institution, "life in Garden Court is shaped by the overlappings, conflicts, resonances, and dissonances. . . . The children play, argue and fight . . . correct, persuade, and help." But so do the dogs that bark, trees that sway, and walls that stand there and resist.

The Mastery level of residents determines institutional Activity. First, Mastery determines the institution's physical en-

vironment. Bars on the windows, doors wide enough to accommodate wheelchairs, or lower sinks to serve young children—the
institution's appraisal of inmates' present Mastery and its goals
for their future Mastery determine the nature of institutional
environments. A direct consequence of certain assumptions
about the moral causes of criminal behavior and the need for
solitude and work to correct them was the nineteenth-century
design of Pennsylvania's Eastern Penitentiary where "prisoners
lived and worked in separate cells, each with its own small exercise yard . . . cells . . . were unusually large [to allow for work-
space] " (Carter, Glaser, and Wilkins, 1972, p. 26).

In addition to the physical environment, the institution's
appraisal of its residents' Mastery influences the psychosocial
environment. Decisions on whether inmates work or not, whether
they are involved in governance, or even whether they should be
permitted or encouraged to associate with peers are determined
by the institution's evaluation of their Mastery and its definition of Reclaiming. It is noteworthy that extreme conditions of
Mastery exert profound influence in determining appropriate
Activity. Both very high and very low Mastery on single dimensions create the need for special or unusual Activity. However,
high Mastery on a single dimension is less consequential for institutional programs than the assumption of low Mastery. Although some persons might have such a high value on one dimension of Mastery that reference to all others is irrelevant, this
occurs infrequently. To be sure, the status of a dying or even
dead religious or political leader may be so high as to continue
to influence others' behavior even though that leader possesses
very low or no Mastery on other dimensions. Yet such cases are
so rare that we can ignore them in discussing the parameters of
institutional care.

However, assumptions of the absence of Mastery along
any dimension—that is, when a member of the institution is
considered socially irrelevant or physically dead—are far more
serious. In humane societies such attributes are, supposedly,
never found among institutional inhabitants. Everyone is to be
considered socially relevant, and no one who is physically dead
remains in the setting. However, some institutional residents are

treated as irrelevant or dead. Any review of Activity at hospitals for the mentally ill, nursing homes for the very old, or institutions for the severely retarded, offers proof that some settings treat their inmates as though they had almost no Mastery on some dimensions (Bagdikian, 1972; Deutsch, 1952; Gubrium, 1975; Rivera, 1972). The ultimate example of Activity based on the assumption that a population had no worth on the Mastery dimension of social value is the Nazi extermination camp.

Low values of Mastery are common in many institutionalized populations since, of course, low Mastery is often the very reason for institutionalization. However, some institutions tend to underestimate or undermine their residents' Mastery. Attributions of extremely low Mastery characterize the most obvious examples of destructive environments that are deliberately, or for lack of concern, operated by any society. Of course, other institutions do seem to improve their residents' Mastery. The deprived and the elite are not always worse off for their institutional experience. The higher echelons of the British Empire's civil service were filled with public (boarding) school "old boys," and in a recent government of Israel three ministers were graduates of institutions.

Similarly positive outcomes have been attributed to the institutions established by Makarenko, Gmeiner, Maher, and others. Anton Makarenko gathered up youthful vagabonds from Russian roads and converted them en masse to "builders of Communism" (Makarenko, 1955). Hermann Gmeiner collected Austrian orphans after World War II and made them into law-abiding citizens, some of whom are now leading a worldwide SOS program of Children's Villages (see Wolins, 1974b). John Maher assembled dozens of ex-convicts, drug addicts, and other undesirables, and his Delancey Street Foundation is restoring them to social utility and self-respecting consequence (Hampden-Turner, 1976). Reduced Mastery is not, therefore, an inescapable outcome of institutional environments. The outcome of institutional residence can be positive, but the outcome is contingent on Activity.

A conceptual scheme for Activity is needed to structure the welter of objects, events, persons, and interactions that compose institutions. Like Mastery, Activity can be depicted as a set of subsystems defined by field and mode (Shye, 1979). Table 2 presents a typology of organizational subsystems and their characteristics as they apply to people-changing institutions.

Internats

Organizations and their labels require periodic revision. Walter Bagehot, a nineteenth-century English economist, had a keen eye for the problems inherent in all types of institutions. "The whole history of civilization," he wrote in his *Physics and Politics,* "is strewn with creeds and institutions which were invaluable at first and deadly afterwards" (1906, p. 74). We are reminded of the hopes attached to Bentham's (1791) panopticon, the Quakers' Eastern Penitentiary (Rothman, 1971), the moral treatment promulgated in mental hospitals in the early nineteenth century by Philippe Pinel in France, Samuel Tuke in England, and Benjamin Rush in the United States (Caplan with Caplan, 1969), or Father Flanagan's Boys Town (Oursler and Oursler, 1949). These *total* institutions (Goffman, 1961) and their names, apparently had within them the same germ of ultimate irrelevance or inutility that Bagehot perceived in all social institutions. Something in their mode of operation was unresponsive to the changing needs, moods, and knowledge of their day.

Decay and inutility may be the lot of all organizations, whether they are intended to sell groceries, make pots, accumulate money, repair cars, or modify people. However, those engaged in changing people seem particularly problematic. Our institutions are, apparently, uniquely troublesome. Unlike groceries, pots, money, and automobiles, the intended end product of total institutions, while pliable, is also reactive. It insists on being not only the object or even the subject of the organization's activity, but, to some extent, also its determining component. Thus, the modes of Activity in total institutions will be like those of complex organizations in general, but they will also be different. As Street, Vinter, and Perrow (1966, p. 3) note, "all complex organizations use people to pursue their

Table 2. Organizational Subsystems

Mode \ Field	Psychological–Behavioral	Physical	Societal	Cultural–Valuative
Expressive	Striving of institution to attain specific declared or implied goals; goals will vary among institutions.	Control of institution over needed physical and fiscal resources and power to manipulate them.	Institution's influence and prestige within general community.	Achievements of institution with respect to general system of values shared by society or significant segments of society.
Adaptive	Interaction between institution's idiosyncracies and its environment; idiosyncracies reflect institution's type, size, policies, inmate and staff behavior, and the like.	Interaction between institution as a physical entity and its environment; appropriateness of institution's physical environment to its members and activities; institution's ability to adjust to existing physical constraints and to secure material means.	Interrelations between institution and other institutions in community, including government, funding bodies, and suppliers.	Interaction between values of institution and those of society; the extent to which values in general society are shaped by institution and those of institution by society.
Integrative	Interaction among various parts of institution; compatibility of members, procedures, and other aspects.	Interaction among various physical components of institution (buildings, grounds) and physical needs and abilities of its members; maintenance of physical plant.	Compatibility of various roles institution plays in relation to society, as reflected by interaction among its own components (members, plant, and so forth).	Consonance of values adopted by institution from society at large.
Conservative	Stability of distinctiveness of institution's characteristics and quality.	Preservation of site, grounds, landscape, buildings, financial endowment, and other enduring material properties of institution's character and identity.	Place of institution within structure of general society, and enduring features with which society endows it.	Commitment of institution to a declared or implicit ideology from which it derives its cultural identity.

Source: Based on Shye and Wozner (1978).

tasks, but people-changing organizations work not only with or through people, but also *on* them. People constitute the *raison d'être* of these organizations, and, as our label suggests, the desired product is a new or altered person."

Not all people-changing organizations are total. Most ply their art upon human subjects on a drop-in basis. Schools, hospital clinics, welfare agencies, and houses of worship are not expected to plan for the total needs of their participants. Residential institutions must do so. In this sense, then, they are doubly different from the usual complex organization: They are both people-changing and total. They should probably be given a categorical name because the term *institution* has outlived its usefulness. We will use the word *internat,* which denotes their peculiarity and connotes certain specific attributes.

Thus the term *internat* denotes a narrower class of organizations than the term *institution,* yet it is broader than such terms as *asylum, hospice, home, training school, residential treatment center, prison, hospital, monastery,* and others. The term *internat* allows us to refer to the entire class of such total, residential institutions and thus examine the common elements of such facilities—those Activities that give such institutions their uniqueness, namely, their contingency upon strong *internal* factors and, at times, their considerable separation from the external community.

To be sure, all institutions have boundaries, but the internat's boundaries are less permeable and more significant than the boundaries of other institutions, leading to a more profound preoccupation with the inside. The term *internat* signifies such constriction to a locality. Furthermore, it makes manifest the relationship between these settings and terms like *intern, internee, internment*—all terms that allude to the phenomenon of an inward orientation that is essential to internat operation. As the Polish philosopher Adam Schaff (1973) points out, terminology is destiny and social instruments, like people, are affected by their labels. Our label should emphasize the significance of *internal* forces in shaping internats' Activities, and it should do so without the negative connotation currently ascribed to *institution.*

Internat is not in itself a valuative term. Some consider the Dutch term *internat* neutral. Similarly, the German, French, Polish, Russian, and Serbocroatian languages designate with it settings and persons who are perceived positively as well as negatively. The Russian *shkola internat* ("residential school") is seen generally positively. By contrast, internment camps (in Polish, *obozy internowanych*) are considered to be bad places. In neither case is the valuation a consequence of their being internats, but is due to the kind of internat they are—the inhabitants and Activities they contain. These internats' specific purposes and methods define public appraisal and, indeed, necessitate a differentiation within the internat category.

The Internat as Totality. Like any other organization, an internat is goal oriented. However, due to its totality, the internat's goals must be a reflection of Mastery demands in all fields, and its Activity must be an expression of all modes. It is usually expected that the "ingredients of the organization [will be] deliberately chosen for their necessary contribution to a goal, and the structures established [will be] those deliberately intended to attain highest efficiency" (Thompson, 1967, p. 4). Important in any organization, this rationally determined link between goals and means is all the more important in the total setting.

A total setting ought to provide total coverage: All aspects of the participants must be considered, and all needs must be served. Goffman (1961) argues that the central characteristic of internats is that all aspects of an individual's daily life cycle, of sleep-work-play, are organized under a single, all-powerful, authority. Such omniscience and omnipotence, however, do not extend to the provision for all needs, as a glance at prisons and nursing homes, hospitals and West Point makes obvious. American prisons rarely provide for the sexual needs of prisoners. Nursing homes show little concern for the social integration of their patients. Hospitals for the physically ill rarely consider the family status of patients in for surgery, and West Point pays little heed to the adaptation of cadets in their home community. In short, internats, though they are indeed total, are nonetheless selective in their Mastery concerns.

Several years ago one of us (see Wolins, 1978) had occasion to test the proposition of totality on a group of some sixty administrators and other personnel of children's internats. They were asked to describe how their staff allocated their time by listing the aspects of Mastery attended to and the percentage of time for each. Their mean responses were as follows:

	Percentage of time
Emotional adjustment	15-20
Social integration	17-20
Intellectual skills	11-14
Social values	11-13
Self-fulfillment	9-13
Physical growth and health	7-12
Abstract reasoning	7-8
Manual skills	6-7
Morality	4-5

The heavy investment in the personal-psychological and the social fields is notable, as is the far more limited expenditures in the physical and cultural-valuative fields, which received only 7 percent and 5 percent, respectively, of the staff's concern. Some respondents allocated no time to physical and value concerns. Neither a clear schema nor a conception of the internat as a totality governed Activity as they perceived it. How different this distribution would be in an internat intended to instill Zionism in survivors of Nazi concentration camps who had just arrived in 1946 Palestine.

Not only do internats face difficulties in attempting to provide for their population's needs, as defined by the personal subsystems in Table 1, they also are beset by problems in trying to meet their institution's needs, as defined by the organizational subsystems in Table 2. Consider the following example. The chief executive of a large childcare organization, which operated several internats, kept a daily diary of activities as part of a cost-analysis study (Wolins, 1958). To his amazement, he discovered that he was spending far more time than he wished on matters of physical plant—sewage plants, kitchens, doors, windows, heating—and not enough time on his goals for the total organization: its values, the integration of its staff, and its adaptation to the community.

The conceptual sources of an internat's problems, then, are two. One set of problems results from the internat's totality as an organization, from its supposedly all-powerful, central governing authority. A second set of problems results from the internat's noncomprehensive nature. Sometimes an internat's omissions are deliberate; for example, satisfying the sexual needs of prisoners is a complicated matter both in terms of internal organization (though the Mexicans have managed) and of community relations. More probably, though, many omissions are really oversights caused by an internat's lack of a comprehensive conception of its organizational subsystems and its residents' personal subsystems.

Energy and Its Use. In their planning and functioning, internats often fail to adequately consider the sources and disposition of energy, that is, the financial, physical, human and other resources that the internat requires to function. The internat is generally assumed to function as a kind of leech on the body politic. Resources that are funneled into the orphanage, hospital, prison, or even elitist boarding school are seen as a form of penance paid by the "productive community" for social and physical profligacy. Internats often are not energy self-sufficient, usually due to a gross underestimation of the institutionalized population's Mastery level. Their energy deficit is filled by resources supplied by the community as the price of Reclaiming performed by the internat.

However, not all internats rely on external sources of energy. For example, when Makarenko collected the bedraggled urchins, vagabonds, thieves, and perhaps even murderers from the roads of postrevolutionary Russia, they had nothing except themselves and built their own community. As his community developed, Makarenko never assumed that one might go outside the internat to seek resources. There were none to be had. A modern executive's fund-raising drive would have struck him as useless and immoral to boot. Ideologically, he perceived of the Gorky Colony as a contributor to, not a consumer of, communal resources. Nearly the same may be said today of Maher's Delancey Street Foundation. The outstretched hand is as likely to signify giving to someone in trouble as looking for help (Hampden-Turner, 1976).

Some internats, then, generate energy, produce some of their own resources, and even produce a surplus. To be sure, most internats we know, from the local nursing home and physical hospital to Spitz's (1945) foundling home in Mexico, operate at a resource deficit. (However, Spitz's nursery inside a women's prison was self-sufficient, and infants there developed normally, while infants in the foundling home were stunted.) Many internats require a heavy infusion of money, people, and ideas in order to engage in Reclaiming ventures.

Perversely, internats often recruit outside resources with one hand, while busily suppressing internally generated productivity with the other. For example, one of us was recently called in as consultant on the subject of prison labor in a rather poor country. The country was plagued by a severe shortage of human services, so we asked whether some suitable prisoners might work in nursing homes or serve as aides in a hospital. We suggested building a daycare center in the prison (or near it) using prison labor. When the local administrators recovered from their shock, they said no. Their reasons ranged from "too much risk" to "we have never done it that way."

But the energy of an internat's population will seek some way to express itself—perhaps by rioting. Even when there is no such explosion, the fact remains that unused, human capability atrophies, whereas used competence flourishes and expands. Internats can choose between more reliance on community charity or internal generation and regeneration. Unfortunately, many modern internats have chosen the former, so that those producing adequate or even surplus energy are a decided curiosity.

Constraints on Activity

It is a popular belief and a sad reality that many, perhaps most, internats have not reclaimed their inmates. In subsequent chapters we discuss four conditions responsible for this failure:

(1) confusion about goals, (2) contradictory goals of various subgroups, (3) lack of clear and consistent information about the consequences of particular Activity, and (4) failure to utilize a tested model of human behavior. When one or more of these conditions is present, the Activity within the internat will inevitably fail to produce the desired changes in the various elements of Mastery.

But even when these four constraints are absent, the variety of human conditions and imperfections of comprehension and control in the internat will preclude the development of a perfect, goal-directed environment. Clearly, knowledge—knowledge of human behavior, of goals and means for goal achievement, of the practices of successful internats—is essential to the internat's success. Its absence leads to equal instances of deliberate and accidental Activity. The charismatic founders of great internats *knew* so well (though at times they could not explain) the goals and sanction mechanisms of their setting that their behavior often appeared instinctive (see, for example, Korczak, 1967).

While *timely* knowledge conceptually organizes the system, it does not reduce its inevitably great complexity. Given the disparate nature of persons, we know that what constitutes pleasure for one may be pain for another. The prisoner wants to escape and climbs the wall of the tower, disturbing the guard on duty. The child has a stomachache and cries while the ward attendant wants to sleep. Goals of differently situated persons within the same setting often fail to coincide. Nor do the sanctions correspond. For an internat to change people in the direction of its goals, the internat's Activity must be delimited by ideological, structural, or operational mechanisms. Let us consider five such mechanisms that constrict Activity.

A *unifying theme* is one approach to defining and narrowing the range of appropriate Activity. When all residents are moved by the same system of belief, their goals and sanctions converge. Those who join a monastic order know what to expect and seek it out. Others choose not to come. To be sure, a unifying theme is often introduced in stages so as not to frighten the novice with its full burden (see the recruitment tactics of

Reverend Moon's Unification Church as described in "Weekend with the Moonies . . . ," 1975).

Second, a *single-dimension focus* reduces the fields or modes of Mastery that Activity need promote. An internat may be designed to pursue some goals along a very limited set of dimensions. It may train runners or baseball players; it may be a "fat farm" or a "heart farm"; it may specialize in promoting academic skills or the excision of gall bladders. By focusing narrowly, the internat produces a clear definition of those dimensions of Mastery that are relevant and along which its residents are to progress.

Third, *homogeneous populations* also reduce the range of appropriate Activity. Along this principle, the chaos of the eighteenth-century poorhouse, where persons with all manner of deficiency congregated, was replaced by the nineteenth-century, population-specific asylums called orphanages, reformatories, and hospitals for the insane. Homogeneity is still the prevailing solution to complexity in regard to all types of problems except the physical, which are tended in settings (wards or hospitals) developed around single components of physical Mastery such as limbs, eyes, hearts, kidneys, and other anatomical subdivisions.

Fourth, *force* may be used in the absence of other means for reducing complexity. Force ultimately reduces goals to physical survival. When prisoners refer to "doing your own time," they identify this reductionist tendency under conditions of force; that is, one keeps close to one's own central goals and judges the sanctions accordingly, while carefully recognizing the same predisposition in other residents, both prisoners and guards.

Fifth, *isolation* is a crucial characteristic of internat settings (Etzioni, 1957). They are surrounded by relatively impermeable artificial boundaries consisting of physical barriers, social prohibitions on entry and exit, coded communication, and other devices that divide the inside from the outside. All these devices serve to reduce the plethora of external goals and sanctions to something manageable within. The assumed utility of isolation applies to all internat models. The Elmira reformatory of the 1870s and the university hospital of the 1970s; West Point, set on a hill overlooking the Hudson, and Sing Sing Prisson located somewhat further downriver; the SOS Kinderdörf in Wienerwald outside of Vienna, and the residential yeshiva in Etzion on the way to Hebron in ancient Judea—all are assumed to benefit from isolation.

Although a reduction of the field by means of these five mechanisms may, in some instances, indicate the patterning of Activity—that is, the actions that will take place and whether they will be rewarded or punished—usually other factors also play an important role. The most significant of these seem to be ideology, values, economics, access to information, and personal idiosyncracies of key internat members. Let us now examine each of these structural principles.

Ideology may be based on subjective intuitions or on objective data. Ideologies based on the former may devolve into political or religious prescription and proscription of goals and sanctions. If an ideological community is well developed and strongly bounded, its dictates may be completely adequate to the creation of a system required for the socialization of new and resocialization of deviant members (see Gollin, 1969; Lawson, 1972; Makarenko, 1955; Munk, 1971). Ideologies based on objective data yield scientific and professional belief systems with their goals and sanctions. Scientific dogma demands that a particular setting should *predictably* yield *observable* and desired changes in residents' Mastery or be abandoned. However, a strongly bounded, well-established internat based on subjective intuitions can persist although it fails in its mission. In fact, faced with ineffective, even destructive state hospitals, most clinical professionals call for more staff like themselves—that is, call for continued and increasing unfocused Activity—inside these internats. (See Joint Commission on Mental Illness and Health, 1961, especially pp. 144-146; Szasz, 1970.)

Societal values may often be embodied in political or judicial decisions that govern Activity. In recent years, rules have included constraints on inmates' labor (Krantz and others, 1977), requirements for treatment (Johnson, 1975; Sandman, 1974), location and physical safety of buildings (Lauber with

Bangs, 1974; Mayer, Richman, and Balcerzak, 1977), and other aspects of Activity. Although many of the precluded and mandated actions have the force of law, others, such as the resistance to even mildly aversive sanctions, are a consequence of social attitudes. Both exert considerable effect on the internat.

The economic situation of an internat clearly limits Activity. Although internats need not necessarily drain public or private treasuries (as witness the monastery, the Kibbutz youth group, Delancey Street, and even some of Gmeiner's SOS villages), most of them are costly and some outrageously so. The cost is unavoidable for internats that define or compel some residents to be helpless and require staff to be well-trained helpers. Thus most contemporary prisons, hospitals, residential treatment centers, and nursing homes generate high costs and concomitant social opprobrium. The dependency of Activity in these settings on economic considerations is best illustrated by their response to outsiders' demands for more positive outcomes: More money. All operators of internats comprehend this variable, including those who have neither the competence nor the intent to run an effective program.

Activity is also delimited by internats' enhancing or inhibiting the flow of information among their residents. Often information is deliberately shared or withheld to produce status distinctions among various persons and in order to preclude or encourage certain Activity. An example of such control is the selective sharing of medical information with a hospital patient, or the general announcement in a prison that good behavior will reduce an inmate's sentence.

Finally, the personal idiosyncrasies of decision makers delimit Activity. The effect of such idiosyncracies is particularly significant in internats by virtue of the isolation in which all members live. Decision makers' personal predispositions, particularly toward power, may quite drastically affect the internat's goals and functioning. Korczak's beautiful humanity determined the significant Activity of his orphanage on Krochmalna Street in the Warsaw ghetto just as surely as Ilse Koch's bestiality governed the Matthausen death camp in Nazi Germany.

A Theoretical Model

Internat environments are complex even when Mastery is restricted by preselection of residents and Activity is limited by the mechanisms we have discussed. Complexity is both natural and challenging. As Thomas (1974) suggests in one of the essays in *The Lives of a Cell,* a full understanding of even the simplest organism would require a prolonged international effort. We are far from fully understanding internats. In our ignorance, static and partial formulations are tempting.

Our model is intended to provide a conceptual orientation that enables us to discuss any population in any type of setting; that is, any combination of Mastery and Activity. By covering the total universe of internat care, the model permits the logical juxtaposition of all categories of populations with all categories of settings. Further, we seek to provide a language within which to discuss this phenomenon but without recourse to stigma-bearing labels. In order to accomplish this goal, we must introduce three terms—*Goals, Consequence,* and *Evaluation*—to complement our vocabulary of *Reclaiming, Mastery,* and *Activity.* Let us first review and formalize our definitions of the latter three terms.

Reclaiming is the outcome of internat intervention that a society intends and perceives. Reclaiming usually has a positive value, even in many settings that are negatively perceived by their inmates, for example, the mental hospital in the twentieth century. The definition of Reclaiming thus is formulated by society, that is, by a community external to the internat, and is formulated to maintain the social system. However, Reclaiming is only sometimes consonant with the internee's personal wishes; for example, forced incarceration satisfies society's needs but not the prisoner's. Thus we may distinguish three types of Reclaiming: (1) social Reclaiming, when societal but not personal needs are met; (2) integrated Reclaiming, when both societal and personal needs are met; (3) personal Reclaiming, when only personal needs are met; and (4) non-Reclaiming, when neither is met. In most contemporary internats, expectations and definitions are vague and amorphous—either due to inattention or perhaps to preclude sharp social evaluation. Reclaiming is often reinterpreted and relabeled to accord with current sociopolitical expediency.

As we have explained, *Mastery* denotes the capabilities of an internat's residents, both those helped and the helpers—traditionally called inmates (patients, wards, or residents) and staff. *Activity* denotes the presence and behavior of individuals and objects composing the internat, and includes all objects and actions with their psychosocial values.

We use the term *Goals* to describe both the stated and implicit objectives of an internat's functioning. Goals may be set by any of at least four groups: the person whose Mastery is to be lowered or raised, the staff working directly to modify Mastery, the administrators whose primary function is system maintenance, and the external society that is to be enhanced or protected.

Consequence denotes the result of an internat's activity: the changes in Mastery and in available resources (costs) that are described (often in technical language) by professional personnel. The comparison of changes in Mastery and the cost of achieving them may well influence each of the four groups of goal setters to continue, modify, or abandon an Activity.

Finally, *Evaluation* is the global, social assessment (usually by groups outside the internat) of all elements of the internat environment: Mastery, Activity, Goals, and Consequences. The consistency of assessment across various constituencies depends on the extent of their agreement on goals and means. In some internats and for certain changes in Mastery, the evaluation will be computational; for example, mortality of mothers and infants in a gynecological pavilion, or the escape rate from San Quentin, or the proportion of West Point cadets who become field officers. In such cases agreement is high. In other cases— for example, recovery rate among inmates of residential treatment centers—evaluation is much more likely to be inspirational, and agreement will be low (see Thompson, 1967; we return to this topic in Chapter Three). Evaluation, as contrasted with comparison of Consequences, is generally, perhaps inevitably, inspirational since it entails comparisons of such noncomparable dimensions as money, societal safety, health, and values.

The social reputation or standing of an internat category

(for example, prisons) or any single facility is determined by the outcome of Evaluation. Since many evaluative criteria are inspirationally determined they need not and often do not reflect actual (or, even more so, potential) changes in Mastery. Disagreements among evaluators often lead to disputes regarding Activity. But although an internat may be analyzed in terms of its Activity alone, this analysis acquires meaning only in terms of Goals and Consequences, and the true outcome variable: the Evaluation of the extent of Reclaiming that may be credited to the internat. However, the meaning of Reclaiming is often difficult to define since the Goals of variously located individuals in society differ. As a consequence, Evaluation must consider Activity in the context of Mastery, Goals, and Consequences.

Our model allows us to simultaneously address these four variables. Our analysis relies on the personal subsystems that specify Mastery, the organizational subsystems that specify Activity, and the concepts of Goals and Consequences that are incorporated in both the personal and the organizational subsystems. We define Reclaiming as a function of Mastery interacting with Activity, Goals, and Consequences. Evaluation, then, is a function of that complex interaction. Using initials and mathematical shorthand, we propose that:

$$R \ [M \ (AGC)] \ E$$

In the following four chapters, we discuss the four modes of Activity (as shown in Table 2) in relation to Mastery, Goals, and Consequences. Specifically, Chapter Three is devoted to goal setting and achievement, Chapter Four to adaptation to the external environment, Chapter Five to the integration of internal activity, and Chapter Six to conservation of the internat, which provides recognition, stability, and security. Each of these chapters is preceded by an overview, which may substitute for the chapter itself as background for the concluding three chapters of the book.

3

Setting, Achieving,
and Evaluating
Internal Goals

Overview

An internat is expected not only to change people but also, more specifically, to change certain kinds of people, along selected dimensions of Mastery, in a predetermined direction. For example, the goals of a monastery (Merton, 1949a, 1949b) are to expand the ideological (religious) commitment of members. The monastery's preoccupation is largely in the value field, and entrants are volunteers, often carefully screened during a novitiate period. In contrast, a Soviet psychiatric hospital designed to contain and modify political dissenters houses a compelled population, and its goals, often covert, are to reduce Mastery in the psychological, social, and value fields (see Medvedev and Medvedev, 1971).

Whatever an internat's goals, it must have some measure of control over resources. The isolation, minimal needs, voluntary membership, and considerable productivity of a monastery give it high control. Not so for the prison whose membership is heterogeneous and largely compelled; whose productivity is restricted by law, custom, and circumstance; and where demand upon the inmates and staff is high because major changes in Mastery have been set as goals (Giallombardo, 1966; Sykes, 1958). Thus achievement is considerably more problematic in the prison than in the monastery because there is less consensus in the former than in the latter.

This discrepancy is further amplified by differences in the authority vested in the internat as a social organization. An internat dominated by a unique expertise, shrouded in the mystery of science or religion, is rarely challenged by outsiders as to its goals, strategies, or techniques. Consider here hospitals for the physically ill (Ferguson and MacPhail, 1954; Owen, 1962) or religious academies such as residential yeshivot (Munk, 1971). In contrast, many challengers arise within and without when expertise is diffuse or nonexistent, or when opinions as to goals and means are in conflict. In such cases critics' actions are guided by what Thompson (1967) calls inspirational behavior, and the internat's control is disputed.

How much control an internat has over goals, means, and even evaluation is a function of its prestige. The status of inmates whom the internat is intended to serve determines its general standing and affects control. West Point and Sing Sing are both situated along the Hudson River, but they have different clienteles and consequently different prestige. Prestige usually has recognized functional implications within a subset of internats—one hospital is deemed superior to another—but it also has implications across subsets. Prestige, as Caplow (1964) notes, is a scarce commodity within and between organizational entities. Society accords differing amounts of prestige to various types of internats (military academies, prisons, monasteries, and mental hospitals), and these attributions of prestige determine the allocation of burdens and resources.

Starting with different goals and very different kinds of people to change, all internats are required to progress toward a general system of values promulgated by society. Although good physical health is relatively easy to define and good behavior is not, ultimately, the criteria of societal approval or opprobrium for internats are similar: adequate or superior functioning of former inmates. Internats charged with reducing Mastery in order to produce social Reclaiming—that is, Reclaiming that meets society's needs but not those of the inmate or resident— are always negatively evaluated, even though their Activity is socially accepted.

The Gordian Knot: Goals

In the internat, as in any complex organization, there are numerous goal makers. But unlike an organization that produces inanimate objects, the internat produces change in people, and those people deserve and insist on voicing themselves. Furthermore, although an automobile factory always produces automobiles, the goals of an internat may be displaced such that the original Reclaiming for which the internat was established is set aside (Merton, 1957) and the internat becomes something quite different—a service organization for the staff, for example. Such goal displacement in people-changing organizations is illustrated by the perhaps apocryphal comment of a Nobel laureate who, admiring the beauty of a university campus, asked "Must there be students here?" Internat residents are well aware of such goal substitution. However, the non-Reclaiming goals, whether of resident or of staff, are not to be declared and surely must not be formal.

Inconsistency and conflict may characterize even bona fide Reclaiming goals, especially since they are set by external agents. For example, an internat for persons whose Mastery of behavioral skills is low uses methods such as residence, association, and therapy to help the inmate (patient) develop socially

acceptable behavior. This isolated setting, however, both protects the external community from behavioral deviants and de-
prives internees of the very environment to which they are to adjust. Deprived of the models and rewards of a normal environment, the inmates are nevertheless expected to acquire normal
behavior. But often the only normative behavior they learn is
that appropriate to the isolated setting in which they live. And
they do that with such skill and persistence that, at times, even
the staff is converted to the normative expectations of the inmates (see Polsky, 1962).

Some internats' residents are perceived not only as behavioral deviants but also as moral or legal transgressors. For
example, prisoners are perceived as bad people, and retribution
and deterrence are often two goals besides Reclaiming. But deterrence is badly served by isolation in that unless potential
transgressors see the quality of internat life they will not know
what they should be striving to avoid. And retribution or punishment may be in conflict with Reclaiming, which must be
based on pleasurable consequences of desired behavior. With their
contradictory goals of rehabilitation and retribution, prisons are
the classic example of intrinsically flawed internats, but they
are not the only one. Simultaneous rehabilitation and isolation
goals (possibly with covert punishment and deterrence goals)
also characterize mental hospitals. Sensitive mental health practitioners attempt to enhance Reclaiming by reducing isolation
(Fairweather, 1964; Jones, 1953), but this is not the rule.

Consider, too, hospitals for the treatment of physical
maladies as examples of internats whose patients are not considered a moral or physical threat to the external community
and whose goal is simply physical health. Foucault (1975), in a
masterful book on the development of the medical clinic, points
out that, initially, the modern physician-dominated general hospital was "the universal solution for the problem of medical
training" (p. 64). That is, such internats were founded to serve
physicians' educational needs, not patients' medical problems.
The vestiges of such a goal are still present. For example, teaching hospitals seek cases with the most instructive symptomatol-
ogy, with the most novel maladies, and with the greatest predisposition to experimental treatment. It might be argued that

such practices serve the community's long-term needs for medical education and therapeutic innovation. But how do such admissions criteria serve an ill person who is turned away by a prestigious facility and sent elsewhere for treatment because his case is not sufficiently instructive for the staff?

Because everyone wants a say in the operation of internats, society is unable to define an integrated, noncontradictory set of goals. Historical development is uneven, as technology changes rapidly, while values follow slowly. The professions involved in the internat are at different stages of their own maturity, and the various participants often have their own goals. For example, consider what happens to John Doe, a prominent citizen who suffers a heart attack while meeting with the board of his corporation. Rushed to the local cardiac unit, he gets devoted and expert care by an efficiently organized and well-rewarded team. Soon Doe is back on his feet, and his corporation donates new, even more modern equipment to the local heart association, which in turn assigns it to the cardiac unit. The pattern of Activity in even this simple case of internat care shows the multiplicity of goals involved: those of Doe, the hospital, the medical team, Doe's corporation, and the heart association. Fortunately for Doe, all these goals were convergent and his care was expeditious and effective.

But consistency cannot always be anticipated and, in fact, exists but infrequently. In Doe's case, the events might have evolved quite differently. His attending physician and nurses could have been tired. The hospital could have refused him admission because he had no health insurance or ready cash. The community could have spent its money on a park in the elite section of town instead of on sophisticated cardiopulmonary equipment. In short, the goals might have diverged so much as to produce a funeral instead of a homecoming celebration. To be sure, neither the consonance (or dissonance) nor the outcomes are usually as extreme as our examples. On the contrary, the goals of the variously located participants lead them in all directions. Because the internat is such a powerful instrument, divergent or dispersed goals inevitably cause waste and injury.

As we noted in Chapter Two, the various participants

(and their goals) can be grouped in four general categories: inmates, staff, organization, and external community. The Goals of an inmate are always defined in terms of the various fields of Mastery. Hospital patients are concerned with improving their physical health, while students entering an elitist school seek to gain an education and perhaps social status.

The goals of staff in the internat are also defined along fields of Mastery but these need not be and often are not the same as the patient's or pupil's or ward's. While helping inmates achieve Mastery, staff members also seek to increase their own Mastery—by receiving a large fee, acquiring a fine professional reputation, or consolidating their authority or power within the internat, for example.

The Goals of the internat as an organizational unit are defined along yet another set of dimensions: institutional survival, pattern maintenance, expansion, and the assurance of community support. While patient Doe is preoccupied with his electrocardiogram readings (if his physician allows him access to such mysterious information), the hospital administrator is reading flow charts of admissions and cost-income figures for the cardiac unit. The administrator is both the person who wrote a policy that refuses admission to uninsured patients and the person who will have to explain this policy to the press, should they question it, and to the community, should they criticize a denied admission.

Finally, the Goals of the external community are expressed along yet another set of dimensions, which include fiscal, humanitarian, and safety concerns. Were patient Doe eligible for Medicare, his bill would concern the community, just as would the escape of a known criminal from the state prison.

These four sets of goals differ not only in their content but also in their degree of formalization and overtness. As an example of formalized, overt Goals, consider the program of the founders of nineteenth-century penitentiaries. They defined their Goal as moral change, expressed it clearly and openly, and formalized it in appropriate Activity—including solitary cells and exercise yards devoted to contemplation. Goals not only dictated the internat's Activity but also specified conditions under which the internat would continue. In contrast, twentieth-century planners, driven by failure and humane concerns, expressed their Goals more broadly but also less specifically and less overtly. As a result, they did not clearly define the dimensions of Reclaiming, and the implications of Reclaiming were never fully accepted by the community. As Goals became formal, they also became more covert. A system that merely muddled through, subject to political skulduggery and public whims, was inevitable.

Goals may be covert or overt, formal or informal. Covert goals are those whose definition and attainment are not public; overt goals are public. Formal goals are those whose definition and attainment are operationally defined by the internat community; informal goals are not.

Many Goals are too fluid to be frozen into regulation, and many are too disconcerting when expressed. An illustration of the latter is provided by the progressive development of the asylum and its remote location. To deal with the incurably mentally ill and retarded, communities humanely resisted the method sometimes used to finally deal with those regarded as incurably criminal—capital punishment. Instead communities housed such persons in the most secure yet least intrusive manner. These mentally ill and retarded persons were subjected to a modern form of banishment. Similarly, the early settlers in Connecticut achieved both safe and invisible confinement by putting their prisoners in an abandoned copper mine. The community's Goals—to feel safe from such prisoners, to feel just and moral in their treatment of transgressors—were well served; the prisoners were not. Indeed, both staff and prisoners were denied the simple joys of seeing the sunshine or green grass.

An internat's Activity results from the combination of the formal and informal, covert and overt Goals of the four participating groups. Any Goal of inmates, staff, administration, or community may theoretically be formal and overt, or formal and covert, informal and overt, or informal and covert. Let us consider several examples of inmates' Goals and their implications for Activity. Formal and overt inmate Goals are expressed when a patient signs a hospital contract, an adolescent applies for admission to a boarding school specifying his interest in learning Russian, or a suicide-prone patient voluntarily signs himself into a mental hospital. An inmate's Goals cannot be both formal and covert because when formalized within an internat they inevitably become overt.

Informal and overt inmate Goals are those informally expressed, such as when a patient tells his male associates that he wants to move to the next ward with the two pretty nurses, or even to have one of them join him in bed. Finally, examples of informal and covert inmate Goals include a prisoner's secret plot to escape or a patient's giving gifts to a nurse, hoping to seduce her.

While some of the combinations of formal-informal and latent-overt Goals do not occur and others—for example, a formal and covert community goal like secret Nazi commands to concentration camp administrators—are quite rare, an analysis of internats must consider most of these combinations. In the ideal case, all the goals are reasonably convergent, yielding an internat that is efficient and at peace internally and with its surrounding community. The yeshiva described by Munk (1971), located in a *shtetl* (see Zborowski and Herzog, 1962, for a description of such a small, religious town in pre-World War II Poland), enjoyed such an existence, as did West Point during World War II. The meaning of convergent goals is illustrated by contrasting the situation at West Point during World War II with the conditions prevailing there during the Vietnam War.

Convergence and Divergence

Full convergence of Goals is rare indeed. It may be approached in highly ideologized, isolated communities composed of faithful disciples. Perhaps hospices of religious orders located on mountaintops or in the desert (for example, Santa Katarina in the Sinai Desert) fit this description. In most internats, however, full convergence is neither expected nor necessarily desired, although arrangements approaching consensus include various types of communes: the Amana and Oneida communities, Father Divine's groups in Harlem (Lawson, 1972), and John Maher's

Delancey Street Foundation in San Francisco (Hampden-Turner, 1976). Goals of participants are most likely to converge in informal, voluntary, communal internats and least likely in formal, compulsory, bureaucratic environments, with free but formally organized internats falling in between.

Freedom of membership in the internat appears to determine the degree of convergence. Only when membership is voluntary can inmates or staff leave if they do not accept the prevalent Goals. In compelled environments, such as prisons and juvenile halls, the Goals of staff, internat administration, and community may converge, but all will be distant from the inmates' Goals. Sometimes, however, one of the other three groups becomes the captive, as now seems to be occurring in hospitals. Interestingly, the captive this time is the community. Given the Medicare program, the community has agreed in advance to accept the Goals of patients, medical staffs, and hospitals. In effect, the Goals of the professional staffs have preempted most of the Goal options of patients, administrators, and the community. The only choice left for the community is to accede and pay the bills or to modify the arrangements. Mounting costs are already influencing changes in Goals and hence in the pattern of Activity (see Luft, 1979). The development of health maintenance organizations (HMOs) is a harbinger of this evolution.

Rearrangement becomes necessary if everyone's Goals cannot be met. When total resources are relatively fixed, their distribution will be responsive to power possessed by each of the participants, and compromise will result. Giallombardo (1966) points out in her study of a women's prison that "the collectivity orientation of the prison [staff and internat Goal] and the goal of economic self-sufficiency [community Goal] generate pressures in the social structure which result in . . . delayed or permanent postponement of rewards for the inmate" (p. 65). The compromising of inmates' Goals to meet those of the other participants is not unusual, because power is usually unevenly distributed between inmates and the others. For example, the choice of Activity is largely the prerogative of the staff, although this prerogative is affected by the social status of inmates. Thus, millionaires on "fat farms," prefects in English boarding schools, and upperclassmen at West Point have goal prerogatives not accorded less prestigious inmates of internats, be they paupers on county farms, lowerclassmen or plebes at West Point, or the prisoners in Alderson Federal Reformatory for Women described by Giallombardo.

Considerably divergent goals, then, characterize most internats. Organizations with such marked divergence of goals should tend toward collapse. Indeed, goal divergence is responsible for the collapse of some internats as Reclaiming systems, although such internats may continue to function as warehouses for residents with gradually diminishing Mastery. The deinstitutionalization drive of the late 1970s, which has been characterized by Etzioni (1978, p. 14) as "a vastly oversold good idea," is in large measure a result of goal divergence. Under the benign guise of the best interests of the patients, the community (usually here the state government) closes mental hospitals to save money. As the cost of care per patient day in New York's state hospital system rose from $3.44 in 1956 to over $20.00 in the early 1970s, the pressure to deinstitutionalize persons increased. The discharge rate rose from 77.7 per 1,000 in the 1955 census to 457.2 per 1,000 in 1974. The trend was not markedly affected by the fact that many of the patients had no place to go and were lodged in welfare hotels. One patient recommitted himself to the psychiatric unit of Bellevue Hospital four times "because I just couldn't stand not having others I could reach out to. I preferred the hospital to my SRO [single-room-occupancy] room" (Siegel, 1972, p. 39; see also Lander, 1975; Santiestevan, 1975; Scull, 1977).

Internats are usually very expensive compared with familial care or total abadonment, yet they survive. They are beset by divergent goals other than cost, yet millions of people remain in internats. Why? We would argue that—despite the divergencies among the Goals of inmates, staff, internat administrators, and society—all participants frequently set Reclaiming above their personal goals. In the case of John Doe's heart attack, everyone's other considerations were *momentarily* set aside. The cardiologist ignored his fatigue and need to rest, the nurse her vacation plans, the administrator his table of organization and ledgers, and the community the cost involved. Had

Doe not been wealthy and insured, however, the administrator might have refused to place Doe's Reclaiming above the hospital's Goal (income). Such an expression of self-orientation, in an attempt to conserve one's own prerogatives at the expense of Reclaiming may, of course, be exhibited by any one of the participants.

In every internat and for every Activity, Reclaiming is encroached upon by such opponent tendencies. In extreme situations, when individual Goals are placed above Reclaiming, Activity is reduced to "killing time." The victims are the caretakers and care recipients alike: cruel or uncaring staff "working" solely to meet their own needs; adult retardates rocking endlessly on the ward floors while sitting in their own feces; lifers "doing their own time"; seniles in back wards of mental hospitals; infants entering anaclitic depression.

Consider the following scenario for failure. A social group worker in a prison describes the behavior of the warden thus: "As a matter of fact I don't think Cokely or for that matter many of the staff is particularly interested in programs which change inmates so that they can stay out of prison. Cokely seems to respond to what society says it wants its prisons to be: places of punishment where men 'learn their lesson.' His major interest is in running a trouble-free, smooth institution, one that doesn't get into the newspapers because of riots" (Manocchio and Dunn, 1970, p. 48).

An inmate of the same prison does not, however, single out the warden. He considers all the staff—including, one supposes, the social worker—to have Goals irrelevant to his own: "Stability and maturity? Jesus Christ! The same tired words given in an unending repetition. I'm so sick of those two goddamn words I could puke every time I hear them. Stability and maturity. What the hell do they mean? These assholes are constantly using the terms but they don't ever bother to tell anyone what they mean. But I think I know what they mean. They mean if you have those things, then you're Joe Square. And if having maturity and stability means I am going to have to be like these assholes, they can keep them!" (Manocchio and Dunn, 1970, p. 79).

Internal opposition to Reclaiming is commonplace: Prisoners riot, mental patients become uncooperative or apathetic, staff become uncaring. Fanaticism in pursuit of Goals is less common but equally harmful. The treatment of prisoners in the nineteenth century and of psychiatric patients in the twentieth provide some examples. The Pennsylvania Quakers were committed to Reclaiming of prisoners through solitude. The fanatic application of this principle produced internats whose silence was as that of a graveyard (Beaumont and de Tocqueville, [1836] 1964). More recently, American psychiatry devised the prefrontal lobotomy as a Reclaiming Activity, and this, in turn, was followed by psychoactive drugs whose full, long-term effects are still unknown. There is little reason to assume that such drastic (fanatical) steps at Reclaiming were ill intentioned. However, these radical experimenters, fired with zeal, served the internat no better than their opponent counterparts.

Most internats, however, strike a compromise between Reclaiming and the Goals of the participating groups. This middle ground is the unifying theme of an internat, a *mind community* (in Tönnies's, 1957, terminology) marked by "co-operation and co-ordination for a common goal" (Hillery, 1968, pp. 77-78), without necessary reference to a place. However, the physical place itself—the internat isolated, remote, self-sufficient—underscores the unifying theme. The Reclaiming theme becomes identified with a setting. Thus, monasteries are the epitome of religious expression. Wartime military camps are the most obvious symbols of national will and mobilization. Medical edifices are the containers and marks of their thematic orientation to health.

While providing a meeting ground for the convergence of Activity around Reclaiming, internats must also fulfill some divergent, personal needs of those involved in the enterprise. Reclaiming and the personal, individual Goals of all participants must coexist. The surgeon must get his rest. The nurse must have her vacation. The administrator must have a sufficient income for the organization. Each of the caretakers and care recipients of an internat must be met part way in order to kindle and expand the spark of Reclaiming that all participants have within them.

Devices for this purpose are many and varied. Often they evolve out of necessity. Harold Skeels placed infants in a home for retarded women. Hoping to provide pleasurable tasks for the retardates and stimulation for the children, Skeels (1966) succeeded far beyond his own expectations. Stotland and Kobler (1965) in their *Life and Death of a Mental Hospital* describe the rewards and pain of the ideological development, flourishing, and demise of an internat initially pervaded by Menninger's teachings. The SOS Kinderdörfer of Hermann Gmeiner (1971) originated out of the devastation of Austria in World War II and the Marian (mother-child) orientation of central European Catholicism. Intended to serve not only orphans, but also unmarried women deprived of probable mates by the exigencies of war, SOS is now a worldwide movement with over 200 children's villages. The SOS Kinderdorf meets well the needs of both abandoned children and the housemothers.

If more staff members support active Reclaiming than oppose it, if some of the care recipients also partake of it, their commitment may lead to the gradual conversion of staff and inmates who do not value Reclaiming above personal Goals. However, if growing numbers of participants do not value Reclaiming, the actual or functional death of the internat is a foregone conclusion.

Is Goal Convergence Possible?

Let us consider more specifically the conditions that promote a convergence of Goals and those that promote divergence. A review of the successful internats depicted by Korczak (1967), Makarenko (1955), Jones (1953), and Skeels (1966) suggests one common underlying strategy: these internats did not rely on any one particular model of internat organization and they did not aim their people-changing Activity *at* inmates.

In contrast, consider medical organizations in which internees are clearly separated from the staff not only because the former are sick and the latter are healthy but also because the former are laypersons and the latter are professionals. Patients are perceived not only as ill but as incompetent to participate in their own Reclaiming. Following this medical model, various professions claim their province of specialty: psychiatrists plan and run mental hospitals, penologists run jails and prisons, and pedagogues run children's institutions. Professionals in such internats aim their Activity *at* the inmates, usually without considering two key components of Reclaiming: the obstructive potential of staff Goals and the participation of inmates in their own Reclaiming.

The traditional medical model assumes that the patient can know nothing of his illness, that the patient cannot function effectively in healing himself or others or in modifying the staff. In the medical setting, the patient is merely an example of an illness-bearing organism that is more or less responsive to professional ministration. Staff, however, are competent and capable to define Activity since they are trained and skilled professionals. Goffman (1961) labels this relationship between the care recipients and caretakers the "binary structure" of an asylum.

Internats that presume their inmates to be incompetent to participate in their Reclaiming then expect those inmates to function competently in order to be considered for release (in the case of prisons) or whenever the internat believes the inmate's Reclaiming is complete (for example, a doctor discharges a patient). The moment of transition from incompetent to competent is deftly illustrated by a patient's discharge from a hospital: Usually, the discharged patient, going home to assume something of a normal life, is brought to the door in a wheelchair. How different this is from the participant healing process of Jones (1953) or Fairweather (1964), the construction of one's own environment by Makarenko (1955) or the communal learning of novice and master in the yeshiva (Munk, 1971) or monastery (Merton, 1949a, 1949b). In all these internats care recipients are gradually led to assume tasks that their roles in outside society will require of them. Furthermore the internees are treated by the internat staff as competent individuals who differ from the staff only in certain specific functions.

In contrast to the medical model, in which Reclaiming is the province of professionals, consider Bockoven's (1963, p. 12) description of the nineteenth-century moral treatment movement in mental illness: "Moral treatment was never clearly defined, possibly because its meaning was self-evident during the era in which it was used. It meant compassionate and understanding treatment of innocent sufferers. Even innocence was not a prerequisite to meriting compassion. Compassion extended to those whose mental illness was thought due to willful and excessive indulgence in the passions." This conceptualization of illness allows for the participation of the ill in their own reclamation. Bockoven calls moral treatment the "forgotten success in the history of psychiatry." What seems to have made it so was *not any specific technique of therapy,* for apparently various techniques were used, but rather a comprehensive way of life, tied together by a strong ideology: "Most of the tasks presented for the patients involved cooperating with others, religious involvement, and doing manual work or intellectual work (like writing plays). . . . The goal was to help the patient enjoy life and take part in society" (Ullmann and Krasner, 1969, p. 127).

The moral treatment model, so broad in scope as to include a concern for every detail of the internat's Activity, soon fell into disuse. Proponents of moral treatment were accused of naivete. Their approach was total, but considered simple. Their goal was straightforward—to help a troubled person. But by 1854, when Thomas Kirkbride wrote his famous work on hospitals for the insane, two other forces were changing the function and operation of such hospitals. First, many concerned social activists, including Dorothea Dix, fought to have persons previously sent to prison now sent instead to mental hospitals for treatment. Simultaneously, physicians were assuming control of these hospitals, asserting that mental illness fell within the professional province of medical doctors. John Gray, superintendent of the largest state mental hospital of the time, and also editor of the *American Journal of Insanity,* concluded that "insanity was *always* due to a *physical* lesion" (Ullmann and Krasner, 1969, p. 128).

Thus the medical model replaced the moral treatment model and, despite its failure, today governs many psychiatric hospitals. The twentieth century has, of course, added new Goals for the modern internat for the mentally ill. On the centennial of Kirkbride's first publication, Stanton and Schwartz's well-received volume, *The Mental Hospital*, offers these Goals: "the protection of the community, the meeting of the general needs of the patients, psychiatric treatment of the patients, education, research, and, in proprietary institutions, profit" (1954, p. 28).

This large array of Goals, stemming from various constituencies, is to be met in a setting that may allow but a small corner to the supposed recipient of help. The goals are "pursued by a complex organization of division of labor embodied in the various roles; the behavior of the particular people in the institution is organized according to these roles" (Stanton and Schwartz, 1954, p. 28).

No vestige of the moral treatment model remains in the modern mental hospital Stanton and Schwartz describe. The logistic requirements of the well-oiled bureaucracy negated the demands of close, intimate interactions—the essence of people-changing Activity. The recipient of care became an object of the bureaucrat's manipulations and was denied control or participation in decisions that affect Reclaiming and Activity. Most serious observers could only share the views of Goffman (1961), Grosser (1969), and others who see the bureaucratic model as antithetical to Reclaiming.

By the middle of the twentieth century, new models for internat care of the mentally ill were proposed, some of which nearly recaptured the achievements of a hundred years earlier. Milieu therapy, introduced to American psychiatric practice by Bettelheim and Sylvester (1948), refocused attention on the inmate. Such therapy entails the organization of the entire internat and requires that all Activity contribute to integrated Reclaiming (Bettelheim, 1950; McCleery, 1969; Redl and Wineman, 1951).

Advocates of the new environment emphasize ego, defined as the *"internal representation of a constellation or sequence of events experienced as part of an environment with a specific affective tone"* (Cumming and Cumming, 1962, p. 32).

Ego components are assumed to have different configurations in healthy and unhealthy persons, and the internat should "provide the patients with practice in the kinds of role behavior that will be expected of them as participating members of society and, at the same time, provide them with a range of problems for solution" (Cumming and Cumming, 1962, p. 75). Additionally, an ego-oriented environment should have a clear authority structure and communication system, both requirements of a well-functioning complex organization.

At first glance, such a model might appear to provide full complementarity between the demands of the organization and those of the patients. But, whereas clear role definitions, unambiguous communication, and other system-conserving mechanisms are relatively easy to define, ego is an undefined concept, invisible and possibly incomprehensible. Thus, although the concerns for organization and for ego were together to govern Activity, it is not difficult to predict which concerns will predominate when requirements of care recipients and of the system conflict. Polsky and Claster (1968, p. xvi) summarize the fate of the milieu model: "The principles underlying the creation of a therapeutic milieu have proved difficult to transmit from one practitioner to another. Administrators of institutions vary in the emphasis they give to personal qualities of staff members or to organizational structure, to managing discrete interactions or to planning daily programs. Efforts to lay down general principles, moreover, fail to provide concrete guidance for creating therapeutic milieux. Accounts of particular therapeutic communities do not present the rationale for therapeutic goals and practices in a form that can be adapted to other settings."

A more specific example of the failure of internats to respond to change is offered by Sommer (1969). He rearranged the chairs of an internat's sitting room so that inmates were able to face each other in conversation or to interact around a small table. Soon the chairs were again all lined up against the walls, where they had originally been put by staff. That arrangement was more convenient for those moving through the room, the janitorial personnel and the supervisors. And the inmates? They, too, preferred the chairs against the wall—an arrangement fitting the self-image of inactive, isolated, nearly asocial objects. It seems that rigidity—often a characteristic of organizations—had also affected the internees. As rules and habits assume preordained qualities and are applied in a universalistic manner, normalcy and convenience replace spontaneity and individualization.

However, despite their difficulties in integrating the fluid needs of a changing inmate population with the conservative demands of the setting, internats based on moral treatment and milieu therapy are clearly distinct from others. The intended centrality of patients makes the internats proposed by Kirkbride (1854) and by Cumming and Cumming (1962) qualitatively different from the community hospital, and all are unlike the usual prison (for example, see Cressey, 1961; Sykes, 1958). In the former, changes in Mastery are to be achieved by the collaborative efforts of caretakers and care recipients. All Activity in the internat is to be orchestrated for such a goal. Theoretically, the energy generated by the entire internat population is to be maximized and aimed at Mastery. Nor are the helpers excluded; they not only change people but also are themselves changed. In short, the internat is operated by and for all its inhabitants.

Compared with this total dynamism, the typical community hospital is engaged in a holding operation. It is a well-run hotel, in which various specialists ply their crafts. The internat itself is inert, a neutral container, sterile, unobtrusive, dominated by rules. The patient does not act, lest he get in the way of treatment. Indeed, to minimize such interference, patients are often sedated even for such normal functions as childbirth. Professional control is total. Although Reclaiming is very much the objective and physical Mastery is the criterion, much of the energy generated by the hospital as internat lies dormant. Fortunately, patients' stays in such environments are usually measured in days or weeks—a period brief enough that most patients do not revolt or fall into total apathy (although Spitz and Wolf, 1946, report depression for infants who have long hospital stays). There are exceptions to this model (see Lindheim, Glaser, and Coffin, 1972; Thompson and Goldin, 1975), but they are far from representing the norm in hospital design or operation.

Now consider internats in which inmate's stays are measured in years, or decades, or longer—prisons. The typical prison proclaims Reclaiming intentions but largely ignores the requirements of inmates. Superficially, the goal substitution that takes place in a prison should make it the easiest internat to administer. Even the inmates accept the primacy of organizational over individual goals in this setting and give rules preference over people. The external community has given up expecting positive changes in Mastery, and Social Reclaiming displaces Integrative Reclaiming as it does in any human warehouse. The inmates' energy surplus, stored over long periods of time, unused in self-reclaiming, stagnates into apathy or erupts in the violence of revolt. The Goal divergencies in prisons—which are expected to punish, deter, and rehabilitate inmates while safeguarding society—are so profound that Reclaiming may generally not be feasible, Stürup's (1968) report of success with chronic recidivists notwithstanding.

Autonomy

The problem of divergence in Goals is confounded by the internats' lack of control over means. Like all organizations, internats need people, money, and ideas. While no organization has full control of all these resources, few have as little as internats for populations who are negatively perceived by society. Physical plant may be used to illustrate. A private, well-endowed clinic for example, has considerable control over its plant. It can select a location, design buildings, and lay out its internal and external space to suit its Reclaiming purpose. But most publicly funded internats control neither their plant nor their residents nor even their staffs. External bureaucracies make these decisions. Governors and legislatures decide on line budgets, divisions of architecture plan and develop plants, and so on.

At times the consequences verge on the bizarre. Willowbrook and the Bronx Developmental Center provide an example and, we hope, an object lesson. Willowbrook is an old, very large, very bad internat for the retarded, located in Staten Island, New York. It entered the 1970s with 5,500 inmates and half as many staff. Under court orders to disperse this human "refuse heap," the state of New York developed several programs including a new physical plant.

Architectural design for the plant was entrusted to an outstanding firm, and the new Bronx Developmental Center, which was to house several hundred evacuees from Willowbrook, achieved immediate fame. Architectural juries and critics acclaimed it an outstanding example of creativity, and it won a top award in architecture. Yet, parents of the future residents and concerned professionals condemned its location and design (Ivins, 1977). Architectural panels labeled the center a work of art, skillfully designed to avoid an institutional appearance. In contrast, human care professionals, desiring that the center convey a message of normalcy, wanted a design that would reflect images of conventional houses. They found the center an ambiguous and austere environment (Goldenberg, 1977). Thirty, not several hundred, residents occupy this monument to external control. The white futuristic buildings have not been a total waste, however. They have recently served as magnificent background for Woody Allen's film *Sleeper* and Marshall Brickman's *Simon*.

Yet another example. One of us was a regular visitor to a youth village in Israel. Overnight lodging was always available in the hospital, and on none of these occasions were any of the young people actually confined in this building. Why had the hospital been built? An anxious and important donor and a distant, demanding bureaucracy felt the village should have it. Neither seemed to care that the village's inhabitants did not want it.

Such irrelevant benevolence often stretches the limits of credulity. Internats are social dependencies and are sometimes colonized by various donors who go to considerable lengths. New York City is well known for the balancing act that public officials, and the bureacuracies they control, must perform between Protestants, Catholics, and Jews. The object is to show fair treatment. In consequence, in the 1950s one Jewish internat was the recipient of an unrequested shipment of school desks, although those in use were considered totally adequate by students, teachers, and administrators. Result: One full warehouse, one sigh of helplessness from a captive director.

The internat's use of its internal resources is also constrained. Consider work as an integral component of internat's internal resources. Work may entail serving oneself, helping others in the setting, or producing a marketable product or service. Given the centrality of work in human affairs, and its key role in the definition of normalcy, it might be expected that work by the inmates would be encouraged. True work—not child labor, nor chain-gang crews—would seem to be integral to increasing Mastery and could also improve the environment of the internat by supplementing its external resources. Work would seem to benefit Reclaiming as well as the individual Goals of all concerned.

Indeed, recall that Freud's twin indicators of maturity are the capacity to love and to work (*Lieben* and *Arbeiten*). Jahoda, surely a reputable interpreter, reports: "In my own studies bearing on the meaning of work for the individual . . . I was helped by . . . a footnote in *Civilization and Its Discontents* that work is man's strongest tie to reality. . . . If work is man's strongest tie to reality, then the absence of work should leave him less solidly in touch with reality. This is indeed the case. Work encourages the continuous action necessary to maintain objective knowledge of reality; work permits the pleasurable experience of competence; work adds to the store of conventional knowledge" (Jahoda, 1966, pp. 623-628).

A good work situation in the internat should provide models and opportunities for competent behavior. By enhancing Mastery in the physical, psychological, social, and value fields, it should contribute to Reclaiming (see Wolins, 1979). Makarenko (1955) used inmate work to build his program. Jones (1953) had patients work to repair their hospital and add to their subsequent employability. In both cases gains were realized by the community, the internat, and primarily by the inmates.

Of course, work is also problematic. Inevitably, risk is

enhanced by the often low competence of inmates and of staff. Exploitation is a definite possibility. Market problems arise. Faced with such problems, most American internats have chosen to prohibit work by their inmates. The community does not support, almost precludes, serious internat work, although it sometimes sanctions busy work or allows inmates to perform unskilled labor for pennies an hour. A recent *Wall Street Journal* survey found that " 'sheltered' workshops paid handicapped as little as 10 cents an hour" ("Minimal Wage . . . ," 1979, p. 1). The application of inmate energy to real work is barred by supposedly humane law, precluded by clinical convention, and treated with much suspicion by all (see Johnson, 1972).

Prestige, Power, and Suspicion. Not all internats are subservient colonies of the communities supporting them. Omaha, Nebraska, owes some of its fame to Boys Town and Father Flanagan. Baltimore is known as the home of Johns Hopkins, Annapolis for the Naval Academy, and Topeka for the Menninger Foundation. And Innsbruck, Austria, is the world headquarters of Hermann Gmeiner's SOS Kinderdorf International. All these internats are relatively independent of external control. They have acquired a degree of prestige, power, and great public support. What distinguishes these internats from most others is the source of their social power (see French and Raven, 1960).

Some sources of power are, obviously, more desirable than others. Trading on its *reward power* the Naval Academy has able recruits, qualified staff, and a handsome budget. At the recommendation of members of Congress, it accepts young men and women and bestows upon them prestigious standing. Like the elitist boarding schools that dictate to the families of students what they may do, the academy enjoys considerable freedom in the disposition of resources. Incidentally, in both the military academies and the boarding schools, self-care is required, service to others is emphasized, and work in and for the community is the very focus of the program.

Referent power determines the position of monasteries and yeshivot. They believe themselves to be authorized by divine authority and thus are usually exempt from the normal bureaucratic tribulations of other group residences. Boys Town and the SOS Kinderdorf initially drew heavily on referent power. Both Father Flanagan and Hermann Gmeiner received major recognition from the Catholic church—a distinction that undoubtedly eased their dealings with the community and increased their prestige and thus their autonomy. However, in the secular state, referent power has been markedly diluted by two other considerations: legitimacy and expertise.

Legitimate power is granted an internat only by the state. For its license, the state exacts a heavy price. It insists on controlling nearly all aspects of an internat's behavior. Buildings and their location, the intake and discharge of inmates, the sources and disbursement of funds—all are subject to external scrutiny. When the scrutinizers know little of either the goals or the strategies of the internat, their decisions regarding rules and regulations—for example, the sprinkler systems, or requirements for certain population mixes (O'Neill, 1974)—may in fact undermine or contradict Reclaiming within the internat.

Those who work in internats may acquire some power by virtue of expertise. *Expert power* precludes the rule by external agencies. In the United States, for example, hospitals, like other internats, are licensed. Their licensing body is the American Hospital Association. Intended to be a self-policing organization, it derives authority from the internats it sanctions. (The association's Joint Commission on Accreditation of Hospitals has had, since 1961, twenty members: three each from the American College of Surgeons and American College of Physicians; seven each from the American Hospital Association and American Medical Association; see American Hospital Association, 1961). Experts are granted such self-regulatory power by the state because they are assumed to know what is good. Expert power is thus the safest source of self-control and freedom from external bureaucratic power. Moreover, the expert may concentrate directly and solely on the Reclaiming without being hampered by concerns of coercion or legitimation. Thus far, however, only those professionals who treat physical illness have achieved expert status in the public eye. Except for a handful of charismatic individuals, professionals with psychological, social, or value goals are suspect. The internats operated by them may have to rely on the least palatable of all forms of power—coercion.

Coercive power is used by internats to achieve a modicum of control. The internat threatens the community with dire consequences unless the internat is supported. Releasing dangerous prisoners or mental patients, or even threatening their release, may result in some grudging community support. Coercion is a weak weapon, but often the only one available to an internat that has neither prestige nor much power but whose inmates are perceived by the external community to bear considerable stigma.

Although not all internats stigmatize, none is above suspicion or charges of being inhumane or elitist. In the public's view, internats are closed social systems, their walls concealing mystery, permitting excess. They nurture doubt, fear, and resentment. Thus, periodic demands for the abolition of this or that type of internat are common: "I should like to see every single institution in the country for dependent children closed tomorrow" (Leonard, 1881, p. 302). "There is only one way to deal with state hospitals or, for that matter, prisons: empty them, close them, then blow them up" (Reding, 1974, p. 7). "There are now four regiments at West Point. . . . Let the regiments be placed . . . in little West Points in San Francisco, Dallas, Minneapolis, and Harlem. . . . West Point, like all old soldiers, deserves a chance to gracefully fade away" (Galloway and Johnson, 1973, pp. 18-19).

The theme is not particularly American or even Western, though it is not as pronounced in less individualistic societies. In societies in which peer group residence is a part of the socialization process, internees are usually treated without stigma (Spiro, 1956; Wilson, 1951). Nor does successful operation seem to be the criterion by which prestige or stigma are assigned. Who has measured the success rate of a monastery, a yeshiva, or an English public school? There are not even any established criteria. And the success of a "bad" internat may make little difference in its evaluation. The English public believed, for example, that "when young persons are sent to Borstal they almost always turn out to be convicts later on" (Hobhouse and Brockway, 1922, p. 433). This view prevailed even though the evidence at the time showed that of the youth who had been in Borstal between 1909 and 1914, 64 percent were not reconvicted and lived in satisfactory condition.

English public schools have shared in the negative image even though they take pride in having educated much of the empire's leadership. They are accused of being "places where class-consciousness is bred and snobbery inculcated. Or they are places where boys learn to rule instead of to serve. There is yet another type of criticism, based on personal memories of unhappy or unsuccessful schooldays, or grim experiences at 'bad' schools in days gone by. Others again attack the Public Schools for perfectly sincere and serious reasons, often based on psychological theory—the deprivation of home influence, the undesirability of sex segregation, the evil influence of fagging [system under which a junior boy acts as a servant to a senior boy], of corporal punishment, or of Public School religion" (Snow, 1959, p. 8).

As to other internats, such as mental hospitals or prisons, the criticism of their effect on inmates is even more severe. "Apathy, lack of initiative, loss of interest, . . . submissiveness, no expression of feelings of resentment at harsh or unfair orders . . . lack of interest in the future, . . . inability to make plans for it, deterioration of personal habits, loss of individuality, resigned acceptance that things will go on as they are" (Barton, 1959, p. 14) are all signs of a pervasive institutional neurosis.

A rather depressing portrayal. Given the accusations, internats as a genre should simply disappear just as Leonard, Reding, and Galloway and Johnson have proposed. But they do not. The number of aged in internats is growing rapidly. The prison census declines, then rises again. The number of halfway houses is mushrooming. The SOS Kinderdorf movement is expanding. Apparently, society cannot meet the abolitionist demands. It seems to need its internats to maintain the social order. Thus, although society does not like the internats as they are, society is reluctant to give them up.

In the past some internats were designed as social disposal

mechanisms for the dangerous, contagious, and otherwise troublesome. Inmates were not expected to leave such settings alive. The programs were *intended* to seclude, ostracize, stigmatize, punish but not to reclaim. An English leprosarium had gallows in the courtyard to remind inmates of the punishment for walking out of the gates. Pinel's hospital kept many patients in chains. These internats were not encharged with Reclaiming their inmates, only with protecting society from them.

Predicated on the unchangeability of man (inherent evil of prisoners, incurable illness of the deranged), such internats needed no models of success and no rewards for accomplishment. They had little concern for stigma and no reason to undertake planned risk in order to permit, even encourage, growth. Some modern-day internats and the public attitude toward them are reminiscent of such perceptions. How else can one explain the modern prisons described by Sykes (1958) or Giallombardo (1966), the hospital depicted by Goffman (1961), the nursing home portrayed by Gubrium (1975)? At most, these settings offer up some lip service to the growth potential of their inmates. At worst, care recipients and caretakers wallow in despair.

There appears to exist a societal conclusion that "the provision of services on any basis other than institutionalization is superior" (Bachrach, 1976, p. 5). This view is supported by the exposés of former inmates (for example, Behan, 1958; Braly, 1976) and by theoreticians of all persuasions. Psychodynamicists like Bettelheim and Sylvester (1948) would not take issue with the statements of behaviorists that "the longer . . . patients remain in the mental hospital, the more severe their behavioral problems seem to grow" (Ayllon and Azrin, 1968, p. 3). Nor would they disagree that "the attendant stigmatization, the patient-role requirements of the mental hospital culture, the limited opportunities to perform behaviors that are necessary in community life, and the development of institutional dependency produce further impediments to successful readjustment to typical environmental demands" (Bandura, 1969, p. 17).

Demand for the abolition of internats that seek only to isolate inmates and not reclaim them appears to indicate a societal awareness of the changeable nature of any person. If people can grow and develop, learn and create and give, then those settings that stifle such tendencies should indeed be assaulted. (This might even apply to a goodly number of family settings as well.) Since society apparently cannot do without its internats, it must consider improving them.

Seclusion and Power. An internat is a "powerful environment" (Bloom, 1964) that provides the focus necessary to excel or to contain. In elitist settings, remoteness, isolation, and concentration are intended to "bring out the best" in the inmates—to produce achievement beyond the social norms. But seclusion is also a useful device for isolating the dangerous and otherwise disturbing.

Whether self-generated or socially compelled, these isolated collectives are somewhat frightening. The high level of energy internats develop may be used in socially lauded ways, but collectively inmates may also do outrageous things. Delancey Street in the 1970s (Hampden-Turner, 1976) or Synanon in the 1960s (Yablonsky, 1965) show how good work is done with criminals and addicts. But, the internat may also assume a negative direction as it did at Synanon in the 1970s ("Life at Synanon Is Swinging," 1977) or in Jonestown's People's Temple even more recently (Kerns, 1979; Krause, 1978). Isolation, a charismatic leadership, a strong unifying theme and effective models can do wonders or wreak havoc.

Nowadays all internats profess Reclaiming goals. But who should be reclaimed and why? Reclaiming is by definition applicable only to those who once belonged to "us"; neither the strange nor the stranger can be reclaimed. Those who are not considered true members of the society are disposed of rather than helped. For example, in ancient Sparta, weak children were destroyed since they were not considered members. In the not so ancient world, human beings who were deemed nonmembers were sold off as slaves, and slavery was considered a legitimate cultural act. Hitler deemed the Jews and the gypsies as nonmembers of the "master race" and destroyed them.

In some cases, society has been willing to Reclaim a part of an inmate—the part deemed to "belong," the soul—while dis-

claiming the body. Spain's Inquisition reclaimed the souls of
Spanish nonbelievers and the conquistadores reclaimed the souls
of those who would not submit to the cross in America.

The idea of Reclaiming the soul, *within* the living body, is
based on the hypothesis that as a society we know how to
change human behavior. Whether *penitentiary* or *reformatory,*
asylum or *treatment* center, the internat is charged with this
task. As the Spaniards and others before them prove, Reclaiming as a goal is not new. The fields of Mastery vary with time
and the technology changes, but every society must undertake
social Reclaiming as an aspect of the pattern maintenance function of society. Preserved by the "normal," every society isolates
its deviants, glorifying or condemning them as the case may be.
Since the internat itself is a rival, and thus a danger, to the most
fundamental of social organizations—the family—it too must be
isolated, glorified or condemned, and always held suspect.

Even the failure to change the inmate has its utility. The
very effort to reclaim—the very declaration "We are reclaiming," serves a societal purpose. Complete success is not necessary; perhaps it is even to be avoided, lest the prison or the psychiatric hospital acquire prestige. Also, the failure of such
internats serves as a warning or deterrent to potential transgressors. This deterrent function of the internat is perhaps as
important to society as its Reclaiming function. Internats—even
for the elite—not only should be uncomfortable but also
should *not* be completely successful. (Where the need for Reclaiming is an objective necessity, as in physical illness, society
does its best to dignify the internat and raise its level of acceptance.) Dangers to society are thus controlled by a symbolic assurance. "We shall reclaim you," reassures the members that
they can undertake exploratory journeys in their urge to explain and master the world. But the failure of reclaiming efforts
cautions members not to journey too far or explore behavior or
activities that society perceives as dangerous.

Consequence and Evaluation

An internat's success in Reclaiming is assessed by changes
in its inmates' Mastery. A hospital for physical ailments is ex-

pected to treat physical problems, and criteria for success are those of physical changes in patients. No expectation exists that a patient recuperating from a heart attack will be a better parent, a more honest executive, or a greater lover of opera. Such, we would be told, are not the goals of a community hospital. Were a community hospital measured by its effect on all fields of its patients' Mastery, its rate of failure would be high.

The internat is an establishment that absorbs resources and yields some kinds of changes in inmates, staff, administration, and community. In other words, its Consequences comprise costs and benefits, both defined very broadly. When costs are compared with benefits, statements of utility may be made. However, the variables comprising costs and benefits are not usually convertible to a common metric. Neither the costs nor the benefits of Reclaiming are purely financial. Furthermore, an inmate's estimate of the costs and benefits of his Reclaiming may differ from the community's assessment.

Although people are fond of saying: "You can't put a dollar value on health" or, we might add, on a classical education or an appointment to West Point, we can somewhat clarify costs. There are five types of expenditures, or prices or penalties, incurred for every Activity: pain, money, trained manpower, physical plant, and tradition. Our sequence is not fortuitous, it denotes the extent of flexibility each investment represents. Pain is subjective and may be transitory. Money may be diverted to other purposes rather quickly and easily. Shifts of manpower are more problematic, of buildings very difficult, and of internat-related traditions almost impossible (see Bakal, 1973; Santiestevan, 1975; Wolins and Piliavin, 1964). Though hard to change, two types of cost—manpower and physical plant—are fairly easily measured by a financial metric. Thus, except for pain and tradition, most of the costs of internat care can be objectively determined by reference to dollars.

The assessment of the benefits internats yield for the several categories of participants is far more difficult to determine. Benefits are measured along the various dimensions of Mastery for inmates and staff, along system-maintenance variables for administration, and along social utility dimensions for the society as a whole. Although some theorists have attempted to convert Mastery values to dollars, such efforts have generally been rejected (see Noble, 1977). We are left, then, trying to compare incomparable terms.

Problems of measurement and comparability should not, however, obscure the importance of Consequences in the life of an internat. For the inmate, anticipated costs and benefits help him to decide whether the gain is worth the investment of personal effort, time, and money. In voluntary internats, such as the community hospital, prospective inmates compare costs and benefits before entering and again when deciding whether to stay. Costs—pain, discomfort, boredom, money—are compared with anticipated changes. Similarly, staff and administration analyze costs and benefits in order to continually monitor Activity. Has the inmate's Mastery changed as predicted (and desired) by the staff? How much did such change cost? These are evaluative questions about Mastery designed to affect the pattern of Activity.

Additionally, cost-benefit analysis provides staff and administration with data for long-term planning. A hospital's mortality rate may indicate the need for additional or more modern equipment, better-trained personnel, or a changed admissions policy that excludes certain cases from the hospital. A prison escape may signal the need for greater vigilance, higher walls, or the transfer of certain cases to a new maximum security prison. Present Consequences inevitably influence future Activity. Too, information about Consequences will reach the outside community and affect the social evaluation of the internat's activity.

Indeed, measurement of costs and benefits is performed by everyone, even those only remotely connected with the internat. Some of these assessments are formal and objective, like fiscal reviews of hospitals or gunnery scores of West Point cadets. Others, like parole board decisions or case conferences, may be formal but based on subjective impressions. Yet other assessments are neither formal nor objective, reflecting the extemporaneous opinions of persons with various expertise.

Thus judges within and without the internat may measure its Consequences. The likelihood of external measurement appears to be related to attributes of Goals and Activity (see Thompson, 1967). When Goals are crystallized and the Activity for achieving them is certain—as, for example, in the prevention of respiratory infections among hospitalized infants—the assessment of Consequences is computational and, we should add, internal. Consequences are expressed numerically along a single dimension of Mastery—illness or health—and verification is simple. No serious reliability or validity issues arise, and an internat's own assessments are accepted by interested outsiders. In situations of this kind, costs are often set aside and only benefits are considered. In contrast, when Goals are ambiguous and Activity uncertain, the measurement of consequences is inspirational, and all interested parties, inside as well as outside the internat, produce their own benefit and cost data. Reliability and validity are major issues, often resolved in the political arena, as the measurement of Consequences for retarded, mentally ill, and delinquent persons has shown.

Four types of cost-benefit analysis may be derived from the interaction of Goals and Activity. (1) *Computational decisions* take place when Goals are clear and a high probability exists of their achievement by selected Activity. (2) *Judgmental decisions* are made when Goals are clear, but the probability of attaining them by known Activity is low. In such a case, assessment relies on the judgment of others (preferably experts) regarding the benefits of Activity. (3) *Compromise* is in order when the Goal is ambiguous but there is high probability that a selected Activity will yield this ambiguous objective. (4) *Inspirational decisions* apply when Goals are ambiguous and certainty about Activity is low. Both costs and benefits are assessed on a purely intuitive basis.

The expression of an internat's comparisons between costs and benefits depends on its Goals, its Activity, and the particular kind of cost or benefit to be assessed. Financial costs are most likely to be measured computationally, while benefits pertaining to ambiguous goals and uncertain means will fall to inspirational assessment. The present trends in the assessment of Consequences may be graphically represented as follows:

← ————— Tendency for measuring costs
Computational   Judgmental   Compromise   Inspirational
Tendency for measuring benefits ————→

These assessment tendencies have their counterpart in the control of Activity. Internats that assess benefits by compromise or inspiration are likely to lodge control over Activity with those who manage incoming resources, that is, administrators and, more particularly, fiscal personnel. In the absence of computational assessment of benefits, the accountants, treasurers, and managers make decisions—even those pertaining to the maintenance and people-changing activities of professional staff. An exception to such control occurs when an inspired, charismatic leadership throws caution (and objective, computationally appropriate evidence) to the winds and insists on implementing its own vision of the good internat. Makarenko, Korczak, Gmeiner, and Father Flanagan all ran programs this way. They also assumed full responsibility for maintaining a flow of resources in order to keep their internats sound, often doing so against incredible odds.

Igor Newerly, Korczak's pupil and biographer, provides a glimpse of the responsibility Korczak assumed during his last days as director of a children's internat in the Warsaw ghetto, before he and the children were sent to the gas chambers in the summer of 1942:

> The life of the Children's Home was . . . concentrated in the big hall on the first floor. . . . By night, it served as dormitory, by day for meals and classes. Ingeniously arranged chests and cabinets partitioned it into classrooms, linen store, reading room, and other special-purpose accommodation. . . . Peace, order, good management prevailed in the house as if the children had long lived there. The Korczakian child community organization—court of peers, self-government, school newspaper, fixed schedule of daily routines and occupations such as monitoring duties, school hours—all were maintained. The children learned, cleaned and tidied

the house, worked in the linen room, the kitchen.
. . . Food at the Children's Home was poor—but by
ghetto standards luxurious. . . . Korczak used to go
out in the morning and return late. . . . He would
make calls at the Jewish Community Office, Cen-
tos, Jüdisches Hilfskomitee, the homes of the rich,
the offices of notorious, utterly compromised col-
laborators. He begged, threatened, quarreled. . . .
He was the father of 200 children and was compelled to provide for them" [Korczak, 1967, pp.
572-573].

The staff of a more computationally-based internat need
not assume Korczak's level of responsibility to achieve authority. In settings in which assessments of benefits tend toward the
computational—such as hospitals for the physically ill—techni-
cally specialized staff control Activity. They not only decide
what models of Activity will be implemented but also select the
ancillary personnel to assist them. Obviously and unequivocally,
physicians run hospitals for the physically ill (even the schedule
of shifts is set to meet their convenience), but the physicians'
control of mental hospitals is far more tenuous even when they
are nominally in charge (see Stanton and Schwartz, 1954; Stotland and Kobler, 1965).

Popular opinion holds computational evidence in high re-
pute, and internats whose benefits are so expressed appear to be
less troubled by external interference, the vagaries of public
tastes and political decisions. Even more profoundly, the scientific community believes that only objective evidence should
control Activity. However, the operations of internats, unlike
the prevention of polio or the construction of bridges, are not
readily amenable to measurement by this direct relationship between Activity, Consequence, and Goal. Usually a good deal of
cost-benefit data are moved into the social sphere for Evaluation and ultimate disposition. Thus the internat that uses inspirational decisions to assess Consequences is in constant risk
of losing its essential community support.

Even internats with diversified support and a high level of
public trust are not insulated against external evaluation. Boys

Town is an instructive example. Through an immensely popular public appeal, Father Flanagan and his staff attracted a very large number of small donations from the American public. Because its Goals were unquestionable and its contributors many, Boys Town was not subject to cost-benefit assessment by external agencies or individuals. But in the early 1970s Boys Town's lack of clear Goals and related Activity was exposed, and Boys Town went into receivership after Americans evaluated it as a non-Reclaiming internat.

Internat evaluation takes place in other ways as well, including grand jury reviews and personal testimonials by inmates. (An early example is Beers's [(1908) 1925] autobiography about life in a mental hospital.) Most modifications in internat Activity that are dictated from the outside are not, however, the result of such spectacular events. Interaction between the internat and the social environment is usually more regular and less dramatic but more significant. It occurs each time any relevant individual or group compares an internat's costs and benefits with the values of the particular society (or any segment of it) at a particular time.

Such instances of comparison yield decisions of several kinds. First, a more or less formal decision may be made as to whether the internat is an effective Reclaiming instrument. For example, San Francisco's late Mayor George Moscone praised the Delancey Street Foundation for "returning its residents to the mainstream of society as responsible and productive citizens" (Hampden-Turner, 1976, p. 7). Such a decision is always provisional, since events inside the internat and expectations outside it are subject to change. Recent reevaluations of Synanon—a progenitor of Delancey Street—provide evidence of how quickly an internat and its public image may change ("Life at Synanon Is Swinging," 1977).

Second, a decision may be made as to whether the Goals of an internat serve integrated Reclaiming or merely social Reclaiming. Third, a decision may be made as to whether the costs of the internat are justified in the light of benefits. Finally, a decision may be made about whether the Activity used to obtain changes in Mastery are socially acceptable. Because internats are remote, unusual, and powerful instruments of human change, they, more than other social devices, are subject to reviews of Activity itself. Isolation cells, prison labor, token economies, aversive therapies, and the total absence of therapy have all been subject to public attention and condemnation.

However, the preceding decisions regarding Reclaiming, Goals, and Activity are not the only assessments society makes. Internats exist not only to Reclaim but also to remove, to dissuade, to serve as the object lesson and as the cracked mirror of society. Thus society may also assess the internat's costs and benefits in achieving covert societal goals. Consider Haley's (1971, pp. 158-159) tragicomic description of a mental hospital:

> The outstanding feature of a mental institution is a kind of formless, bizarre despair overlaid with a veneer of glossy hope and good intentions concealing a power struggle to the death between patients and staff, coated with a quality of continual confusion. The basic art of schizophrenia lies in a genius for dealing with power struggles, and of course in a mental hospital the problem of power is central. It should not be thought that the struggle between patient and staff is unequal. True, the staff has drugs, tubs, cold packs, shock treatments (both insulin and electric), brain operations, isolation cells, control of food and all privileges, and the ability to form in gangs composed of aides, nurses, social workers, psychologists, and psychiatrists. The schizophrenic lacks all these appurtenances of power, including the use of gang tactics, since he is essentially a loner, but he has his manner and his words and a stout and determined heart. He also has had extensive training in a family made up of the most difficult people in the world.

The psychiatric hospital accepts the schizophrenic and thereby relieves the family and society of his care. But it knows no more how to heal this type of disturbance than do experts or professionals on the outside. The schizophrenic's lack of Mastery is increased, not ameliorated, by the hospital. What is it that society expects? Some proponents of deinstitutionalization, according to Haley (1971, p. 175) "have created a slogan which can be seen on the signs they carry as they picket mental hospitals, 'Let's get the patients off the back wards and back home into the back rooms!' " Other critics accuse internats of various real and imaginary inadequacies. Bad internats are what society wills them to be, affirming Thomas's (1928, p. 572) view that "if men define situations as real, they are real in their consequences." The definition of Goals, the conception of Reclaiming and Evaluation, the significance of Mastery, Activity, and Consequences are the complex realities of internats in our society. Performing within this framework, internats live up to society's actual—though perhaps covert—expectations.

4

Adapting to Society's Expectations

Overview

Internats, like all other social organizations, do not exist in a vacuum. Even the most remote monastery, the most isolated prison or mental hospital, is part of a social matrix to which it must adapt. Compared to other organizations, internats are both more capable of isolated survival and also more suspect and vulnerable to attack. Whether supportive or hostile, an ongoing transaction between internat and environment is inevitable, and this transaction takes place across the full complement of fields.

The family and the internat are the only organized units of society that are expected to provide for all needs of their members. In fact, as family functions have been relegated to other social institutions (education to schools, socialization to peer groups, and feeding to cafeterias) any internat is compelled to meet more needs than a family. Internats supplement or replace family functions that are unexercised or inadequate. Hospitals treat sicknesses that exceed a family's capability. Orphanages care for parentless children. Prisons hold persons for whom family socialization has failed. Military academies and boarding schools offer instruction and environments conducive to higher Mastery than a family can provide. Internats are the familial apposition: from the family, in time of need, internats take members and to the family most internats are expected to return them. (Of course, some internats—for the aged, for the severely handicapped—are not expected to return their inmates.) In order to return inmates to society, internats must conform to the society that they serve. A difficulty arises since by designation, internats are collectives of members set apart from society for one reason or another.

Internats are aggregates of persons who are in some way different than others—be they monks or prisoners. To house large numbers internats require special physical forms. Larger buildings, unusual in shape, with easier or more difficult access and containing people different from most, are, at the very least, disconcerting to neighbors. The institutional building and the group inhabiting it are both rejected by the society that established the internat. The community wants a hospital, but no one wants it in his neighborhood. The community wants a prison, but no town wants to house it. With the decline of religious influence in America even establishments for monastics are a bone of contention (see Lauber with Bangs, 1974). Critics raise the issue of zoning and ask, interestingly enough, whether members of a monastic order residing together may be classed as a family. Similar, though sometimes less vehement, resistance is faced by small internats like halfway houses, nursing homes, and group homes.

Yet the internat must be geographically and socially part of the community it serves. Models, resources, and clients come from the community, and discharged inmates are intended to rejoin or build their families there. The inside of an internat ideally should be attuned to the outside in its physical style (clothing, food, space), its social values of authority and communication, and its ethical values. Adaptation requires that internats operate like other social organizations in the open community, but the people they work with are deliberately unlike those in the community.

The internat's adaptation problem also poses difficulties for the community that must adjust to its unusual neighbor. Some communities respond positively. West Point provides a major source of income to the merchants of its neighboring town. An isolated prison or mental hospital is often located with the express intention of providing employment for nearby residents. Certain internats become so famous or infamous that they and not the surrounding communities set the tone of adaptation. Usually, though, the imposition is mutual. A community suspects and is discomfited by its internats, but it may have little choice but to make peace with them.

Primary and Secondary Customers

Aristotle is quoted by Diogenes Laertius: "Society is something in nature which precedes the individual. Anyone who either cannot lead the common life, or is so self-sufficient as not to need to, and therefore does not partake of society, is either a beast or he is a god." Neither the internat nor its subjects can "lead the common life." Reclaiming, by its very nature, implies action on the uncommon. The internat is a collective of those who cannot or will not lead the common life.

An internat is an uncommon social entity, yet it must find its place in the social system. The internat's activity touches and is touched by the community in several ways. Members of the task environment—customers, suppliers, competitors, and regulators—come from the community, representing both society's contributions and its demands.

The primary customers of people-changing organizations

like internats not only come for a product but may themselves be the product. Inmates, wards, patients, and cadets come because their community is unable to cope with their Mastery ambitions, needs, or problems. To have its effect the internat must, by definition, be unlike the outside world from which the inmate has come. Were the mental hospital like home, it could not hope to improve upon the family's performance.

The first Activity of the internat is to isolate its members from the external community. Fences and visiting hours, uniformed staff and guarded records denote deliberate separateness from the outside. Prisons, monasteries, military academies, and isolation wards are extremely isolated, while group homes, halfway houses, and open hospital wards are more accessible. Access determines "the degree to which the social standards maintained within the institution and the social standards maintained in the environing society have influenced each other to minimize differences" (Goffman, 1961, p. 119).

Some internats require that a new internee's initial withdrawal from the community be total and immediate. Others hold that gradual immersion is less traumatic and produces greater long-term effect. Thomas Merton (1949a, 1949b), in a penetrating analysis of the process he experienced in becoming a Trappist, describes the gradual approach. Prisons, boot camps, and most hospitals practice drastic immersion. The rapid separation of the inmate from prior environment may serve a useful ritualistic purpose—to indicate the start of a new life—or it may bolster the internat's power. It used to be customary in American orphanages to subject a new admission to total stripping. Old clothes were removed and symbolically burned or discarded, toys and other private "treasures" were similarly disposed of. A bath and close haircut completed the orientation.

In most settings, though, the shock effect is substantially modified by unpremeditated moderating forces. New inmates and staff bring with them pieces of the outside. So do the media and the visitors, no matter how limited their access, and the suppliers and regulators also contribute their share. In short, while an inmate's entrance into an internat does denote and connote his maladaption to the general community, the internat cannot totally exclude the effects of external forces. The external world is present both in an inmate's memory of the past and hopes for the future. It is a symbol of the expected, ultimate adaptation most internats intend for their inmates. Prisoners, according to Wheeler (1969), are oriented to the external world at the start and conclusion of their terms and to the internat during the middle.

Before an internat can begin Reclaiming, it must adapt the inmate to internat life. Although many, perhaps most, internats structure their internal operations to resemble those in the external community, their success is limited and inmates must learn the internal rules. Vocational programs, for example, endeavor to teach job skills useful on the outside. But consider one prisoner's assessment of a vocational training program:

> The clothing manufacturing is part of what they call their "vocational training" program. But what they teach you is how to get along in the penitentiary. They teach you a lifetime penitentiary trade so you'll always be useful to them when you come back the next time, and the next time. They won't ever have to retrain you. They only manufacture maintenance materials and supplies for themselves and the other state institutions. On paper it looks good. They are able to say they're teaching trades to convicts: trades like the textile mill, clothing manufacturing, and furniture manufacturing. . . . The only problem is after you've learned the trade here you can't get a job doing it outside. . . . Of course, they have displays of "prison-made" articles in prominent places for the public outside of the prisons, but they're just cream, individual efforts, and the system neither wants nor encourages excellence [Manocchio and Dunn, 1970, p. 31].

Staff, too, recognize that inmates' successful adaptation to the internat does not necessarily prepare them for adaptation to the external community. A social worker in the same internat as the prisoner just quoted depicts the situation:

But there is nothing that members of the staff like better than to put in a man's file glowing reports of how much the inmate had benefited from a specific part of their program. The academic people are ecstatic if an inmate completes the high school program and finally receives his diploma, and the vocational people are particularly gratified if an inmate completes the year or two-year course. The fact that some of the trades being taught are technologically outmoded, or that there is little demand for some skills, or that in some instances the training is too rudimentary to enable him to get a job at the trade has apparently little to do with it [Manocchio and Dunn, 1970, p. 104].

Even in the most carefully planned and well-intentioned internat programs, the problem of inmates' readaptation to the outside community appears. Therapeutic communities that plan considerable outside work for internees (Jones, 1953) and even halfway houses located in the community (Fairweather, 1964) find adaptation problematic. Why?

The adaptation problem appears to have two components. First, Activity in the internat can resemble ordinary community life in only limited ways if the internat must exert a powerful force to modify an inmate's dimension(s) of Mastery and thus accommodate the inmate's or community's wishes. Often this extraordinary attention to a single dimension of low Mastery affects the staff's general perception of the inmate as incompetent in many ways. The inmate's incompetence is generalized such that a hospital patient suffering from gall bladder problems is treated as though he cannot think or a retarded person is considered unable to perform normal physical tasks. Risks ordinarily assumed by persons in their everyday life are thought inappropriate for the inmate. Yet risk taking constitutes the nature of normal experience. Without risk there is no growth.

Second, adaptation is problematic because the capability of inmates, even on the dimension at issue, is highly varied not only at time of entry but throughout their stay. And change is gradual. A model program to effect full adaptation would, therefore, have to pace performance expectations in accord with changes in each inmate and the proximity of his return to the external community. But most staff have neither the skills nor the time to plan such individualized programs. However, even if they could, they would be unable to implement such gradual changes in an inmate's program because to do so would disrupt the ordered patterning of the internat. The stability of fixed staff-inmate hierarchies and prerogatives would be challenged should some inmates be encouraged to become too competent, should their competency approach or exceed that of the staff.

Even if these and similar internal obstacles could be overcome, the community would object since it wants clear distinctions between the disabled and the able. Anyone who tries to blur such distinctions may be advised to leave town, as happened to Cumming and Cumming (1957), when they attempted to persuade the inhabitants of a Canadian town that the difference between the townspeople and the patients of a nearby mental hospital was merely quantitative. The community, though it posits that an internat's task is to achieve normal competence in deprived inmates, does not really assume that such an objective can be reached. Released convicts, mental patients, and even returned and rehabilitated veterans are only reluctantly allowed to enter the mainstream.

Within the external community is a group we may call the *secondary customers* of the internat: the inmate's family, future employers, relatives—all have their expectations of the internat. For every inmate, or primary customer, several secondary ones stand in the wings. They, too, engage in mutual adaptation with the internat.

Secondary customers have few problems adapting to an internat that operates with a unifying theme that is characteristic of the well-ordered outside community. When the English nobility ruled the social structure, famous public schools accommodated society's expectations and successfully trained rulers of the empire. Only the advent of socialist thinking and power ultimately disturbed their peace. The same relationship of internat and secondary customers could be observed in the Catholic church. When the priesthood was strongly disciplined and centrally directed, there were no basic conflicts between the internats for novitiates and their ultimate parish superiors. Most internats, though, neither develop from nor carry on a unifying theme. The Goals of varying secondary customers may then differ from those of the residents and of the internat itself.

Of late, communities have shown a greater readiness to accept released inmates. Severely handicapped, moderately disturbed persons, criminals with impressive records are released into the community—a development lauded by many as evidence of less rigid distinctions between the ill and the well, the disabled and the able. Secondary customers are said to now be more receptive than before because communities are more open (Kleinfeld, 1979). However, this pattern of "skimming" the internats for their most competent inmates leaves in its wake two other problems—multiple readmissions (the revolving-door phenomenon) and lack of competent role models for the internat population.

Early release from the internat is, no doubt, laudable, but it also leads to a high incidence of readmissions when the inmate's adaptation or his acceptance in the community is incomplete. Second, skimming removes the most competent of inmates, leaving those remaining with few models for acceptable behavior. In the process of producing evidence of its effectiveness ("Our inmates are being discharged"), the internat also reduces its capability for inducing change.

The revolving-door phenomenon offers an additional perspective on the mutual dependency of internat and community. Few internats are now perceived as proper permanent domiciles for anyone other than the old, monastics, and the terminally ill. Any other person who voluntarily remains in an internat is considered a failure; the blame is usually ascribed to the inmate and the internat, yet not to the community. When one looks at individual cases, though, responsibility is not so easily attributed:

> Ralph Lobaugh walked out of the Indiana State Prison in August after serving thirty years be-

hind bars for three murders that authorities were fully aware he didn't commit. But he had spent so much time in the maximum security institution that he could not cope with the freedom he had sought for fourteen years, and after only two months outside he returned to his cell. Lobaugh, sixty, told officials he could not relax on the outside, and went back behind the gray walls a week ago. He was reassigned his old cell and prison job. "He just got nervous and real excited and wanted to go back to prison," said Harold G. Roddy, director of Indiana's inmate work release program. "The man is institutionalized—he's just been locked up too damn long" ["Back in Prison," 1977, p. 30].

Prolonged internat residence is undesirable because it produces institutionalization, but early release is criticized for returning to the community persons who are not capable of living independently. In each instance, the secondary customers could conceivably be helpful by becoming "the strong friend outside" (Allerhand and others, 1966; Edgerton, 1967; Taylor and Alpert, 1973) that every person leaving an internat must have if he is to succeed on the outside. Fairweather (1964) attempted to build such a bridge as part of the internat, and Delancey Street Foundation is deliberately detached from any former place of incarceration (Hampden-Turner, 1976), but in both instances, one central task is to change the internee's image and self-image. Neither can be achieved if the internee's relevant others do not also change their image of the internee.

The full reintegration of former inmates is in considerable measure dependent on community imagery over which the internat has little control. Even secondary customers may perceive the internat as stigmatizing and consider the discharged inmate branded by disgrace. In addition to whatever stigma an inmate carried because of his initial low Mastery, the released inmate also takes home the mark of his internat. Insightful inmates understand that adaptation to the community requires a denial of one's former (and ongoing) self: "When I try to get a job they always ask me where I'm from. I don't tell nobody I'm from there [Pacific State Hospital]—I say I'm just an 'outsider' like anybody, but I've been working in the East. They want to know how long I've been away and I say that it's been pretty long. I don't tell anybody where I'm from, or I'd never get a job" (Edgerton, 1967, p. 151). Should they choose or be unable to deny their past, former inmates may partially integrate themselves into the community by accepting second-class citizenship. There are always jobs others do not want, employers for whom most persons choose not to work. Braly (1976), who spent many years in prison, never found it hard to get a job if he accepted these conditions.

Professionals who follow up on the released internee may not be helpful in adaptation, since they "typically do so by identifying the patient as a community deviant who entered his inferior status when he was diagnosed as mentally ill. [Or, we may add, as a criminal or retarded, or deficient on some other dimension of Mastery.] This is a particularly effective social device for sustaining the stigma because the patient tends to be seen in terms of a psychiatric label which too often stresses the pathological aspects of his behavior while overlooking his capacities and potentialities. By treating the ex-patient as a 'special' case needing further psychiatric attention, the patient is supplied with additional justification for various kinds of failure in the community" (Fairweather and others, 1969, p. 16).

Finally, a former inmate must have accepted in some measure the dependency created in the internat. Had he rejected such dependency he would have been considered overly troublesome and would most likely not have been recommended for return to the community. The long-time inmate, particularly a "well-adjusted" one like Mr. Lobaugh, found his niche in the internat. The outside world may indeed be a burden harder to bear than the inside. When the community provides justification for returning to the internat, including even a label such as recidivism or chronic illness, then why not take it at its word? Perversely, and despite professed discomfort with such an outcome, everyone gains. The primary customer returns to a familiar place, the secondary customer is rid of a difficult burden and discharges responsibility for failure to the internat, and the internat staff has continued rationale for their employment.

Suppliers: Labor and Money

Understandably, caretakers in internats find themselves on both sides of the deinstitutionalization argument. Formally, they must identify with the usually announced goals of moving every capable inmate to the community. Covertly, they desire to ensure job security as well. Thus, "the health workers' union —The American Federation of State, County and Municipal Employees—continues to support community-based care, provided *all workers' job rights are protected*" (Santiestevan, 1975, p. 34; italics added).

In tying their objection to closing internats with job security, staffs inadvertently confuse the issue. Central to the argument is the inevitability of some form of restricted environment for a certain proportion of a community's population. Many of the patients who are released during deinstitutionalization campaigns end up in other internats or even back in their own. The sad fact is that jobs will never be scarce in people-changing internats, no matter how many transformations in form and names they undergo. Objections to deinstitutionalization from the public-employee sector would have more credence as a defense of inmate rights if internats were not heavily *understaffed*. A reduction in the number of inmates should therefore lead to improved service.

Furthermore, as the example of Willowbrook—a New York internat for retarded persons—shows, these same inmates often are transferred to smaller, local units that still require staff. As a result of the court decision to reduce the population of Willowbrook, a major, well-financed, well-staffed effort was undertaken by an especially constituted agency. Several years after its establishment this agency—the Metropolitan Placement Center—reported that of the 5,300 Willowbrook residents in 1972, 70 percent were in internats and another 11 percent in ten- to fifteen-bed group homes—that is, small internats (data from personal communication by Carla Perlman, Feb. 2, 1979). About 9 percent of the population had died in the meantime— the only really final deinstitutionalization for some categories of internat residents.

Possibly part of the staff's concern about deinstitutionalization of inmates reflects their response to their own institutionalization. The more competent staff are likely to leave since they can find other employment. The less able remain, seeking shelter in the asylum. Though it was intended for others, *some* of the caretakers quietly and informally join the ranks of care recipients. As a prison group worker observes, complaining about another staff member, "What do you do with a guy like Harris? The system protects him. Under the state Civil Service regulations you can't even fire him for being incompetent" (Manocchio and Dunn, 1970, p. 52). Anyone familiar with internats knows that along with many care recipients there are also some caretakers who are unable to cope with the outside world (Rosenblatt, 1970). Rotenberg (in a personal communication) argues that perhaps some seemingly normal persons in democratic societies should be given the *right* to be dependent.

Many internats are unable to attract adequate personnel, and the understaffing of internats for stigmatized deviants is universal. The higher a position is on the competency and pay scale, the more acute the shortage appears to be. A U.S. presidential task force survey of 220 juvenile correctional institutions provides the following evidence (adapted from Carter, Glaser, and Wilkins, 1972, pp. 61-63):

	Number Needed	Number Available	Percentage of Deficiency
Psychiatrists	282	46	84%
Psychologists	282	182	36%
Caseworkers	1,413	926	34%
Teachers	2,827	2,495	12%

Even chaplains seemed to shun certain internats. The 220 state internats surveyed had sixty-two vacant chaplaincies. The report offers no data about the need for and availability of cottage staff, except to note that "under present salary schedules . . . even persons having not more than a high school education . . . are virtually unattainable. . . . One state report[ed] that some of its cottage staff [were] on public welfare" (Carter, Glaser, and Wilkins, 1972, p. 65).

Vacant positions are probably also a mark of high transiency. In the mental hospital described by Stanton and Schwartz (1954), "the problem of the loss to the hospital of experienced psychiatrists was generally recognized as a serious one, and was reflected in anxiety about a full-time staff, . . . [the nurses] were much more transient than the psychiatrists . . . [and] if the turnover of nurses was high, that for aides was much higher" (pp. 104-106).

High rates of staff attrition from certain internats is understandable. Personal care is psychologically very demanding. Even physical proximity among unrelated persons is considered awkward and uncomfortable in many cultures, particularly Northern European and North American (Hall, 1966). Yet, in the internat, be it prison or nursing home, hospital or developmental center, physical contact of the most intimate kind is part of the staff's function.

Few community members realize that to prevent prison riots or murders, a prison guard may well have to "go through all [an inmate's] clothing, from the sweaty socks and shoes, go through the lining of his shorts, the inside of his shirt and the lining of his trousers. Then to start on [the] body . . . the *entire* body! The armpits, spread his cheeks . . . look up there, into his ears, his mouth, . . . his hair, have him raise his balls to make sure he had nothing hidden there" (Manocchio and Dunn, 1970, p. 54).

Nor do people outside the internat really comprehend the meaning of working in a ward with profoundly retarded or markedly regressed aged like Mrs. M: "Mrs. M is totally incontinent. Came in to put her to bed and found her already in her nightgown. She had not been dressed all day. Her nightgown was soaked. Her urine had run down her legs, through her stockings, and into her shoes, which were now soaked also. . . . All she does is sit in her urine-soaked clothing all day, watching television" (Townsend, 1971, p. 59). Such an experience is not only physically unpleasant but also often emotionally draining in that a staff member's efforts are not reciprocated by inmates. Those with whom contact is rewarding are usually not found in internats for the mentally ill or severely retarded.

Besides manpower, adaptation of internat and community requires a well-moderated flow of yet another resource—money. Competition, regulation, and uncertainty govern this aspect of supply as well. Internat costs are very high. The annual cost of a child's residence in a well-supported correctional setting for juveniles or in a residential treatment center is now several times the mean wage of a factory worker. Mental hospitals, nursing homes, prisons, hospitals for the physically ill—all such settings, which characterize their inmates by disability, are costly. Not surprisingly, the community, in its anxiety over expenditure, advocates the earliest possible release of inmates.

On occasion, such concerns are well motivated. Gradual progression from labor-intensive, dependency-producing internat experiences to protected, but more demanding, settings has proved to be helpful (Fairweather, 1964; Miller, 1964; Wozner, 1965). However, although transitional settings are far less costly than internat care, many such settings cannot acquire sufficient funding. As a result, internats either prolong an inmate's stay—at great expense and to the inmate's disadvantage—or release the inmate to cope as best he can. Numerous recent studies of deinstitutionalization report this problem (Lander, 1975; Scull, 1977; Segal and Aviram, 1978). Santiestevan's (1975) title, *Deinstitutionalization: Out of Their Beds and into the Streets,* is more than merely a colorful, journalistic label for a serious social phenomenon of the 1970s and early 1980s. The current allocation of public funds for internat care does not provide well for halfway houses or other quasi-institutional settings.

A similar phenomenon was noted by one of us in Israel. Considerable resources were made available in order to contain and train a very aggressive population of youthful offenders. The method used was a *token economy,* under which behavioral acts carry rewards and penalties such that by accumulating sufficient tokens for good behavior an inmate can buy his way out of the closed internat. Many inmates responded quite well: Aggressive acts declined markedly, and a facility previously so dangerous that it had to be closed became manageable. Although inmates accumulated enough tokens to leave, they had nowhere to go except the streets. But most were no longer willing nor able to survive on the street. Yet the government refused to fund a transitional facility, a kind of open internat (Wozner and Lev, 1975).

At present, the public understands and funds total-care internats but appears not to understand the need for way stations, possibly functioning as transitional satellites of total internats, whose programs are more permissive yet still supportive. Funding is scarce for internats with open gates and without high walls, whose residents have reasonably high Mastery and need a structured transition to community life. Perhaps the public needs to be educated about the value of halfway houses, or perhaps the concept of halfway houses is disturbing in that it challenges clean distinctions between the normal and abnormal, the sick and the healthy. Perhaps, merely, transitional facilities do not yet have a specifically defined role in society. Somewhat like families, they are, nonetheless, not families. Like other social institutions (hotels, schools, lodging houses, Salvation Army dormitories), they are, however, intended to be protective. As they allow their residents greater independence than an internat, they also carefully increase the risk of failure to both inmate and society. As such, all operations of this kind are perhaps even more suspect than the internat.

Competitors

The internat's major competitor is the family, the only other total environment for care and growth. Nearly a century ago, Folks (1896) summarized the rationale for preferring family care to internat care for children:

> In the family there is an ever changing variety of interest; in the institution there is comparatively unbroken monotony.
> In the family, there is a gradual transition from the complete dependence of infancy to a larger measure of freedom and independence. . . .
> In the institution, on the other hand, there is of necessity a measure of restraint and repression which tends to obliterate individual distinctions, to discourage originality and inquiry.

>In the family there is an ever present con-
>sciousness of the necessity of making both ends
>meet. . . . In the institution . . . the children have
>practically no opportunity to learn the value of
>money.
>
>Another feature of life in the family . . . is
>that the child develops local relations and attach-
>ments which are a safeguard and an assistance in
>starting out in life. . . . The boy who is suddenly
>transferred from an institution . . . is an isolated
>unit.
>
>But perhaps the most important feature of
>family life . . . is the development of affections.
>Young children particularly need fathers and moth-
>ers [pp. 140-143].

Under normal circumstances families do indeed perform
all the functions an internat may assume and do so far more effectively and at lower cost to society. A family can care better
for the common cold than a hospital. It can usually control a
child so he does not play truant or steal from the corner market. It teaches the young, succors the aged, protects the somewhat retarded, and understands the somewhat disturbed. A
problem arises when demands for care exceed familial capability, either because the care recipient needs a great deal or because the family resources are limited. Thus a family's ability
to provide care is quite uneven over the various Mastery areas
relative to which internats socialize, conserve, heal, train, or
store people.

Socialization is usually needed by the young and by those
entering a new cultural milieu. The purpose is to give the novice
the values, behaviors, and attitudes he will need to be a member
of society. During socialization the novice is usually exempt
from a full member's responsibilities, but the general condition
is not perceived as deviant. Most socialization is, indeed, performed in familial settings.

Conservation is usually needed by the old or otherwise
debilitated. Conservation attempts to maintain the highest Mastery achieved by the individual, and capacity is retained through

functioning. A continued assessment of such individuals is necessary, and the setting must assume responsibility for risk and for compensating the deficiency. The declining size of modern families, the increase in the number of families in which both adults work, and the increased longevity of the aged seem to make such care difficult—there are simply not enough family members to help. An increasing number of old persons are in internats of various types.

Healing is necessary when a breakdown occurs in natural development and functioning. Persons with physical and mental illnesses and, by some definitions, criminal behavior require healing. Most healing functions in Western society are granted to internats. However, as we noted earlier, the peripheral areas are fuzzy and may be allotted to the family with outside assistance.

Training is considered appropriate when rapid modification is to be achieved in specific, often quite limited, dimensions of Mastery. Usually, training is necessary for the performance of certain tasks. When a career such as the priesthood, military, or civil service in the British Empire is sought, persons often enter an internat for training. Other training is usually accomplished by attendance at schools or institutes while the student resides with his family.

Storage is a covert but ever present function of both families and internats. In the most positive sense, storage is useful for the individual and society. Storage is necessary for individuals for whom no other social niche is available. Families hide their retardates, disturbed, and misbehaving. Internats also do so. Most inmates of prisons and many patients in mental hospitals are in storage while we learn how to help them or await their expiration.

Since families do socialize, conserve, heal, train, and store their members, every internat resident is a sign of some sort of familial inability to meet the needs of its special member. The family may be a willing customer—as are the families of future priests or military officers and those of the acutely, physically ill—that readily recognizes the superior capability of internats in meeting its unusual needs. However, families of reasonably

capable old, mentally ill, or retarded persons may be reluctant
or critical customers since the skills offered by internat staff are
little different from what they themselves often possess.

The family has good reasons to be suspicious of the internat, a family substitute. Despite their substantial capabilities,
internats may be deficient in caring, as Folks pointed out. Bettelheim (1950) is undoubtedly right that "love is not enough,"
but its absence from a socializing, treating, teaching, conserving,
or storing environment should be cause for great concern. All
such environments produce a measure of dependency of the
care recipient on the caretaker. The unequal relationship offers
opportunities for negligence, cruelty, abuse, and exploitation
(see Wolins, 1974b). To prevent such, society regulates internats.

Regulators

Formal regulatory groups are part of every internat's task
environment. Internats are licensed by state governments. They
are often required to have boards of directors as prerequisites for
joining prestigious bodies such as the Child Welfare League of
America or the American Hospital Association. They must meet
standards set by these organizations to qualify their programs
for reimbursement by state or national treasuries. Internats are
also regulated as to where they may locate (Lauber with Bangs,
1974), whom they may admit (Thomas, 1975b), what they
must or must not do while the inmate is confined (Johnson,
1975), whom they will employ, and what the conditions of employment will be.

Interaction between the internat and its regulatory
groups yields programmatic decisions. Standards produced by
certain national organizations provide examples. The executive
director of the Child Welfare League of America introduced its
1963 *Standards for Services of Child Welfare Institutions* by re-
ferring to the standards' purposes: "an opportunity to *think*
about what we are doing . . . [to] represent practices which are
considered to be *most desirable* for continuous improvement of
services. . . . The standards are directed to all who are concerned

with improvement of services. . . . The general public, citizen groups, public officials, legislators, and the various professional groups" (Child Welfare League of America, 1963, p. viii). In order to achieve their objectives, standards must be specific and operational and address every aspect of personal and organizational functioning.

To the extent such ground rules are defined and agreed upon, the interaction of regulators, customers, suppliers, and internat is made easier. The power to write such rules may be granted to a group representing the internats; the Joint Commission on Accreditation of Hospitals is a case in point. Such associations of internat representatives write their own rules, which are then accepted by all other actors in the task environment by virtue of the power and prestige of the rule makers. Training internats, monasteries, and military academies usually make their own rules largely because they claim exclusive expertise in their own areas.

In contrast, socialization, conservation, and storage internats are subject to considerable intrusion. Outsiders—the courts, state officials, legislators—usually write their rules, at times without consultation. In recent years court actions have shown that such intrusiveness causes serious operating problems (see Glazer, 1978). The courts decided who may or may not remain at Willowbrook, an internat for retarded, and what activities are proper. In 1973 the U.S. District Court (357 F. Supp. 752 [E.D. N.Y. 1973]), ruling in *New York State Association for Retarded Children, Inc.* v. *Rockefeller,* prohibited seclusion of residents, required a staff-to-resident ratio of 1:9, ordered the immediate hiring of at least eighty-five nurses, thirty physical therapy staff, and fifteen physicians, and ordered the immediate repair of inoperable toilets. Similar external regulation of prisons, nursing homes, and mental hospitals is common.

Society generally imposes regulation on dependent individuals and social organizations as part of requirements for support. However, modern developmental theory holds that individuals and groups tend to achieve more independence, individuation, and growth when external regulation is minimal. We see that, for example, external control over the behavior of families

who receive public support has been declining, yet regulation of
internats has increased. Greater public intrusiveness into the activities of internats—licensing, standards, reporting, and inspec-
tions—is viewed as responsible action to improve the quality of
internat care. In this sense, the internat is treated as yet another
bureaucracy, whose behavior must be carefully monitored so
that untoward activity will not occur. Such controls constrain,
often drastically, the freedom of action within the internat.
Thus regulation serves two somewhat contradictory effects: it
protects inmates from potential exploitation or abuse by an
internat, yet it also constrains the internat's freedom to effect
Reclaiming.

Several particularly troublesome external activities result
from (and also further) internat dependency in its adaptation to
the environment: unrequested beneficence, unreasonable demands for reporting, requirements for overly rapid change, and
structural rigidity. In Chapter Three, we noted two examples of
unrequested benevolence: the design of the Bronx Developmental Center and the gift of totally unneeded school desks to a
Jewish internat in New York to maintain political balance when
a Catholic facility was sent desks it requested. Moreover, since
the ultimate suppliers of goods and services to the internat are
in the market economy, it is not unusual for large political contributors to promote decisions irrelevant or even inimical to an
internat's goals. To locate a new hospital, prison, or other internat in the jurisdiction of a powerful legislator or in an out-of-
the-way tract is to allow political needs to defeat social needs.
Only recently was a federal hospital located in a Louisiana
parish because its congressman chaired a powerful committee.
The hospital stands nearly vacant.

Regarding reporting, certainly a dependent system should
report on how the public largess is spent; however, the volume
of paperwork now required is prodigious. By analogy, regular
review by social workers was at one time a requirement for welfare families. Although a most ineffective way to produce accountability, the system persisted for many years. It ended not
because of the inconsequentiality of data produced but because
of the massive manpower needed to produce it. The relationship

between reporting and activity is aptly expressed by Cohn's law, developed by an insightful officer in the Israeli Air Force, "The more time spent on reporting what is being done, the less time there is to do it. Stability is achieved when all the time is spent reporting on the nothing being done."

Rapid change is a third aspect of internat's adaptation. Rapid change is demanded of internats when theories of care and treatment shift. When knowledge is inadequate and theories of intervention fluid, the proscription of one era may become the prescription of another. Builders of the Bronx Developmental Center experienced such a shift when the stylistic standards for a desirable building changed during construction. Theories about how best to change Mastery are notoriously unstable. But internats guided by these theories cannot quickly adjust to changing trends. Change would require retraining of staff in the new theory, retraining of inmates to new routines, and even redesign and reallocation of the internat's physical plant. Internats cannot change their coloration in instant response to an environmental or theoretical shift.

Reporting and controlling call for uniformity. When some "higher" authority decides it knows what is good and what should be done or reported, it should, and logically does, press for such activity. In the recent past social workers made up budgets by reviewing the needs of welfare recipients. It was not unusual in America for Anglo-Saxon dietary habits to be used in determining the market basket of California Chicano families or retired, indigent Jews in Miami. Individuation, the very heart of a good developmental setting, was thus undermined. This is no longer practiced with families, but it is still the pattern regarding many internats.

Finally, the effect of external rigidity on internat Activity is illustrated by the following example. A state agency recently decided that a central kitchen would provide meals for five internats located in one city. The internats included in this arrangement were two halfway houses for delinquents, a residential treatment center for the severely retarded, a training college for counselors, and a classification center for neglected and wayward girls. The internats' directors argued that each internat needed different food, different spacing of meals, and different involvement of inmates. Additionally, one internat's program required that residents pay for their meals. The state made some adjustments; but the major adaptation was made by the internats. Subsequent revisions of meal arrangements had to be abandoned because the contract could be renegotiated only once a year. The internats adapted at a cost in lost individuality, increased dependency, lower creativity, and public criticism.

Standard specificity, while protective of the inmate, carries the risk of rigidity, toward which internats have a natural proclivity. Consider a rule that says that, in the interest of safety, children not be permitted to work in the internat kitchen. Although the rule seems reasonable, it prohibits a child whom the staff find capable of handling the risk and who wants to become a chef from entering the kitchen. An attempt to modify the rule to exempt such a child would require negotiations with numerous and remote regulators. Most internats would have neither the time nor the resources to do so; surrender is safer and simpler. The authors know of one internat for disturbed and disturbing adolescents whose staff decided that the best placement for one of their wards was an elegant, elitist boarding school nearby. The cost to the state would have remained the same, and the internat's responsibility would have continued. The ward's consent was obtained, but state regulators vetoed the proposal on the grounds that their rules did not authorize placement in a private boarding school that was unlicensed to accept dependent children (and of course the school had no desire for such stigmatizing licensing by the state's welfare department).

Professionals

While forced standardization is the lot of many internats, some are successful in asserting their individuality. Their assertiveness is usually the result of outstanding leadership: Aichhorn, Makarenko, Korczak, Bettelheim, Menninger, Kirkbride, and John Maher were not confined by the models of their times. These creative and forceful leaders not only developed fresh ideas about the internat but also used their individual settings as firm platforms from which to produce programs of general social utility. In their creative internats they tested knowledge that affected the surrounding communities. Leaders like Makarenko, Korczak, or Bettelheim, though primarily known for the internats they developed, also had a good deal to say about the family, the other form of total care.

Such leaders, however, are rare. At best, internats have a strong professional staff who, aware of new work within their professions, bring new ideas and knowledge to the internat (see Hage and Aiken, 1970). However, except for hospitals treating the physically ill, where continuing education is considered essential to competent practice, most internats do not usually exchange information with professionals outside the internat system. Professional staff is often not of the highest quality. Turnover is high, and contact between the professionals and other caretakers is variously impaired (see, for example, Piliavin, 1963; Polsky and Claster, 1968; Stanton and Schwartz, 1954).

Administrators of such settings, having a difficult course to navigate in any case, tend to fall back on the easiest alternative—the smallest change tolerable. Hopkins, who attempted to introduce a new technology into an internat for the mentally ill, illustrates this: "After our project had been underway for a year, the head of the service called a meeting to discuss the special educator's program. Although the ostensible purpose of the meeting was to 'evaluate' the program, the director terminated the program without even looking at the data. . . . We invited the director of the service to share the data . . . [but] he was always indisposed on any available date. Similarly, he could see no value in teaching behavior modification techniques to attendants—'You don't want to bother with them' " (Hopkins, 1970, pp. 363-364).

Yet internats can make a contribution to general knowledge and practice. Ayllon and Azrin (1968), for example, tested behavior modification principles in mental hospital wards, and their findings suggested the possible use of such principles in families (Patterson, 1971). Bettelheim (1950) tested techniques for dealing with autistic children. Aichhorn (1935) experimented with various approaches to misbehavior. Neill's (1960) educational theories of self-determination have been widely adopted, and Pestalozzi's ([1801] 1915) philosophy and methodology of child rearing have been applied by others. All these theoretical and technical formulations, first developed within an internat, eventually found applications outside the internat.

On the contrary, external technology and particularly outside professional behavior, although acceptable in the community, may well be dysfunctional within the internat. Professionals tend to categorize problems in a way that leads to negative labeling and firm segregation of treaters and treated. Within the close confines of an internat, such marked separation of various subgroups through labeling undermines the program by reinforcing the negative image of inmates (see Goffman, 1961; Trieschman, Whittaker, and Brendfro, 1969).

Even professional behavior that is perceived by inmates as posturing will meet with considerable resistance, as a prisoner's description of a prison psychiatrist illustrates: "He hates it when I call him Louis, or, even worse, Louie, especially when others are present. He feels that as a psychiatrist he should always be addressed as Dr. Palow—not even just plain Doctor. The first few weeks he was here, he wore a long, white coat while conducting interviews in his office. Maybe they still do that in Europe, where he was trained. At any rate, the white coat sure kept the inmates at a distance, although some were impressed and loved it. Finally, one day, the white coat disappeared. . . . I feel he is a phony. But the department has something going about window dressing their institutions with psychiatrists in order to impress the public and the legislature" (Manocchio and Dunn, 1970, pp. 91-92).

Finally, the ties that an internat's professionals maintain outside the internat are problematic in yet another way. A unifying theme is essential if an internat is to model and reward goal-oriented behavior. The definitions of acceptable and unacceptable behavior must be standard throughout the internat; they cannot individually be subjects of prescription or proscription. But an internat's unifying theme may be undermined if the primary orientation of staff is to individual disciplines, professions, or associations.

Deterrence, Exclusion, and Permeability

The builders of old English prisons adapted them to their assigned tasks in the community. Heavy cornices, small windows with bars, a few massive and well-guarded doors set in tall, impenetrable walls were their prescription. A prison was to be foreboding, casting fear upon the potential transgressor. To be an effective deterrent, the prison was located in the center of a city ("Prisons," 1826). The legacy of such thinking persists to our times, for physical structures are far more permanent than the social expectations governing their use.

In the nineteenth century, though, the internat's deterrence by its physical presence was outweighed by its nuisance value to the good citizen. Symbolic deterrence was judged sufficient. With the additional rationalization about the benefits of the pastoral idyll, the prison and mental hospital, internats for retardates or orphans, and, of course, the contagious tubercular were dispatched to the countryside. There, they joined the leprosarium, banished much earlier. The internat's isolation from the community was almost complete.

Although in recent years internats have gradually, often stealthily, moved back into town, only the smallest and most innocuous have been granted a modicum of acceptance. Here is the dilemma in the planning of internat environments: While social proximity enhances adaptation, physical proximity of an internat arouses community hostility. Following a study of internat acceptability in Green Bay, Wisconsin, Knowles and Baba (1973) concluded that even group homes (perhaps the least obtrusive of all internats) are viewed negatively by some 20 percent of their immediate neighbors. Rate of rejection declines with distance; few people object to an internat in someone else's neighborhood. Most communities write their zoning ordinances so that internats are excluded from good residential areas (Lauber with Bangs, 1974).

The recognition that setting and structure are important to adaptation has not changed since the London planners proposed their prison, but consequences have. Although location within the community is now considered optimal, exclusion is the almost universal practice. The public recognizes that buildings are used in the transaction between inmate, staff, and community but resents any undue intrusion on the prerogatives of the able, the well, and the law-abiding. To adapt to such constraints internats are sometimes compelled to a certain amount of deception and self-deception.

Both internats and the public understand the effects of setting and structure on an internat's public image and self-image. Both are concerned with the way in which an internat's architecture labels its inhabitants. Recent tendencies, as the Bronx Developmental Center shows even in its name, are toward mainstreaming, the integration of persons with various handicaps into environments normal for their age group. Mainstreaming has also been applied to site and structure. As an English publication on design stresses, "all residential establishments will in the future be known as *community homes*" (Advisory Council, 1971, p. 6; italics added).

Inconspicuous architecture does not stigmatize inmates, whereas unusual architectural features—bars on windows and locked gates—indicate that inmates are a danger to the outside (or, on rare occasions, that the outside is a threat to them). Ramps, railguards, and special signs indicate that residents have limited competence. Slum or remote location of an internat suggests that the residents may be ignored.

Of course, locational and structural labeling may also be positive. As Delancey Street members found out, residents of a mansion in a prestigious neighborhood of San Francisco are not perceived as criminals. In short, we all resist cognitive dissonance—a phenomenon often ignored in planning the design and location of internats. Delancey Street may be unique, but it is not alone in using site and structure to carry a positive message to the community outside. A children's internat, the very type of facility receiving much of the abolitionists' wrath, can do likewise. The lovely cottages of SOS Kinderdorf at Wienerwald, the well-kept lawns, the ornate but open gate—all constitute invitations to the outsiders' visits and, in turn, invite a positive evaluation of what transpires inside.

The open gate at Wienerwald is both reality and symbol. It stands for permeability. An internat's residents can model their own behavior on that of the external community only through contact, which is a function of physical proximity and the absence of barriers. The Bronx Developmental Center is again a case in point. The site of this expensive facility is bounded by industrial buildings and a highway—neither likely to provide models of behavior for the residents or opportunities for relating to the outside. Furthermore, the architects focused the building around interior courts. Thus, the available models are those interior to the setting, narrow in their range and external appropriateness.

Planning for contacts is essential, but unilateral and bilateral permeability require different physical constraints. The prison and military academy represent the extremes of unilateral openness. In the prison, screened and supervised outsiders may come in, but the exit of prisoners is very restricted. In contrast, the military academy, wishing to maintain a powerful internal environment, is more inclined to let inmates out than to permit visitors. Such control over access, while projecting exclusivity and mystery, also reflects a fear of physical, behavioral, and moral contagion. In settings for handicapped persons, control over unilateral inflow is particularly difficult because of the inmates' physical or psychological incapacity. If contact is desired outsiders must be admitted within the internat, which reduces its control and power.

Allowing each of the three populations—patients, staff, outsiders—their individual and proper ranges is more complex, yet paradoxically, less troublesome when bilateral flow is desired. Structures allowing the bilateral flow of persons are based on the assumed capability of inmates to sustain it. A strong integrative structure allows the internat to control both the behavior of outsiders when they come in and any contacts by insiders with the outside. The openness of Delancey Street is a case in point. Control is not lodged in physical design but rather in social mechanisms (Hampden-Turner, 1976). This inevitable relationship between the physical and social fields is often ignored by architects.

Even physical risk may be controlled by social devices. Next to a large boarding school in the Soviet Union was a beautiful lake, an alluring place to swim during the summer and to skate in winter. But some accidents had occurred; swimmers had ventured too far, and skaters had set out on ice too thin. The administration considered fencing the lake, but decided rather to make it a focus of explanation and instruction and, if that failed, to apply social sanctions against transgressors. Sadly, many internats choose physical restrictiveness rather than devising social rules.

Moreover, when organizational and individual evaluations of risk and its consequences are divergent, organizational considerations usually prevail. As Sommer (1969, p. 93) points out, "the shelters mental patients would design for themselves differ markedly from what society has provided or is likely to provide in the future to meet its own needs." Risk is a major issue in this divergence. Consider the building regulations governing almost all internat facilities: "These regulations involve special plan arrangements, special exit requirements, the use of special building materials and special construction. The resulting 'specialness' adds another stigma to an already difficult life" (Sokoloff, 1976, p. 329).

Why is the internat resident denied the usual, normal dignity of risk taking? Because "officials want to be sure that no one comes to harm. . . . They are understandably concerned with their own legal and moral liability in case of accidents" (Sokoloff, 1976, p. 329). Planning for risk is particularly problematic when the internat serves individuals of progressive Mastery. Sokoloff proposes that residents, upon passing a proper "escape time" test at a level customary in the community be allowed to use a facility without, for example, special fire safety provisions.

A physical plant always implies both danger *and* growth-promoting opportunities. The administrator's perception of risk is often merely a matter of accelerated or otherwise increased consumption of facilities. Since substantial numbers of internat residents are confined by virtue of intolerable behavior, designers are encouraged to use appliances and materials able to withstand abuse. Such high-tolerance design is, nevertheless, also a source of difficulty. Sokoloff (1975, p. 21a), designing for retarded populations, emphasizes that unnecessary hazards should be avoided, but "the facility should not be designed to withstand intolerable behavior which then allows such behavior to be tolerated."

Design that assumes reasonable behavior of inmates requires high maintenance, repair, and replacement and higher risk if the inmates are aggressive or disabled. However, designed risk is sensible only if used to promote developmental gain. Baseboard-level electrical outlets in a toddler's environment or double swinging doors in a home for the aged are risks that carry danger without gain. Other opportunities for exploration can be offered the child, and less capricious instruments to test the agility of the aged are also available.

As illustrated by the preceding examples, considerations of personal and organizational risk lead to different design consequences. In most instances the former tend toward choice, normalcy, and simplicity; the latter toward standardization, elaboration, and constriction. To be sure, every environment, and internats in particular, must have some features designed to compensate for failures in individual Mastery (Lindsley, 1964). Unfortunately, the heterogeneity of its population and changes in population over time predispose the internat to create an environment suited to the lowest competence level. Although such an environment meets the internat's organizational needs, it serves badly the more competent inmate who needs exposure to greater risk.

For individuals capable in all but one dimension of Mastery, the overly restricted environment is a particularly serious impediment. Consider an adolescent hospitalized for a physical illness: "Just . . . when the adolescent has achieved a degree of independence and is not restricted territorially . . . he finds himself in a hospital where activity, time, and space are structured for him. . . . [He] may express his fears and anxiety through excessive assertions of independence from routine, violence and damage to hospital property, or defiance of rules relative to school work, sex, smoking, or drugs" (Lindheim, Glaser, and Coffin, 1972, p. 90). If the restricted environment is perceived by the inmate as an overly protective cocoon, he may strike out against it in self-defense.

An opposite reaction may occur in the aged, the mentally

retarded, or severely disturbed. Lawton (1974) posits an "environmental docility hypothesis," implying a correlation between Mastery and the physical environment. Whereas the adolescent may rebel, the geriatric or psychiatric patient may show apathetic acceptance—a passivity often called hospitalitis, prisonitis or institutional neurosis. Again the internat sets the limits and its organizational needs prevail, while the individual's need for growth is ignored.

Given the internat's responsibility for its inmates, some risks in plant design cannot be allowed, and the physical consequences of such restrictiveness are unavoidable. A warden's task includes preventing prisoners from escaping. The aged, very young, or disturbed may easily fall prey to exploitive intruders, and the internat should be designed to reduce such risk. A benevolent asylum—which prevents the inmates' coming to harm and provides opportunities for contact, manipulation, improvisation, and adaptation—is difficult to achieve. Lack of security in physical design is unacceptable. Maximal security may be stifling by its constraints.

Societal Aspects of Adaptation

As the recent deinstitutionalization drive illustrates, society's attitude toward its internats is often uneasy. Not all internats are criticized, however. Gmeiner's SOS Kinderdörfer have worldwide support at the very height of fervor in opposition to childrens' internats (see Wooden, 1976, for an example of outcry against "institutional child abuse"). Understandably, as social circumstances change, society's expectations of internats also shift, and changed expectations of childrens' internats reflect the evolution of interest in all internats.

Even the briefest historical review shows that as societies became more humane, they changed the means for dealing with deviants. Having abolished most executions and banishments, societies resorted to various forms of controlled group environments for deviants. The object was detention and possible treatment of the disturbing one. The dungeon, which earlier functioned to exaggerate punishment or to permit long-term neglect, now became the prison, the mental hospital, and the medical hospital—where a goal of improved Mastery was announced. The new social institution resembled the old elitist establishment in that both tried to produce changes in the personal characteristics of inmates. The monastery and the eighteenth- and nineteenth-century prison strove for a higher moral level. The new orphanage provided for cognitive growth, like the distinguished, centuries-old public school or yeshiva.

Gradually the methods of internats for the elites and those for the deprived or even for the deranged also seemed to converge. Only the entrants and end products did not. Benevolent methods could now be used for people of whom society disapproved. Society demanded, yet at the same time could not accept, equal treatment for persons with such different pasts and probably different futures. Society's claim that the goal of all internats is maximal expansion of Mastery sounds hollow against the clear separation, on many levels, between the elite boarding school, the juvenile hall, and the residential treatment center.

Although the primary public image of today's internat is that of a failing instrument of Reclaiming, the internat has at least one additional declared social task: control. One may argue that all Reclaiming is no more than a device of social control. Foucault (1979, p. 231) describes the evolution of the prison farm to make this point: "The prison farm antedates its systematic use in the penal system. It had already been constituted outside the legal apparatus when, throughout the social body, procedures were being elaborated for distributing individuals, fixing them in space, classifying them, abstracting from them the maximum in time and forces, training their bodies, coding their continuous behaviour, maintaining them in perfect visibility, forming around them an apparatus of observation, registration and recording, constituting on them a body of knowledge that is accumulated and centralized."

Maximal control over unwanted, disturbing members could be achieved by using the internat instrumentality. Szasz (1970) argues that control has been a primary function of mental hospitals. Daniel Defoe, in his time, agitated against the use

of internats as a means of controlling wives. Defoe objected to
"the vile practice now so much in vogue among the better sort,
as they are called, but the worst sort in fact, namely, that of
sending their Wives to Mad-Houses at every Whim or Dislike"
(Hunter and Macalpine, 1963, pp. 266-267). (This is yet another example of the reciprocal relationship of internat and
family.)

Control if carried to an extreme reduces Reclaiming to a
mere caricature. The isolation cells of nineteenth-century penitentiaries may have changed the morality of some inmates. How
many actually made peace with their Creator we will never
know, since many went raving mad in the process (Beaumont
and de Tocqueville, [1836] 1964). Similarly, the prison execution, following a session with clergy, saves the soul, as a last act
of desperation over the behavior of the inmate's body. The
saved soul signifies social Reclaiming, which for some is tanta-
mount to integrated Reclaiming.

All internats aim to transform. Physical constraints may
be the most obvious means of affecting behavior; social pressure, threats, and inspiration are less blatant, but to the extent
they are employed in the people-changing process, their intention is the same: "The whole history of human development has
engaged man in an endless struggle for control. . . . Control of
individuals has not been easy though, especially control of their
inner lives, where hope and will reside" (London, 1969, p. 3).
Control of any attribute is more easily achieved in an internat
than outside. All forces within such a setting may be directed to
transform and reclaim. Granted such power, the internat inevitably must control. The intensity of its control depends on the
combination of agent and controlling mechanism. There are
four such combinations, presented in an ascending order of
preference in an open democratic society:

1. An external agent and tangible control amount to coercion.
2. An external agent and symbolic control signify persuasion.
3. Internal and tangible control may be seen as self-discipline.
4. Internal, symbolic control manifests itself as conscience,
   conviction, belief.

The move from control of the body through external
agents began, according to Foucault (1979, p. 16), toward the
end of the eighteenth century; over the last 200 years the soul
has increasingly become both the locus and the means of control. But control by internal forces and symbolic mechanisms is
less tractable and possibly more to be feared than earlier forms
of control. We no longer make spectacles of public execution,
but we do have psychiatric patients dazed by large doses of
thorazine. The advent of chemical and surgical means to alter
convictions, influence conscience, and affect belief makes internal, symbolic control as fearsome as physical coercion. While
some internat operations have reflected the efforts of their or-
ganizers (and a more humane society) to move from physical
coercion to other means of control, who can tell what will be
acceptable as each of these is, in turn, discarded.

Preparation of Elites. Most discussions ignore the very
significant function of internats in preparing elites. The social
expectation for the elite internats is that they lead but do so
within the framework of an accepted social order. The English
public school and West Point are both examples of social control exercised through the training of elites: "The official statements of the [English public] schools, at Speech Day, in chapel
sermons, and in brochures, still emphasize the necessity of training boys in a Christian way so they will be able to bear the privilege and responsibility of rule" (Weinberg, 1967, p. 55). The
leadership mission of West Point is well depicted in a statement
by General Westmoreland, who assumes that cadets "have a
sacred trust to provide the dedicated leadership and service to
our nation which is so essential to our national security. I certainly view this, and I'm sure you [the cadets] view it, as a very
high calling and a noble cause" (quoted by Furgurson, 1968, p.
288).

These internats have had no difficulty in meeting the expectations for leadership. Rather, they become suspect as
potential dangers to presumably egalitarian societies. Of late,
both the boarding school and the military academy have come
under attack: "Some of the great publicists on the Left, such as
[George Bernard] Shaw and [H. G.] Wells, call for the abolition

of the public schools as citadels of privilege" (Public Schools Commission, 1968, p. 19). Similarly, critics of West Point claim that "these idealistic youths are taught a set of values and attitudes designed to produce an officer who believes he is morally and intellectually superior to those he is charged to protect . . . whose self-imposed mission is to determine our country's destiny. . . . Should Americans trust an institution that produces men who don't trust them? We think not" (Galloway and Johnson, 1973, pp. 17-18). Among the elitist internats only the religious ones—monasteries, yeshivot, and the like—seem to be immune from the contradictory expectations of simultaneous elitism and conformity.

Unclear Definition of Reclaiming. Any lack of correspondence between social Reclaiming and integrated Reclaiming is a major source of difficulty in modern internats. A definition of Reclaiming that involves a consideration of inmates' well-being came late in the evolution of internats. It was an act of grace. Reformers like Philippe Pinel and Dorothea Dix saw a possibility for humanitarian Reclaiming that combined control and preparation or treatment. Society's need for control and the individual's needs could both be addressed under carefully guarded circumstances. The medical model was helpful here. Limits were to consist of place (the hospital) and of time. Troubled and troublesome were to be saved like the physically sick in the hospital and prepared like the elite in their academy. For a *limited time only* they were to have the rights of human beings and few social obligations. This humane attitude epitomized the spirit of the nineteenth-century reformatory and the moral treatment hospital.

Foucault (1979) observes that the transition from the scaffold and other inhumane treatment to incarceration was an act of humanity. So also was the transition from a social definition of Reclaiming to an integrated definition that included the best interests of inmates. This was, indeed, progress over the premise that "terror acts powerfully on the body through the medium of the mind, and should be employed in the cure of madness" (Rush, [1812] 1962, p. 211). However, progress in the internat was uneven. Control by any means, including torture and death, gave way to preparation for social utility and emphasis on the rights of inmates. Social expectations were changing regarding acceptable outcome *and* tolerable process. Yet, some previous goals remained to be incorporated in the new expectations. Control is still a significant component of Reclaiming. But in process and outcome, more emphasis is placed on the rights of inmates.

Once only mechanisms for social control, reformatories, hospitals for the mentally ill, and prisons are evolving into means for enhancing the individual. The societal intent for the "graduates" of internats is indeed as John Stuart Mill demanded in his treatise *On Liberty* ([1859] 1955, p. 18), that they be "the proper guardian[s] of [their] own health, whether bodily, or mental and spiritual." So long as they do not infringe on socially fixed boundaries, we should add. But progress has been uneven: Some American psychiatrists still practice electroshock therapy, and terror as a means to Reclaiming has not been completely abolished.

The definition of integrated Reclaiming also affects conditions of confinement. Personal rights are defined more broadly. The inmate is offered more choices, even when they imply greater risk to others, as societal safety is balanced against inmates' personal freedom. Folks, that most insightful of nineteenth-century social reformers, foreshadowed this development: "The reformatory is, first and foremost, a place to which criminal children are sent to be reformed; and the implication is, in the case of every child thus committed, that the community was obliged in self-defense to place it behind bars. Just as the criminal discharged from prison finds it difficult or impossible to reinstate himself in society, so the boy discharged from the reformatory finds himself branded with the trademark of crime" (1891, p. 137). In Folks's formulation of Reclaiming, society owes not only protection to itself but expansion of Mastery for the reformed boy.

More recently, American jurisprudence has further specified the definition of integrated Reclaiming by dictating criteria for admission and requirements for Activity. Inmates have rights. They may demand their freedom, and they may demand treatment. "On June 26, 1975, the U.S. Supreme Court ruled in the case of *O'Connor* v. *Donaldson,* that a state cannot constitutionally confine 'a nondangerous individual who is capable of surviving solely in freedom by himself or with the help of willing and responsible family members or friends' " (Thomas, 1975b, p. 3). In short, anyone whose Mastery is high enough and is not considered dangerous may not be forcefully incarcerated. If admitted to the internat, he must be treated. Criminals are not covered by this ruling, in that they may be perceived as dangerous, but the rapidly climbing probation and parole rates (Scull, 1977; U.S. Department of Justice, 1977) indicate that those who are considered nondangerous and responsible are not being confined. Moreover, confined persons "have a constitutional right to receive such individual treatment as will give each of them a reasonable opportunity to be cured or to improve his or her mental condition" (*Wyatt* v. *Stickney,* 325 F. Supp. 781, 784 [M.D., Ala. 1971]). Recent legislation (H.R. 9400, labeled "A Bill of Rights for the Institutionalized") allows the U.S. Attorney General to file suit on behalf of care recipients of nursing homes, mental hospitals, and other facilities for the chronically ill.

The dual expectation of protecting individual rights while Reclaiming inmates poses some serious dilemmas for the internat. For example, an inmate may by right be entitled to the shortest residency possible, but public outcry results should a released inmate commit antisocial acts. Internats are supposed to shelter those unable to live in the community and reintegrate those who are able to do so. But to shelter individuals is to isolate them and thus impair their adaptation. Overly restricted inmates revolt or, more likely, abandon themselves to total dependency. Although prison revolts make headlines, institutional neurosis is the far more prevalent and more consequential phenomenon. When inmates surrender to apathy, staff become omnipotent and may exploit, rather than treat, inmates (see Deutsch, 1948, on mental hospitals; Wicker, 1975, on prisons; Wooden, 1976, on internats for children.) As we noted earlier, some staff members themselves surrender to total dependency (see Rosenblatt, 1970, pp. 135-136).

Deviance and Normalization. However, the definition of who cannot be returned to the community is always fluid. Ordinarily, this group includes the fully disabled, the depraved, and the physically dangerous. At times, however, persons of truly high Mastery are similarly perceived. Of necessity, such collectives of the unwanted develop their own lifestyle quite distinct from those outside. When the lifestyle results from deliberate choice—as in monasteries or academies—the difference may be carried as a badge of honor. For both compelled and self-selected exiles, the relationship to the world outside is marked by hesitancy and even fear, feelings particularly intense at the time of exit.

In a survey of released retardates Edgerton (1967, p. 147) notes that "release from the hospital was indeed the beginning of their right to live like anybody else, but it was emphatically not the end of their problems, nor of their need for passing and denial. They now had to face the multiple challenges of living independently in the 'outside' world."

And even within the internat the inmates with higher Mastery attempt to make themselves wanted on the outside by claiming to be "normal": "I never belonged there [an internat for retardates] in the first place, and then they made me stay eighteen years with all those crazy people and people that had to be taken care of. It was terrible, it was like they thought there was something like that wrong with me" (Edgerton, 1967, p. 59).

The line between those deemed to require institutionalization and those deemed able to live within the community is very thin. Criteria change constantly. Who must stay in and who may come out are determined by forces outside the internat. A recent example pertains to the physically disabled: "They see themselves as an oppressed minority. They demand access to America. . . . More and more of them are joining forces against a society they feel prefers to treat them as patients or charity cases—and deny them their rights" (Gliedman, 1979, p. 59).

If internats are to prepare more of their residents to lead independent lives in the community, they must gradually reduce the dissimilarity between the inner world of internat and the outer world. Competent inmates must be allowed to develop their roles as workers, or spouses, or parents—the roles that normal adults assume. Internats must reduce the distinction between caretakers and care recipients, between the abnormal ones inside and the normal ones outside.

If the inmate is to achieve normal behavior both he and society must be transformed. A reliable technology must help the inmate, and society must feel secure enough to accept former inmates into the community. Neither of these conditions obtains at this time for almost anyone but the physically ill. In few communities do former and potential residents of internats press for full access as they do in Berkeley, California where the Center for Independent Living helps physically disabled persons who wish to live in the community and organizes political activity within the community for public transportation, jobs, and housing for the disabled (Kleinfeld, 1979). And even fewer communities respond constructively.

In rising to meet society's conflicting expectations, internats are frequently accused of failing at their goals and perpetrating unacceptable or inhumane methods. Society wants its internats to reflect social concern, the humanity of caring—not rejection, fiscal niggardliness, punitiveness, or confusion. Society's message to internats is somewhat similar to the schizophrenic message often found in family situations: "It's not that you should *do* something different; you should *be* different. Only in this way can you help me to be what I'm not, but what I could be if you were not what you are" (Palazzoli and others, 1978, p. 36).

Adaptation and Values

"Man's chief purpose," wrote Lewis Mumford, "is the creation and preservation of values: that is what gives meaning to our civilization, and the participation in this is what gives significance, ultimately, to the individual human life" (1940, p. 208). As an instrument of society, the internat is charged with transmitting and preserving values. Whenever an internat accepts someone for care it may either continue and reinforce the resident's values or attempt to change them.

Monasteries and yeshivot are, basically, devices for continuation and reinforcement. Values propagated in the community are brought to their fullest blossoming—a luxury that no society could extend to the many but that every society bestows on a few. Similarly, Khrushchev's interest in developing a cadre of *stroiteli Komunizma* [builders of communism] fueled the massive drive for *shkoly internaty* [boarding schools] in the Soviet Union during the 1950s (see Weeks, 1974). Underlying even these efforts to purify and reinforce values is value change. To some degree the monastery, the yeshiva, and the Soviet boarding school engage in conversion. True, most of the entrants come voluntarily for reinforcement, but the system as a whole continuously reaches out, accepts nonbelievers, and educates them in its values.

Not all potential converts enter voluntarily. Stealth, deception, and economic pressure have been used to coerce people into such environments. For example, the Turkish Janizaries were small boys taken as war booty and forcefully inducted into internat life. Indian boarding schools in early twentieth-century America were incomparably more open and more voluntary yet, to some extent, pervaded by a conversionist zeal: "Removal from home and tribe was viewed as necessary for diminution of Indian identity" (Fuchs and Havighurst, 1972, p. 224). Opportunities for reinforcement and change are offered by every internat. Although West Point cadets enter voluntarily and prisoners enter Sing Sing under compulsion, both enter internats that are intended to defend society and particularly its values.

Although designed to defend social values, internat life may be seen as a danger to society by virtue of its otherness. This danger is not attributed to internats for a minuscule and morally exemplary elite, but internats intended to help deviant inmates achieve normalcy promote a collectivism that conflicts with the individualism lauded in the Western world. In any society, collectivist assumptions undermine familial values because collectivism places the good of the collective above loyalty to the family. For example, both Nazi and communist collectivism turned family members against one another. Soon after the Russian Revolution, some of Lenin's extreme followers, led by

Aleksandra Kollontai, advocated the abolition of the family in favor of collectivist child rearing, food preparation, and housing. But all such collectivist movements have been short lived. Even the far milder collectivism of the Israeli kibbutz as depicted by Spiro (1956) or Darin-Drabkin (1962) has gradually developed some of the features of the family structure (Gerson, 1980).

The family experience denied by an internat's collectivist mode is considered essential to individual and societal survival. "The more the family and community become foreign to the individual, so much the more does he become a mystery to himself, unable to escape the exasperating and agonizing question: to what purpose?" (Durkheim, [1897] 1951, p. 212). An internat, remote from family and community, may be seen as antithetical to the very survival of society its Reclaiming functions are intended to foster. Some evidence supports this view and the inevitability of such an outcome. Spitz and Wolf's (1946) institutionalized infants, deprived of maternal care, developed anaclitic depression just like Durkheim's adult subjects, who suffered anomie.

Internats threaten a society's values in yet another way. All internats are, by definition, collectivities of unusual persons. Both persons of unusually high Mastery and those of unusually low Mastery may be perceived as threats to society. Both extreme believers and disbelievers tend to congregate in internats. Believers do so because they require the isolation and mutual reinforcement to bolster their extreme positions; disbelievers, because they too seek such group shelter or are compelled in this direction by "normal" society.

The processes of internats are also enmeshed in value conflicts. Although Bentham ([1789] 1907, p. 171) contended that "all punishment in itself is evil," he nonetheless thought it admissible "in as far as it promises to exclude some greater evil." The use of internat residence as punishment is still practiced, primarily in dealing with criminals but also in dealing with political prisoners (Bloch and Reddaway, 1978) and sometimes the mentally ill. Prison epitomizes the value conflict: "Penal imprisonment, from the beginning of the nineteenth century, covered both the deprivation of liberty and the technical transformation of individuals" (Foucault, 1979, p. 233). Almost two centuries later, it is clear that prison usually accomplishes only the first. Significantly, the transformation that does occur tends to move most prisoners further from society rather than closer to it so that not even social Reclaiming is attained.

However, "the history of imprisonment does not obey a chronology in which one sees, in orderly succession, the establishment of a penality of detention, then the recognition of its failure" (Foucault, 1979, pp. 264-265), followed by the testing of other methods and their acceptance or rejection on the basis of evidence. Instead, society suspects the instrument and its procedures, but does not cast them aside. The prison is "the detestable solution, which one seems unable to do without" (Foucault, 1979, p. 232).

Objections to internats' collectivism or methods may both be suspended when socially desired objectives are demonstrably attained. The English public schools have not only functioned as carriers of cherished values—now somewhat derogated by a more socialist bent—but also provided the society's leadership. "Only five prime ministers have been educated outside the public schools. . . . Old Etonians have dominated the beginning and end of the series" (Bamford, 1967, p. 233). Moreover, "The public schools not only socialize and educate a significant proportion of the British elite. They also perform what may be described as a custodial function. They conserve within themselves and protect from corruption the norms and values of elite behavior which are to be passed on to successive generations. Because of this custodial function the norms of elite behavior, and the value system associated with them, have been retained to a remarkable degree within the social structure" (Weinberg, 1967, p. 8). Weinberg also notes that the values preserved by the public schools are not the patrimony of only the wealthy: "Their norms of reverence for the past, of gentlemanly behavior, and insistence on rule obedience . . . are often ideal modes of behavior emulated by perhaps the whole middle class, and perhaps a large section of the working class as well" (p. 7).

Isolation of the setting, divergence and exclusivity, cruelties of the strong over the weak, homosexuality—all have been documented for elitist settings as they have for prisons and mental hospitals. Army camps, monasteries, and academies have had their scandals, but as collectivities they represent an ideological and professional elitism. A society may fear their elitist stance or mistrust their methods, but must also admire and respect them. Societies seem to need outstanding models, and thus as we cannot do without our prisons, we cannot do without our elitist internats.

A society's values will always influence its internats, and internats always reflect their society's values. When society points to an internat and accuses it of being dehumanizing, it is accusing itself. Society cannot ignore or ameliorate its less admirable characteristics by banishing them in the internat: "The organization of the hospital [as of any internat] is influenced by, and forms one special manifestation of, the general culture of which it is a part" (Caudill, 1958, p. 18). We ultimately confront a paradox. Although internats are intended to be environments unlike external ones, both staff members and inmates continue to do in the internat what they have learned outside; they continue to bear their "background norms" (Belcher, 1965). Thus the inside is both quite different from the outside and quite similar to it.

5

Integrating the Various Components of the Setting

Overview

Every social unit must achieve a measure of cohesion in order to survive. Given their seemingly strong boundaries, resulting from isolation and the performance of special tasks, internats are often assumed to be well integrated. Even the designation *total institution* conveys an impression of consistency, coherence, and purpose.

Many characteristics of internats, however, challenge or prevent integration. First, inmates' inclinations often diverge from those of staff. Inmates' goals, personal styles, or desires may differ from the internat's program, and rather than accept

117

the program, inmates may be resistant, uncomprehending, or passively docile and withdrawn. To gain submission, attention, and cooperation the internat may engage the newcomer in behavior designed to reduce or even eliminate past influences and replace them with new ones. Ideally, the behavior presented to the novice as laudable or improper will be consistently reinforced as such by all members of the environment. Normally, though, settings reflect multiple cultures of inmate and staff subgroups, and novices receive mixed informal signals concerning standards.

Second, the integration of an internat is often impeded by crisscrossing lines of authority and expertise among the caretakers. The introduction of new technologies may promote an efficacious approach to some problems but also may lead to inconsistency and misunderstanding. Complex, crossing lines of authority may lead inmates to wonder who is in charge. When inmates are asked who is their single, regular, available friend within the internat, they often answer with names of other inmates and not those of staff.

Third, physical plant also may pose obstacles to the integrated functioning of an internat. Physical plants are more stable than either the intervention theories they are aimed to implement or the populations they are built to house, and they appear to discomfort their inhabitants. Risk levels that are set too high evoke criticism and expose residents to avoidable injury; levels set too low constrain development and the inmates' return to "normalcy." Buildings, furnishings, and grounds affect self-image, promote or retard social intercourse, increase or reduce individualization and opportunities for privacy.

Fourth, the internal social structure of internats may not necessarily be integrative. Organizational size and a priori definitions of competence are reflected in divisions of labor that often have sharp and impermeable boundaries. Progression, reflecting increasing competence, may be limited by definition as well as by inadequate opportunities. Though inmates are supposed to be gaining Mastery needed for their ultimate adaptation outside, they may have few opportunities to learn or practice the roles they will be expected to assume once they leave the internat. For example, most inmates do not assume or role play the parts of workers or parents during the residency.

Finally, values may enhance or hamper integrative processes. In pluralist societies, which emphasize individual expression, value-consistent internats are a rarity. Religious orders and communes of political ideologists are outstanding exceptions. Therapeutic ideologies based on strong theory and supported by empirical evidence and an elaborate technology, as in hospitals, may produce similar value consistency. But most reclaiming internats, be they prisons, mental hospitals, juvenile homes, or residences for retarded, operate in an environment of confused values.

The Feeling of Togetherness

The massive, impenetrable walls of a penitentiary and the physical organization of a nursing home around a central administration unit give the impression of an inner wholeness. The internat appears as a system contained within a unifying physical force, turned upon itself and acting as one body. Within the internat, however, are divergent inner constituencies, the forces of individual parts, all straining for expression and realizing themselves in some manner. Undoubtedly, a good deal of internat life, as seen from the outside, is reflected in a sentiment expressed by a fourteen-year-old girl in an English boarding school: "You tend to lose your being one separate person and become part of everyone else, their expressions of speech, the way they laugh, the things they do" (quoted by Lambert with Millham, 1968, p. 394). Or, in the words of a boy with a bit more experience in such a setting: "This place is like a thirteenth-century monastery, except those old monks *wanted* to be cut off from the world and we do not" (p. 377).

Although the boy appears to be an unwilling member of an internat, he nevertheless notes the monastic components of it. Like the girl, or the outside observer, he emphasizes the unity, the integrity of parts. Desirable or not, the place is one.

The physical nature of an internat gives the impression of a unitary, powerful, all-consuming environment. Yet the psychosocial reality of these settings reveals them to be more divergent, more complex, and less powerful than they seem.

Internats are useful when they press upon the individual a clear and consistent line of development. Annapolis is very effective in training officers of the type desired by the U.S. Navy. Similarly, the planners of Johns Hopkins Hospital have been reasonably successful in organizing a healing internat. However, some fairly well integrated internats accomplish the opposite of their intended goals. The internat in Polsky's (1962) *Cottage Six* was effective in maintaining and even reinforcing delinquent behavior. Moreover, a careful survey of internats as a lot dispels the illusion of high integration. Serious studies—even including Goffman's (1961), which popularized the label *totality*—show inner confusion, conflict, and contradiction.

Prisons, which probably have been studied more than any other internats, are a case in point. More isolated than most other residential settings with clearly defined populations, allegedly the home of a "criminal culture," they might be expected to epitomize an integrated environment. Yet their binary structure—of inmates, on the one hand, and staff on the other—reduces integration. (Clemmer, 1940; Garabedian, 1963; Giallombardo, 1966; McCorkle and Korn, 1954; Schrag, 1954; Sykes, 1958; Sykes and Messinger, 1960; Wheeler, 1961—all provide evidence of this dichotomy.) Integration is also reduced by individualism and personal isolation (Glaser, 1964; Morris and Morris, 1963) and by considerable value divergencies among both inmates and staff. The "Square Johns" (inmates who follow the prison's formal norms) identified by Schrag (1961) and the inmates with noncriminal orientations noted by Irwin and Cressey (1964) do not fit into the criminal subculture of a prison. Yet they are there, and their actions are part of the internat's environment.

Similar conflicts of orientation, interest, and practice are to be found in all internats. Only their prevalence and significance varies. Caudill (1958) describes such conflicts in a hospital; Stanton and Schwartz (1954) in a mental internat; Street,

Vinter and Perrow (1966) in correctional settings for juveniles; Wolins (1974b) in internats for abandoned and neglected children; Gubrium (1975) in a nursing home for the aged. Even perception of the same action may be different depending upon whether it is held by the treater or the treated:

> [The treater:] On the way back from the group meeting, held where the men live in the five-hundred man cellblock that I'm responsible for, I pick up Dunn's file from the Record Office. I am reading it when he sticks his head around the doorway and says, 'You sent for me?' [Manocchio and Dunn, 1970, p. 66].
>
> [The treated:] The bull at the downstairs station checks my ducat and unlocks the grill gate for me. When I get to the top of the stairs, the bull at the other grill gate has me pass my ducat through to him, reads it, gets my I.D. card with its picture to make sure I am the one who is supposed to pass, and unlocks the gate for me to come into the inner sanctuary of the quack staff they have here. After the bull lets me inside, he has me empty my pockets on a table and assume the shakedown position: legs spread and arms held horizontal from the body. Then he begins the familiar shakedown. He starts at the nape of my neck, feeling the seams of the collar. . . . He makes certain to feel the cuffs of the trousers. At least he doesn't make me take off my shoes and socks, as some of the bulls do. . . . The hallway is dull and cheerless, and I am alone sitting there. I sit there for five minutes, and because Murray's [his social worker] door is open, I decide to stick my head in and let him know I am here. . . . 'You sent for me?' 'Yes, Jimmy,' he says. 'Have a seat. How've you been doing?' He always gives me this bullshit, as if he cares how in the hell I've been doing [Manocchio and Dunn, 1970, pp. 159-60].

These two passages describe a simple meeting, held for a supposedly well-established reason, by two persons who know each other and are not new to the setting. Murray, the social worker, who is generally depicted by Manocchio and Dunn as a concerned, caring staff member, nevertheless does not seem to understand the grotesquely onerous task he imposed on Dunn in order to "help him." Dunn, after all, was not scheduled for a "treatment session" in order to be "ducated," or "shaken down"; yet this is *his* most profound experience. Very likely, both Murray and Dunn know that the procedures intended to prevent smuggling in the prison are an unmitigated failure in any case. Even more significantly, Murray and Dunn, although members of the same internat, approach each experience from the perspective of their status—social worker and prisoner.

Consider another example. The descriptions by two seventeen-year-old boys in an English public school show the divergence of imagery and actions within an internat such as theirs. One says, "I . . . like the atmosphere in the school—it is an atmosphere in which one can both work and play very easily —one feels that the masters, especially the headmaster, are really interested both in the boys and in the school. Also the fact that the whole school, and all its activities, are fitted into a religious shell, however thin that may be at times, and however many times that that is criticized, does very definitely help" (quoted by Lambert with Millham, 1968, p. 363). The second says, "I hate the place—being spied on and one's life being pried into by housemasters and others" (p. 376).

The views of Dunn and his social worker, or those of the two boys at the boarding school, suggest something quite distinct from a total environment, which would by its very nature be integrated. An internat operated by an omnipotent ruler—or based on a long-established and unquestioned tradition—with a clear sense of purpose, and a logical tie between means and ends would be internally consistent—the platonic ideal of its species. Authoritarian prisons in totalitarian societies and Trappist monasteries (Merton, 1949a) come closest to this ideal. Within such environments individual discretion is limited, and few aspects of daily life are amenable to negotiation. Most behavioral standards are preordained by a high level of coercion or of consensus. Neither is characteristic of Dunn's prison, the boys' boarding school or, for that matter, most nonreligious and nontotalitarian internats.

Coercion is repulsive to a society that values human rights. It is also very difficult to sustain, even in isolated environments. Counterpressures build up and periodic explosions occur—as at the Auburn Penitentiary (Wicker, 1975)—a regular reminder of the pent-up energy contained within the internat as well as its lack of totality. Full consensus, however, can be a feature only of voluntary association and computational behavior, resulting from a high agreement on goals and consistency of means. No serious observer of the people-changing enterprise would assume this to be the state of the art. Some consensus does, however, prevail. All operating internats have staff that agree to work in them and to carry out assigned tasks. Nor are inmates in continuous revolt or total surrender. However, since the interests and perception of staff and inmates tend to differ, a dichotomy will evolve. Such a binary structure seems to exist in all internats, reinforced by the distinction between care recipient and caretaker.

Although such a dichotomy reduces the totality and integration of an internat, it may nonetheless still be functional. An "inmate culture" diverts the internat from its professed goals in delinquency settings (see Polsky, 1962; Sykes and Messinger, 1960) but not in the military academy or in the elite boarding school (Ellis and Moore, 1974; Weinberg, 1967). In military academy and boarding school alike, the inmate culture provides the individual with an understandable, proximate model and a reward-laden structure that replaces the distant caretakers and yields some negotiating power toward an internat consensus.

All efforts to change people when stripped of their niceties, involve a struggle of will between the treater and the treated. Within an internat, the struggle may assume a brutal form. Merton (1949a) describes the contest of wills that occurred at his entry to the monastery, even though by then much of the battle was being fought within himself. Other novices, less ready perhaps, whether for the academy or the prison are subjected to initiation rites in which inmates and staff demand the novices' allegiance. Ultimately, each learns a more-or-less

workable division of the allegiance among staff, mates, and his
own self. Inmates teach one another the arts of survival. They
are the best trainers in the internat, teaching criminal behavior
(Clemmer, 1940), developing an insiders' argot (Schrag, 1954;
Sykes, 1958), teaching one another how to adjust to the inside
and also how to get discharged (Bateman and Dunham, 1948).
They develop leadership (Polsky, 1962) and are aware of what
is going on among the staff (Stanton and Schwartz, 1954).

If all else fails, if self-conservation becomes impossible
and Reclaiming is not the practice, the inmates may respond
with self-destruction or mutiny. In the Nazi extermination
camps inmates threw themselves on electrified fences. In nursing homes some patients "just give up" (Gubrium, 1975; Townsend, 1971). Even an apparently Reclaiming environment may
produce a rash of suicides when the staff become confused and
agitated over reorganization and financial changes (Stotland and
Kobler, 1965).

Administrative Integration and Reclaiming. A tour of
Auschwitz or of a well-run prison should be sufficient to con-
vince anyone of the *administrative* integration that can be attained in settings that lack any psychosocial integration. The
order such environments attain promotes social Reclaiming but
not integrated Reclaiming. Let us consider several characteristics of a well-administered setting and see how such administrative integration affects inmates.

For example, an internat that has precisely scheduled activities to conserve costly treaters' time will have inmates who
wait in boring lines, missing pleasurable activities, and who complain of rigid schedules with inconvenient hours. An internat
that is organized to address groups of similar persons with uniform and standardized procedures will fail to provide more
capable inmates with challenging models, and relationships between inmates, staff, and administration may seem uniformly
impersonal.

Similarly, internats that have a fixed organizational hierarchy, with a fixed chain of command and responsibility designed to preserve the organization, may fail to provide inmates
with opportunities for individualization and progress, and their

administrators may refuse to consider changing rules and routines to meet individual needs. Finally, a hierarchy that clearly separates the roles of treaters and treated may lead to the treatment of problems but not that of persons.

Administrative integration is not without benefits. It gives security and structure to the administrators, staff, and a sizable proportion of inmates. It fulfills the requirements of internal "opponents," those members whose critical attitude serves to check overly hasty innovation. However, administrative integration may miss the object of rehabilitation. As Segal and Moyles (1979, p. 164) found regarding mental patients: "A strongly interrelated pattern of dependency is produced in settings that emphasize a controlling management-centered environment." Integration that promotes rehabilitation must emphasize the inmates' needs and concerns, not the management's interests. Polsky's (1962, p. 182) prescription could probably be used as a guideline: "The fundamental task of the residential treatment center is not only to rehabilitate individual youngsters but to create a *therapeutic youth culture*; the latter mediates institutional values and exerts a profound influence upon each boy" (italics added).

An integrated Reclaiming culture must comprise the various operating needs of the setting, including the social Reclaiming expectations of the outside community as well as the personal needs of residents. Such integration of societal and personal Reclaiming requires the internat to have the following attributes:

1. A comprehensible unit of residence and membership. Large settings with faulty communication impede Reclaiming (Porter and Lawler, 1965; Stanton and Schwartz, 1954; Szurek, 1947).
2. Individuation rather than uniformity. Standardized approaches that admit no exceptions impede development (Freud and Burlingham, 1943).
3. Frequent redefinition of the treated's role as the individual's Mastery increases. Unilateral, total dependency does not permit growth (Fairweather, 1964; Main, 1946).
4. Specific and limited periods of *defined* low Mastery. In-

determinacy and prolonged stay appear to be counterproductive (Clemmer, 1940; Hobbs, 1974; Wheeler, 1961).

5. Reduction of the dichotomy between treater and treated, caretaker and care recipient. Realistic tasks and considerable demands on inmates promote growth (Caudill and others, 1952; Sanders, Smith, and Weinman, 1967; Sykes and Messinger, 1960).

6. Participation of inmates in determining their own future. Such participation is the foundation of a therapeutic milieu (Bettelheim and Sylvester, 1948; Jones, 1953).

7. Consensus among the various orders of treaters. A major source of difficulty for inmates, highly correlated with their level of dependency, is disagreement among staff (Piliavin, 1963; Zald, 1962).

8. Models of the attainable, desirable, and rewarded. "Skimming off" the most competent inmates—that is, releasing them and retaining only the least competent—has a detrimental effect on the internat (Devereux, 1944).

Integrated Reclaiming requires the internat to consider personal as well as organizational aspects. The internat is to be perceived as a small, relatively complete universe in which "any action ... [is magnified because it is as] a rock tossed into a bathtub of water, whereas the effect ... in a community is more that of a pebble thrown into a lake" (Caudill, 1958, p. 322). Activity by treater or treated will affect the whole system. Its meaning will be judged by the integrative criteria likely to come from inmates and staff alike. Integration that is solely the result of a bureaucratic structure or of a treatment instrumentality is ineffective. An internat must have both. System maintenance and system change must move in tandem with emphases on personal development and relationship. Organizational demands will result in a tendency toward order, clarity, and control. Personal development will call for autonomy, practicality, and problem solving. Relationship will require involvement, support, and expressiveness (Moos, 1974, pp. 337-340).

Social learning from observable models provides some

measure of internal integration. In a confined setting the models to be emulated by the care recipients and caretakers alike may be preselected. Newcomers, stripped at least in part of their outside identity, have no option but to emulate the veteran inhabitants (see Vinter with Newcomb and Kish, 1976). Only the psychologically most powerful (for example, Gandhi, Solzhenitsyn, Victor Frankl) can resist.

Stripping and Reshaping. Certain activities may be undertaken with particular effectiveness in the internat because external distraction is excluded. With the aim of transformation, a first order of business, also one of the most condemned internat functions, is stripping new residents of certain old influences, patterns, or habits. Lewin (1951) postulates that change involves three steps: unfreezing, moving, freezing. *Unfreezing* means loosening the individual's ties to former and current behavior. Such cathartic abreaction—that is, the imaginary reliving of past experiences for the purpose of reconstruction—is also considered essential for change in the psychodynamic model. Although behaviorists like Wolpe (1958) and Homme (Homme and others, 1970) are willing to dispense with this precondition of change, most settings devote considerable energy to it. Novices are "denuded": everyday clothes are removed, personal possessions prohibited, hair shorn, as a way of preparing them physically, psychologically, and spiritually to begin a new life. The prospect is a scary one—to enter the unknown without the comfort and security of the familiar—ancient Egyptians and Chinese understood this so well that they tried to furnish the nether world with the earthly possessions of the departed. Modern internats often insist on discarding all ties to the past.

The internat can denude an inmate mercilessly, crudely, and rapidly. It may do so as a therapeutic procedure to induce the desired change or as a means of furthering its own interests. The two purposes usually coexist; for example, the stripping process employed with West Point plebes is assumed to expedite and improve their performance as officers as well as ease administrative tasks for staff. Evidence is limited on how much stripping is necessary to achieve change. Stripping, like any surgical procedure, is painful and dangerous and should possibly require the equivalent of the signed consent hospital patients give prior to surgery.

Reshaping occurs in tandem with stripping. Internats are particularly suitable environments for reshaping, which is based on new stimuli. The internat's control of an inmate's experiences is intended to yield new behavior and, consequently, a new self. Again, the isolation and omnipotence of internats provide an opportunity for Reclaiming but also for abuse. Opportunities are developed through tolerance of failure, acceptance of the temporarily awkward and even bizarre, shelter from ridicule, and proximate examples of others who have surmounted similar or greater difficulties to achieve Mastery. However, an internat's tolerance of the unusual entails the risk that the inmate may never overcome such behavior and never become ready for the outside world. Consensus among administrators, staff, and inmates on the dimensions and direction of Reclaiming as well as the means for attaining it are required in order that inmates know the desired behavior and are consistently reinforced when they perform it.

Reshaping may even require induced regression. Many theorists proclaim the utility of induced regression as a step toward a new identity. For example, Freud trained his patients to relive infantile experiences; Bach and Wyden (1969) had patients regress into infantile and aggressive acting out; and Janov (1970) trained patients in the "primal scream." All internats are well suited to induce an inmate's regression as a step in the reshaping process. Regression is expected in a hospital for physical illness, but for the other internats it is a risky business— above all, because regressed individuals are engaging in bizarre behavior. Unless a trusted authority, with expert powers, requires it as a necessary step in Reclaiming, this behavior will meet with strong outside disapproval. Significantly, the "expert power" so successfully employed in the hospital for physical illness, has no equally powerful analogue in other internats. Although the medical profession has succeeded in colonizing the mental health field, here the physician's professional mystique has been punctuated by confusion, dissension, and persistent failure.

Two other risks of enforced regression are that the regression itself will be seen as evidence that Reclaiming is not taking place and that if the models of high Mastery are absent the regressed inmates will determine behavioral norms of the internat. If regressed behavior becomes a norm reshaping will proceed in a direction opposite from that desired as the social learning that occurs will be counterproductive.

Evidence abounds on the teaching effectiveness of internats. Experts and the public agree that prisons are excellent schools of crime, mental hospitals increase many patients' deviant behavior, internats for the retarded effectively teach incompetence even greater than that inmates possess at entry. Why does this happen? Bandura (1969), probably the most influential writer on the subject, proposes five conditions under which behavior change will occur. Unfortunately, each of these therapeutic conditions can be subverted by an inmate culture that is hostile to social Reclaiming. Let us consider each of Bandura's conditions and their subversion. First, Bandura suggests that the new behavior should have no serious negative consequences. A hostile inmate culture translates this to mean that any behavior may be tolerated; a motivated group of inmates, cadets at West Point, understands this to mean that initial failure is part of acquiring higher Mastery.

Second, benefits should be immediately apparent. Motivated inmates will be encouraged by good results; hostile inmates will see the benefits (approval, privileges) as a manipulative game. Third, there must be no fear of moral or value sanctions against the new behavior. Motivated inmates will thrive on this freedom; hostile inmates will abuse it. Fourth, persons in position of authority should not oppose the new behavior. A hostile inmate culture will take this to mean that the doctors, nurses, guards, and attendants are not in charge—that the inmates, particularly the veterans, can do anything and get away with it. Fifth, optimal conditions for promoting change include ever present models and regular reinforcement. In a hostile inmate culture the models are hostile to the internat's goals, and hostile behavior is regularly reinforced by other inmates.

Because it meets Bandura's requirements best, the inmate

culture—hostile or motivated—dominates all social learning. All inmates—prisoners or West Point cadets—modify their behavior to suit peer norms. Such norms may either complement or defy the internat's official norms. Although concentration and isolation permit the internat substantial control over social learning that promotes Reclaiming, they do not assure it. Only premeditated selection of treaters and treated, behaviors and sanctions, leads to a well-integrated setting that will promote Reclaiming. More and better staff or better buildings may perversely exacerbate internat problems by introducing greater interference with, but no ultimate victory over, the direction established by the inmate culture.

Experimentation and research on the effective utilization of group environments for behavioral control have been minimal. Nearly a half century ago, August Aichhorn, the father of modern juvenile delinquency theory, studied his own internats and noted that, "in more modern institutions, two efforts are being made: (1) to separate the children into the smallest possible groups, and (2) to compose these groups in such a way that the group life will favorably influence the behavior difficulties" (Aichhorn, 1935, pp. 143-144). Although he discusses groups, Aichhorn does not propose group work; his recommendations pertain to group structure and the use of "group life," along with professional and other resources, to favorably influence the behavior of internat residents. This self-evident prescription is ignored by the planners and operators of most internats today.

Treatment by Specialists. Behavioral control in internats may also be achieved through specialized techniques, often referred to as therapeutic intervention. Any storage facility may, of course, be a convenient receptacle for inmates, providing ready and economical access for caretakers. Some settings focus exclusively on specialized techniques, ascribing to them the change achievable while in residence. An internat so used is a vessel, a more or less good hotel in which the inevitable power of the social environment is ignored as irrelevant and in which certain technology is conveniently applied. Sophisticated technologies alone cannot produce an integrated setting for Reclaiming.

Nevertheless, all internats offer excellent settings for specialized techniques. For example, complex medical ministrations requiring high levels of competence, expensive and rarely used equipment, and intensive supervision are most conveniently, safely, and efficiently administered in a hospital. The internat is also a logical setting for techniques that require isolation—treatments that are possibly dangerous or abhorrent to the public, such as radiation therapy or executions.

Aside from providing a good setting for certain therapeutic modifications, an internat may also benefit from such technical intervention. A severely disturbed patient may be calmed through therapy; a very dependent one may be helped to function at a higher level of Mastery; a novice, converted to the new rite, will become a caretaker. True symbiosis between technology and Reclaiming may therefore exist. However, the integration of specialized techniques in the life patterns of an internat faces several obstacles.

Perhaps the most serious problem in integrating specialized techniques is one of conceptual unity. If there is no conceptual unity regarding the means to achieve Goals among the operators of specialized techniques and the usual caretakers, inmates perceive the technique as merely an isolated episode in their internat experience—a fifty-minute interlude is not an integral part of their lives. The treatment may be a digression from, often even a contravention of, the social learning occurring on the ward. Unsurprisingly, Moos (1974) has found that professional staff (physicians, psychologists, psychiatrists, trained nurses, and others) are interested in developing treatment programs, and they favor such programs over maintaining the existing system. They tend to experiment and innovate. They do not seem to strongly influence the quality and intensity of the relationships among patients, and they have some effect in diminishing the emphasis on system maintenance" (p. 332).

Pattern maintenance is, of course, much more important to those who remain within the system and have developed a means of operating within the patterns than to occasional, even if high-status, interlopers. Indeed, experts who bring their special techniques to the internat are resented and often undermined by the permanent generalist staff, as Piliavin (1963) found in studying the relationship between cottage parents and social workers. Similarly, experts and professionals complain about the generalists' skills. A psychologist feels that "many of the cottage parents have worked out rather simple schemes for dealing with behavior problems. It apparently makes them more comfortable, even though it may be harmful to the boys. It's difficult to approach them about these things because you are apt to break down whatever relationship you have" (Weber, 1969, p. 429).

Such tensions between the full-time caretakers and the occasional specialists are fewer in an ideologically or theoretically integrated setting. For example, Stotland and Kobler (1965) credit an institution-wide belief in Menninger's intervention philosophy with providing unity to their hospital. Similar integration appears to have characterized the ward operated as a token economy by Ayllon and Azrin (1968). Whether authoritarian settings directed by the occasional but powerful professional can achieve the same results is unclear. For the present, it appears that "whether the influence of professional staff is more beneficial or more harmful is a moot point" (Moos, 1974, p. 332).

Daily routine and specialized techniques may even collide, as they did in an internat for delinquents that had a firm rule prohibiting smoking. Staff were required to report all violations. Of course, clandestine violations were commonplace, and periodic rule-enforcement campaigns were held. In this setting several therapists formed a treatment group with the following ground rules: "In this group you can say or do anything whatsoever without getting any punishment, any warnings, or any reprimands. We will keep everything you say and do a secret. We want you to feel free to express yourself in any way you wish. If we desire to set up rules, we will do it democratically. We will be like a little independent island" (Corsini, 1957, p. 95).

The consequences were immediate: "At this point one of the boys took out a cigarette, deliberately lit it, and took a great puff, . . . looking right at the speaker. The other boys . . . began to beg for a puff. As the therapist went on, the cigarette moved from mouth to mouth, and no attention was being paid to his statements. . . . The therapists did nothing about the situation, except to indicate in the vaguest terms that everybody should keep secret what happened in therapy, but very shortly other inmates began to ask to enter the group, stating quite frankly that they wanted to enter so they could smoke. At this point, the therapists dissolved the group" (Corsini, 1957, p. 95).

This incident highlights not only the inadequate comprehension specialists may have of internat life but also the sporadic nature of their contacts. Unless practitioners of specialized techniques are aware of the organization's total dynamics, their actions will not contribute to, and often may detract from, integration. Consider the surgeon who makes the rounds at nine in the morning and finds a well-ordered ward, carefully prepared charts, cleaned and fed patients, and no visitors in the way. To accommodate the surgeon, patients were awakened at six; the charge nurse has been up since five-thirty in order to be on duty before seven; and visitors are anxiously waiting outside. The internat's staff and inmates arrange their schedules and routines to suit the specialist's convenience. Similarly, a cottage parent caring for delinquent boys comments about the professionals working in the same internat that "it's fine and easy for you people working up in the administration building to come at eight o'clock, leave at five, and have a half-day off on Saturday, but we cottage parents are with the boys all the time" (Weber, 1969, p. 429).

In an internat's relationship with scarce and prestigious professionals, the internat may have to play the toady to the prima donna. Nothing is more disruptive to the internat's integrated functioning.

A House May Not Be Home

From the most immediate surroundings of bed, closet, table, chair, and toilet to the outer reaches of the community, the space of an internat is of major import. The internat building and its interior arrangement are part of a service system that "touches a diversity of professions and specialized fields, from sociology and psychology to esthetics and physiology, from recreation and planning to politics and architecture" (Pastalan and Carson, 1970, p. 215). The internat's physical space determines Activity and thus the outcome of intervention.

Yet the planning of internat care appears to involve little

awareness of design. Even universities, with their ready access to available knowledge of both human development and design skills, have done little to make their physical surroundings life enhancing. College dormitory housing is, on the one hand, quite distinguished from most other types of internats in that "literally thousands of studies of use satisfaction have been completed" (Sommer, 1969, p. 132). Yet, on the other hand, as in most internats, little of this material is used in planning and designing new facilities.

The advice of consultants who specialize in the design of particular types of internats and prescriptions to be found in the literature have recently shown an increased tolerance for risk in order to permit progressive normalization of residents' lives. With normalization come reduced supervision, increased privacy of the care recipients, and also greater exposure of the caretakers. Internats designed along this principle, for example, offer private rooms for inmates, open supervisory stations, and even dining and leisure facilities for integrated use by caretakers and recipients.

In the past 150 years, the theoretical or ideological basis for the design of internats has taken a full swing of the pendulum. The same compassion that led Kirkbride and other planners of moral treatment hospitals to design facilities "materially different from ordinary habitations" motivated the President's Committee on Mental Retardation (1970) to enunciate the "normalization principle," according to which those requiring extrafamilial care are to be given conditions as close as possible to those of mainstream society.

The intentions of many modern internats are identical with those of Kirkbride, who was profoundly concerned for the well-being of his patients and their reintegration in society. Present theorists, however, believe that such social integration requires opportunities for normal behavior. They would, therefore, abandon Kirkbride's isolated hospital in favor of its community-integrated predecessor and successor. Both Kirkbride and present theorists agree on the definition of Reclaiming; the difference is a matter of which mechanics are presumed to be most effective.

The Therapeutic Physical Environment. In the most successful internats, the physical environment encourages activity, creativity and awareness while responding to the needs and be-havior of residents (Sommer, 1972). In an internat the physical environment is deliberately used to prevent regression and breakdown, while aiding recovery and growth of residents. But even a cursory view of the physical environment of most inter-nats shows how far they are from serving such goals. As encom-passing environments, internats are expected to meet a wide range of human needs, some of which are contradictory in their implications.

How, for example, should one solve the problem of toilet and sink height and location in an internat for children? Nine children, ranging from infants to adolescents, live in one house at the SOS Kinderdorf (Gmeiner, 1971). To deal with the child at his own level, the Kinderdorf provides three sizes of toilets and sinks; but mindful of the importance of modeling and pro-gression, it has them placed in one room. This arrangement re-duces privacy but also increases assistance to and supervision of the youngest ones. In short, satisfying all demands of progres-sion, modeling, privacy, and supervision was not feasible even in this creative and concerned internat.

The broad range of particular settings necessary to meet all the needs of residents defeats some planners. Spivack (1973) lists eighteen types of spaces specifically appropriate to particu-lar behaviors, and argues that each of the archetypes is needed: "Humans living in an archetypally incomplete and rigid environ-ment lose behavioral opportunities, or behave maladaptively" (p. 227). Yet, how many internats provide specific space for sleeping and meeting, working and learning, worshipping and mating, healing and nourishment? Many of these spaces are merged, fused, or simply ignored in internats. "When settings are thus forced to handle an overload of functions . . . the re-sulting incongruence between behavior and place may appear bizarre and chaotic. The individual may become disoriented, and may respond with a variety of . . . maladaptive measures" (Spivack, 1973, pp. 242-243). Considerable evidence supports the significance of environmental inadequacies in the creation of aberrant human behavior (see Hebb, 1961; Spitz, 1945; Wit-kin and others, 1962; Zubek, 1969).

The contradictory requirements of a single population

are another challenge to design and planning. For example, a stable physical environment appears to be generally preferred by both residents and staff of internats for the aged. In the face of reduced sensory capacity, the residents tend to rely on conservative features of their environment. Lipman (1968) describes the near-ritualistic patterns of chair occupancy in homes for the elderly, and Sommer (1972) notes a similar attitude among staff. Yet these comfortable (and often desired) physical-social arrangements reduce the variety of stimuli, constrict social interaction, and generally infringe on any opportunities for personal growth. Such stability may induce both comfort and stagnation.

Perhaps the most significant reason that planners and operators are relatively unaware of the therapeutic effect of space is the lack of adequate inmate and staff response during both the planning and occupancy periods. Many residents are economically, physically, socially, and psychologically handicapped in a manner that prevents them from expressing an opinion. Many staff are transient occupants of establishments whose long-term operation is directed by others. As Sommer (1972, p. 90) observes, "The susceptibility of institutions to obsolete design lies in the lack of responsiveness of both designers and client representatives to user inputs. Since they have a captive market, they are not concerned about loss of customers or even consumer resentment unless it is organized politically."

Inmates are not only deprived of control over the space but also sometimes stripped of personal possessions. The rationale for such rules varies: therapy requirements, control over infection and contraband, lack of storage space, the need for equal treatment with no exceptions. Whatever the organizational reasons for such rules, the inmates' extent of choice is limited by considerations of ownership. Since choice is generally more constricted in an internat than outside, the absence of ownership options is a serious matter: "People like spaces they can call their own and make over; they reject an alien environment that is built according to . . . a standard model of impersonal humanity in the most durable and antiseptic condition" (Sommer, 1969, p. 171). By preventing inmates from personalizing their settings, creating their own niche, internats constrain inmates' adjustment to their environment.

Space, Status, and Models. There is ample evidence of the powerful influence models exert in internat environments. The most effective modeling occurs when the model is proximate, of higher status, attached to the learner by affective bonds and, in turn, reinforced by a third, authoritative party (Bandura, 1969; Bronfenbrenner, 1974). Exactly such a situation is offered by the design of rooming-in maternity wards "where in groups of four the patients learn from one another, new mothers from mothers who have had other children, or a new mother on her first day from a mother who has already seen and tended her child for two days" (Thompson and Goldin, 1975, p. 318).

While the utility of modeling has been documented systematically only in twentieth-century learning theory, its principles were understood by the builders of internats in the eighteenth and nineteenth centuries. They realized that effective modeling requires at least visual and auditory contact, both of which can be encouraged by the physical environment. They were also aware that the environment conveys status and can be used to shape any kind of behavior. For example, a quality building in a good neighborhood signifies high status and encourages its residents to dress and behave accordingly. Although the builders of nineteenth-century reformatories, like their twentieth-century colleagues, primarily focused on the negative implications of modeling, and therefore preached and practiced various degrees of segregation—that is, removing persons under treatment from negative influences—some child welfare specialists, including Folks (1891), pursued integrationist policies.

Inasmuch as visual and auditory contact are an essential condition for modeling, site selection and physical structure affect modeling. Internat planners who selected isolated, pastoral settings in which to heal or reform the mentally ill and delinquent believed that distance from corrupting environments (usually implying the central city districts) would decrease the effects of the corrupting models. These planners, however, failed to consider that inmates within the isolated internat, an aggregate of deviants, would be able to model themselves only on one another. The internat's distance from the community precluded inmates from modeling themselves on normal community members.

Modeling and attachment are related to proximity. Proximity is particularly important in populations of limited mobility such as the aged, the very young, or the ill. In a home for
the aged, Friedman (1966) found that the new inmates, randomly assigned to various floors, established friendship patterns
mainly on their own floors. Similar observations have been
made of the inmates of a women's prison (Giallombardo, 1966),
a nursing home (Gubrium, 1975), and student housing (Festinger, Schachter, and Back, 1950). Location determines opportunities for contact, and incidental contacts lead to friendships
and a measure of behavioral modeling. To isolate the improved
from the improving and the entering is, therefore, likely to impair rather than promote Reclaiming.

For optimal effectiveness, the available models must be
examples of progressive growth of Mastery. Access to models,
even though often not well controlled, shows the inmate an
acceptable behavioral repertoire. The best models for novices
are those whose Mastery is improving and who are similar to the
novice in terms of their field of low Mastery and developmental
history. Novices need opportunities to observe the effort and
accomplishment of others similar to themselves. Behavioral distance must be small and demands of the environment and capability of inmate models progressive, leading to a changing division
of tasks between care by others and self-care. Since each stage
in this division of responsibility has different implications for
equipment and for staffing, a hospital for physical illness would
have to abandon the heavily staffed and equipped single-unit
system in favor of "three or four different inpatient units where
patients might be housed within the hospital in the course of a
single illness" (Thompson and Goldin, 1975, p. xxviii).

To permit some self-care and allow patients to help one
another "many hospitals combine infants with toddlers and preschoolers in one nursing unit. . . . The advantages lie chiefly in
the additional attention and stimulation afforded to the infants
by the presence of slightly older children who can both talk to
them and provide . . . interesting activity to watch. Some older
children in turn benefit from the experience of helping with the
babies" (Lindheim, Glaser, and Coffin, 1972, p. 21). Similarly,

double rooms are useful in certain cases: "Dan, an eighteen-year-old with a long-term spinal problem . . . stated that a good roommate made the hospital experience worthwhile. His roommate, Carl, was seventeen and in the hospital for the first time for a spinal operation. Dan, who had already had the operation, was able to comfort Carl with realistic information, sympathy, and humor" (Lindheim, Glaser, and Coffin, 1972, p. 82).

Models representing progressive competency find favor with some professionals whose perspective is based on learning theory, but the operational implications of such modeling are generally resisted. Kleemeier (1961) found that programs for the aged are usually segregated by competence. Weiss (1969, p. 26) notes that "large nursing homes separate their patients according to their physical and mental condition" into five categories, ranging from minimal to protective care. Segregation of prisoners is also common (Nagel, 1973), as is the separation of persons by age, capability, and gender in most reclaiming internats. "Administrators are likely . . . to segregate whenever feasible, since administration problems are fewer where one set of procedures fits most patients" (Lawton, 1974, p. 64).

In part, such separation may well be justified on the grounds of drastic need, tolerance, and behavioral differences between groups such as, say, teenagers, infants, and the aged in a hospital setting: "A suitable environment for young children in no way meets teenage needs. In like manner, the teenager's pattern of life . . . can be upsetting to adult patients" (Lindheim, Glaser, and Coffin, 1972, p. 79). With due consideration for such differences, we all realize that families are not segregated by age; integration of this kind is possible—for example, Hermann Gmeiner successfully integrated infants, adolescents, and one or two adults in every cottage of the SOS Kinderdorf.

The physical structure of an internat must also account for the cultural attitudes toward spatial distance held by its inhabitants—care recipients and caretakers alike. For example, Hall (1966) notes that the amount of distance between two individuals has different implications for the Scandinavian and the Indian, the North and the South American. What the former perceives as uncomfortably close the latter may find normal or even coldly aloof. Similar discrepancies in the perception of distance are reported by DeLong (1970) particularly in care settings for the bedridden aged. Although staff members are most comfortable at a distance between approximately two to four feet from an inmate, that distance is beyond the touch and olfactory range of the elderly, who therefore perceive such distance as representing aloofness. While distance may not create a serious barrier to interaction among mobile individuals, for the bedridden it does. DeLong (1970, p. 85) suggests that "the elderly prefer densities . . . that are nearly intolerable for the normal American populations." In such environments, stuffed with objects and people, the partner to a social transaction is more proximate, less able to withdraw. If DeLong's observations are confirmed for various populations, they may form a basis for integration in which physical distances are deliberately manipulated in order to achieve social, psychological, and even valuative effects.

Even distance may be overcome when the physical plant is integrated by value theme. In Manchester, England, a home for the aged includes a very handsome synagogue, which was planned to encourage community interaction in various rituals and celebrations. Similar reference to religious values, and their integrative capability, is apparent in the cruciform construction of ancient hospitals. Intended to give the largest possible number of patients good visual and auditory communication with the central chapel, the crucifix design also conveys religious symbolism. The hospital builders believed religious practice to be an important part of the cure; although they could see the illness in the physical field, their interpretation of it extended to the valuative. With such a perspective, physical deficiency was to be compensated not only through a good bed and clean air but also through communal religious ministration.

Any plan for the physical integration of an internat must also consider the needs of the staff. The environment must offer staff a certain amount of privacy but also must encourage the staff to interact with inmates, to minister to inmates' needs and to provide models for the more advanced. An internat must offer neither too many hiding places for staff nor too few. Recent tendencies in planning are in the direction of greater staff exposure. This design increases staff effectiveness by emphasizing the unity of care recipient and caretaker, hence the humanity and personal quality of care. However, open nurses' stations or easy inmate access to the private space of staff also carry the risk of a higher burnout rate and loss of expert power.

Actors and the Play: Internat as a Social Unit

Within the physically limited space of the internat a full play of life is enacted. The play is complex, filled with contradictions and conflicts. In prisons the staff's roles as custodians and therapists often conflict (Cressey, 1969). The inmate culture may elicit and reward behavior that counters rehabilitation (Sykes and Messinger, 1960). The roles of inmates and staff may be defined such that antagonism, not cooperation, predominates. And even when all actors are working together, the number of roles is considerable and their interrelationship complex. Yet, bakers and nurses, secretaries and psychiatrists, all have their roles and tasks. Several types of conflicts result from unclear or contradictory goals, vaguely defined responsibilities, and divergencies of perception and attitude among specialists and generalists.

First, internat specialists act in accordance with standards and principles of practice developed in the external professional community. A dentist may decide that Johnny, the model for good class behavior, should come for orthodontia exactly in the middle of the daily math lesson. The teacher, needing Johnny's performance to stimulate an unmotivated class, would decide differently. Similar conflicts also occur outside the internat, as a professional makes judgments and decisions according to the criteria of the profession, but such conflicts are amplified in the internat's smaller, more resonant environment. In most internats, the conflict is resolved in favor of the specialist, even at the expense of Reclaiming.

Second, generalist roles in the internat (aide, cottage parent, prison guard) are defined vaguely, admitting both confusion and conflict.

Observations of generalist roles in different cultures lead us to suggest that the problem lies less in the generality of expectations than in the limits of corresponding authority. Neither the Russian *vospitatel'* nor the Israeli *madrich/mechanech,* who had both full responsibility and much authority in their settings, experienced the lack of clarity about expectations and the conflict with professionals characteristic of American cottage parents or ward attendants.

When conflict is among generalists, resolution by expertise is not feasible. In an internat for juvenile delinquents, described by Zald (1962), teachers experienced far less conflict with cottage parents than did social workers. This difference is partly due to frequency of contact, but it is also attributable to lack of expert power (even of the limited kind held by teachers) on the part of either cottage parents or social workers. Resolution could only be obtained by recourse to supervisory and administrative personnel.

Role conflicts also result from ambiguity in the Reclaiming process. With the exception of the professionals, only a few staff members or inmates clearly understand the relationship between the roles they are assigned and Reclaiming (Street, Vinter, and Perrow, 1966, pp. 177-188; Weber, 1969). Inmates are ordered to do certain things and prohibited from doing others, but they are rarely told the rationale for such rules. Nonprofessional staff often are unsure of how their tasks and roles are to contribute to Reclaiming. The consequence is a ritualization of behavior and roles. Activities are pursued without all the actors knowing how these are assumed to promote Reclaiming.

Only the professionals seem to understand, yet even most of them rely more on faith than on empirical evidence. Both routine and intuition play a part in governing Activity. Routine diminishes contradicting roles. Intuition resolves the conflict to satisfy situational (or even ideological) contingencies as illustrated in the following incident, told by a counselor at an Israeli internat for children who recently immigrated to Israel.

We were sitting behind the dining room, leaning on the wall, eating fresh figs "liberated" from the nearby orchard. I had about half of the group (twenty boys and girls) with me. I was telling them stories about how I arrived in Israel, by myself, being not much older than they. The time was 11:30 at night, long after "lights out." The village was fast asleep. We sat close together against the evening chill. Then one of the boys whispered in Arabic—his mother tongue—"Brother, the Director is coming." We left everything: figs, buckets, blankets, and sneaked back to our rooms. Next morning the Director approached me at breakfast: "You know, Y., you were foolish last night. As the counselor (*madrich*) you should have stayed there with the kids and met me. I came to see what was going on. I did not mind you were staying with your group." I told him that I felt like a transgressor, doing something against the regulations which we had recently decided to enforce more stringently. Ignoring my discomfort he said: "Pick up the blankets at my office so the storekeeper (*machsanai*) won't know about it" [Wozner, 1955].

The counselor's official role was to enforce the internat's rules, but he felt his role as a brother to be more important. The director's official role was to ensure staff unity in the internat, yet here he "conspired" with the counselor against the storekeeper.

"Sociofugal" and "Sociopetal" Caretakers. Role definition may be used in a "sociofugal" or a "sociopetal" manner (Osmond, 1959). All internats appear to assign staff tasks so that a staff member near the inmate coordinates and represents to the inmate everything that the internat purports to be doing. In the hospital for physical ailments, for example, a physician and nurse fill this role, with the nurse acting as a surrogate for the doctor, explaining the doctor's orders to the patient and taking responsibility for the implementation of those orders.

In other types of internats, the allocation of authority and responsibility is much less clear, especially in large settings or whenever prestigious specialists are involved. When responsibility and authority are decentralized, both inmates and staff may be confused, as the following situation illustrates: "When the cottage mother attempted to participate in the planning for John's program, she indicated that she conceived of herself as having responsibilities for planning delinquents' programs. The professionals, reserving this role for themselves, rejected the cottage mother's participation. The cottage mother retaliated by ignoring the job assignment for John that the professionals arranged" (Weber, 1969, p. 439). Decentralization can thus leave both inmate and staff wondering who is formally responsible for selected aspects of Activity.

Several other consequences are likely to result from a broad decentralization of roles. First, some essential aspects of an inmate's needs may fall between the defined responsibilities of the various task-oriented—rather than person-oriented—specialists. Second, the specialists may be more interested in resolving one particular problem than in considering the entire range of the inmate's needs. Finally, the locus of responsibility for any one inmate is so diffuse, that no one can be held accountable.

To avert such conflicts, some internats grant central authority to one generalist. In some children's internats, for example, house parents have full responsibility and authority for all internat activities that pertain to their child. Specialists work with the children through the house parents' intercession and under their control (Caudill, 1958; Gmeiner, 1971; Korczak, 1967; Wolins, 1974c).

Some theorists suggest that good treatment facilities are composed of many small, highly staffed behavior settings (Barker, 1968). Perhaps this plan would indeed be functional, giving the treated and treaters responsibility and authority. However, such settings would not function to the inmate's advantage unless a staff member or the patient himself were assigned a centralized role. Proposals for greater specialization of internat roles may sound appealing, but increased expertise in settings for delinquent, mentally ill, retarded or otherwise severely dependent persons has yielded neither exemplary care nor desired outcomes.

Significantly, the English language does not have a term

that designates the status and corresponding role expectations for caretakers. The French *éducateur* (Linton, 1971), Hebrew *madrich* (Carlebach, 1971), Japanese *tsukisai* (Caudill, 1958) and similar terms in Polish, Russian, and German simply have no English counterpart. Reissman and Miller (1964, pp. 34-35) suggest that the linguistic omission reflects a psychodynamic world view that is "primarily concerned with individual, non-social methods of change." Linton (1971, p. 168) ascribes it to the lack of an ideological base in the treatment process. Whatever the explanation, the problem is more than a semantic one.

Having a firm, caring, knowledgable, powerful staff ally and model is particularly important when the inmate's Reclaiming demands a continuous and progressive role change. One may be sick, confused, misbehaved, incompetent, or untrained when entering an internat, but such deficiencies in Mastery are to be remedied. The inmate's behavioral changes will be a response to contingencies and will be legitimized by the social norms of the setting. Progress will be impeded if the ascribed roles and responsibilities of inmate and staff are not clearly defined or well understood.

The Inmate's Role. Since their Mastery is to be modified, inmates may be defined as in need of treatment—a role best exemplified by the patient in a hospital for the physically ill. But the role expected of an inmate is rarely a well-defined one. Conflicts arise, for example, if an improving inmate begins to assume some caretaker's duties for a less competent inmate or when an inmate is to receive both therapeutic and custodial care. Internats usually reduce such conflicts by ignoring some of the troublesome roles. A patient who is also a nurse is simply not permitted to help other patients as he improves.

A patient may not carry out the patient role for other reasons as well. Inmates who were coerced into the role may refuse to accept it. Voluntary inmates may have second thoughts about their admission or may find it difficult to understand what is expected of them. "Very disturbed individuals and those with poor prognoses, if they are 'difficult to treat' or are 'untreatable,' may precisely be so *because they do not assume the patient role.* That is to say, they do not accept the conditions and limitations of the treatment relationship. They appear to suffer from a general inability to differentiate among role relationships and to behave in accordance with the specific expectations that varied social situations require" (Lennard and Bernstein, 1969, p. 153). Often, the first step in treatment is to teach the inmate how to accept his status in the therapeutic relationship: "Teaching a person who comes for treatment how to be a patient . . . is a necessary part of what must transpire during psychotherapy" (Lennard and Bernstein, 1969, p. 147). The only role that an internat must teach all inmates is that of inmate.

Other roles can, and often do, remain in abeyance despite the internat's Reclaiming task and staff need to produce contingency situations that reinforce Reclaiming. The conditions conducive to Reclaiming must include recognition of effort, reward for minor or even disingenuous achievement, and tolerance of failure. In such a Reclaiming context, any action may be interpreted in two ways. First, "the same response pattern may be diagnosed as 'sick' or may be normatively sanctioned and considered emulative by different groups, at different times, or in different environmental settings" (Bandura, 1969, p. 62). Second, an act may be clinically interpreted as a manipulative put-on, representing a clever ruse or a mere intellectual exercise rather than truly reflecting an internal state. Unless a staff member knows an inmate well enough to carefully interpret the inmate's actions, those actions may unfairly and uncritically be consigned to one of these two categories. Braly, who spent many years in prison, describes such a situation, a conversation with a member of the parole board.

> "Very well," he began in a tone that sounded like the prelude to my exit music, and I interrupted desperately. "Mr. Fitzharris, doesn't it mean anything to you that for the first time in my life I've been able to earn my own way? I had a job where I made decent money." "That's noted. In this one area you've done well. But this writing business comes and goes, doesn't it?"

I could hardly say it didn't. "And you're an old con. How can we trust you? How do we know what you've been up to? You vanish for months at a time. Then there's this violence in your record." "That was twenty years ago." He had the grace to look down. "I know. But that was you out there in Nevada, not someone else." "It was not me. I am someone else. In the twenty years since that happened I have never stopped trying to change myself." "How can we know that?"

That was it, wasn't it? They didn't know. How could they know? And since anything I might find to say was selfishly inspired, designed to free me, it had to be discounted. Only the file could be trusted, and here the ink never faded.

When I played this scene over, as I did again and again, the feeling that came over me was the horror of total impotence. There was nothing I could do. No way to demonstrate my sincerity. I had moved beyond the usual pattern and was now abandoned there [Braly, 1976, pp. 360-361].

Unless the internat provides inmates with opportunities for behaviors normally performed outside it, inmates' competence to live outside the internat cannot be evaluated; Braly will not get his chance and Fitzharris will have no evidence. In many internats the existing roles and role models are irrelevant to both the external world and the inmates' needs. No prison inmate can even attempt to identify with the guard's role, and a disturbed resident modeling himself on the psychiatrist would be assumed to be sicker than he is. Bureaucratic or professional personnel often represent unachievable models, which leaves the resident only those models provided by the inmate subculture.

The absence of significant role progression in many internats is underscored by its presence in others. West Point and the English boarding school are hierarchically structured, providing a behavioral ladder an inmate may climb. While distinctions between inmate and staff are preserved, performance expectations of an upperclassman at West Point or a prefect at Eton put him between the plebe, or new boy, and the instructors.

The upperclassman's behavior is a model of how the plebe is expected to develop. Performance associated with the progressively advancing status is explicitly and approvingly modeled by upperclassmen *and* staff, signifying continuity rather than dichotomy of role expectations (see Astrachan, Harrow, and Flynn, 1969; Almond, Keniston, and Boltax, 1969).

Apparently, progressive role modeling is more readily accomplished in small units. As internat size increases, the staff-inmate ratio decreases, and mutual help among residents, staff supportiveness, consensus about the treatment milieu, and encouragement to openness of expression by inmates all decline (Moos, 1974, p. 132). Larger internats are more likely to be integrated by formal, bureaucratic principles; their structure is more rigid, control and management are stressed, and there is less emphasis on inmates' independence and spontaneity (Moos, 1974, p. 137). Integration to advance Reclaiming is surrendered when necessary to system maintenance, and personal needs yield to organizational considerations.

In the extreme instance of such an environment, an inmate's choices are passivity and revolt. Neither is particularly conducive to Reclaiming, but revolt is less frequent and more obvious, therefore also less dangerous for the inmates' long-term well-being. With no role ladder to climb, no encouragement of individual achievement, no sense of progress, inmates have little incentive. Settings integrated around organizational needs prefer inmate inaction to inmate revolt. Their motto could well be "less behavior, less trouble"—the antithesis of Reclaiming.

Involvement and activity occur when inmates' actions are accorded external and internal significance by community, staff, and peers. The former is contingent on their being related to Reclaiming (Moos, 1974, p. 153), which symbolizes the outside world and its expectations. Internally, actions have significance when they bear on one's own fate and that of others (these are the earmarks of milieu therapy). When all primary members—inmates and staff—influence the course of Reclaiming, then all are, in a sense, therapists. All are subject to significant role expectations in the changing and self-changing process.

Believing and Changing

Every internat is an artificial construct. Nothing in the nature of man or his basic social organization requires internats to be formal structures. Were families able and willing to care for their weak, sick, old, and demented, were they capable of elitist training and discrete but effective storage, such a social institution would be unnecessary. Artificiality has its consequences. Grouped together under a single roof, the members may have no common ground. Even in voluntary internats the diversity of entrants is substantial.

The internat exists to provide a level of Mastery for all its inmates. Its Goals may be related to common values or an ideology. Hospital staff and patients are expected to value health. Members of a smoking-abatement retreat are unified by their dislike of smoking or its consequences. The values that unify reformatory boys and their ill-paid staff are more ambiguous and less clearly related to Goals, Reclaiming, or Mastery. Some unity is afforded by the common values of survival under adverse conditions and discomfort with certain aspects of the internat as an institutionalized setting. Seemingly, more than successful technology distinguishes the hospital and retreat from the reformatory.

Many internats' arrangements are antagonistic to the inmates' acquisition of new skills and behaviors appropriate to Reclaiming. The inmate has no chance to move from his status to a different one, and the staff members' opportunity for mobility is also greatly restricted. The result is either a confusion of values or a tendency toward an inmate culture of rejectors and renegers whom staff may join or oppose. In this manner, an internat becomes an interactional battleground. A daily struggle goes on between those determined to promote Reclaiming and others prepared to settle for a simple meeting of organizational needs. Inmates and staff in the former group must continually ask themselves whether their effort is worth the strife, whether they should just yield to the prevailing forces of an internal counterculture or to organizational demands.

Apparently a community of inmates and staff sharing

common values can achieve its objectives even in the absence of technical or professional competence. Cohen and Filipczak (1971) argue that an effective technology not unlike that used in smoking-abatement programs can be successfully used in the reformatory. They show that a method of systematic reinforcement of specific goal-directed behavior yields results when value consensus is not readily apparent. Too, some internats whose technology is amorphous, claiming no expertise or *professional* competence in people changing—for example, monasteries, yeshivot, the Delancey Street Foundation, the SOS Kinderdorf—are apparently also achieving their objectives.

Both the local hospital that treats the physically ill and Delancey Street, which works effectively with ex-convicts and drug addicts, affirm the principle that change appropriate to Reclaiming can occur only if the gratifications following new behavior are greater than those surrendered. As Parsons (1951, p. 60) notes, "No actor can subsist without gratifications, while at the same time no action system can be organized or integrated without the renunciation of *some* gratifications which are available in the given situation." Gratifications—their definition, availability, or renunciation—are determined by the values of each system. The effectiveness of a gratification as a motivator will depend on whether it is "couched in terms of significance *for this particular actor in these particular relations with these particular objects*" (Parsons, 1951, p. 62).

Inmates may be induced to undertake some actions without understanding their corresponding values, but such actions will be insignificant to or even contrary to Reclaiming. A patient may be compelled to accept a salt-free diet, but unless he wants to live and understands how salt raises his blood pressure and causes cardiovascular problems, he will forsake the diet once he leaves the hospital. A prisoner may work in the metal shop because it is less boring than his cell, but unless he learns to value work and productivity, he will not enter the labor market upon his release.

Sanctions within the internat must thus be related to the inmates' value system, but they must also resemble the values of the external community. Failure to meet the latter criterion is an operational (not theoretical) defect in many token economy systems. Sanctions in an internat cannot merely represent internal consensus on value orientations or merely motivate all participants to meet the internat's organizational needs. Sanctions must be based on a definition of Reclaiming; they must encourage inmates to improve their Mastery, and they must have recognizable counterparts in the external world.

Most internats have several sets of sanctions, whose power varies considerably. First, there are clear, strong sanctions with observable criteria for the nonprofessional staff. Second, similar sanctions apply to the professionals but only regarding their administrative duties. Third, weak professional and ethical sanctions with unobservable criteria are applied to the professionals' other duties. Fourth, strong, formal sanctions with observable criteria apply to inmates' formal behavior. Fifth, sanctions relative to the Reclaiming behavior of inmates are diffuse and weak, since the criteria are relatively obscure. Sixth, there are strong informal sanctions of acceptable inmate and staff behavior; these are usually covert but well known to all. In many internats, the two behavior sets most directly applicable to Reclaiming—that is, the third and fifth sets—are also the weakest.

In principle, a number of sanction systems can simultaneously function as long as they share in, and do not contradict, a goal-directed theme. But there is no noticeable common theme in running an orderly ward, gaining insight into an Oedipal conflict, being on time to a workshop, and not being a stool pigeon. Even if a commonality could be found, its links would be weak and disputable.

Inevitably, diverse people have their own reference groups and different sanction hierarchies. The question is whether an internat can develop a single system of graded sanctions manifestly related to Reclaiming. In such a system, only activities functional to goal achievement will be positively sanctioned, while dysfunctional activities will be ignored or negatively sanctioned. When goals are agreed upon and means are specifically prescribed, sanctions are computational—in Thompson's (1967) terms—as in medical settings; for example, a doctor can calcu-

late that if a patient does not have surgery he has a 50 percent
chance of survival. When neither the goals nor the means are
agreed on, a graded sanction system is unlikely to evolve until a
consensus is introduced by an ideology or the powerful intervention of charismatic leadership.

When actors agree only on changes along some dimensions of Mastery, several outcomes are possible. The internat
may ignore other dimensions of Mastery, as a hospital usually
ignores some physical and most nonphysical attributes that are
not directly related to its conception of Reclaiming. Authority
may be invoked in the form of expert power or even coercion as
in prisons, for example. Or the internat may plan for the integration of the various value orientations under an ideological
umbrella or an open interactive process.

Unclear or inconsistent Reclaiming values do offer benefits to participants. Staff members have to work less, may sneak
away earlier, bribe the inmates and feel less threatened by them,
moonlight, prepare themselves for new careers, and get along
better with fellow staff members. Paradoxically, the same is
true also for inmates. Many internats are structured in a way
that punishes inmates or staff who are intent on Reclaiming.
The easiest solution under these circumstances is collusion between inmates and staff to do the minimum necessary for joint
survival. Most prisons, psychiatric hospitals, and homes for the
elderly or retarded function in such a value wilderness.

Different dynamics are found in internats that offer their
membership a highly congruent value set—a clearly defined
ideology. This ideology is sometimes presented in the guise of
high technology or precision professionalism, as in the hospital,
for example. More often, though, the ideology represents a way
of life potentially attainable by the internat membership. When
such ideology exists, it imbues the hardships of Reclaiming with
endurable—indeed, even enjoyable—acceptance. Ideology within
the internat is, therefore, more than a cosmetic or veneer. It is
the essence of the Reclaiming process, a harmony of ideas and
actions (Feldman, 1966; Festinger, 1963).

An internat's ideological consistency will be reflected in
its Activity. Weinberg (1967, p. 45), for example, observed the

teaming of games and religion in the English public school: "Games reinforced the chapel because the ideal of moral integrity and self-control could be practiced on the playing field. The public schoolboy was not to be a sheltered cleric, but an active and dynamic Christian." The integration of Activity through a unified belief system appears to yield a more profound acceptance of that Activity by inmates: "Public schools not only generate relatively more conformity, wider acceptance of their purposes and basic means among their senior pupils, and to a wider range of ends than other schools, but the *quality* of that acceptance is . . . deeper. . . . Conforming pupils do not simply accept, they are deeply committed to the school's aims, values, and structure" (Lambert with Millham, 1968, p. 363).

Clearly, the best modeling and reinforcement is derived from such commitment. Inmates can apply their development in one field to another, as the schoolboys converted the symbolism of religion to self-denial and fair play in sports. New meaning and new values can be learned through the application of such symbols (Rose, 1962, pp. 5-9). This kind of learning can be accomplished in settings other than the boarding school. Astrachan, Harrow, and Flynn (1969) demonstrate that introduction of values (by way of modeling by research personnel) to a psychiatric ward influenced both staff members and inmates in the modeled direction.

Gesellschaft and Gemeinschaft. Parsons (1951, p. 349) describes the relationship of an ideology to goals and to the evaluation of behavior: "An ideology . . . is a system of beliefs, held in common by the members of a collectivity . . . which is oriented to the evaluative integration of the collectivity, by interpretation of the empirical nature of the collectivity and of the situation in which it is placed, the process by which it has developed to its given state, the goals to which its members are collectively oriented, and their relation to the future course of events."

Goals, then, are a step in the conversion of values to Activity. An ideology will yield integrated goals, as it defines and, in some respects, confines goals. A Soviet *shkola internat* [boarding school] will not teach entrepreneurial behavior, and a monastery will not teach familial skills. What need not be taught in an orphanage or a mental hospital is, however, more difficult to determine, and what ought to be taught there is more difficult still.

The distinction between the *shkola internat* or monastery and the orphanage or mental hospital is that the former (as ideal types) are collectives of people sharing similar values. They are communities bound by bonds of common values and beliefs, mutual interdependence, and commonly recognized stratification; Tönnies (1957) calls this arrangement a *Gemeinschaft*. In contrast, *Gesellschaft* characterizes those internats with formalistic, bureaucratic structures that resemble factories, government offices, and other production enterprises. Following Parsons (1968, pp. 687-689), we can itemize six basic differences between these two patterns of human organization.

Gesellschaft	*Gemeinschaft*
1. A community based on the rational pursuit of individual members' self-interest.	1. A community of fate in which the parties act and are treated as a unit of solidarity.
2. Relationships between members are mechanistic. Typical relations are exchange and the voluntary limited-purpose association.	2. Relationships between members are organic. Members share benefits and misfortunes in common, not necessarily equally.
3. Members' obligations to each other and to the community are specific.	3. Obligations are unspecific and unlimited.
4. Relationships between superiors and subordinates are delimited by the rules of the organization.	4. Relationships between members may be hierarchical and functional.
5. Contingent rules and sanctions govern behavior.	5. Sanctions are applied with attitudes and not specific acts.

Gesellschaft	*Gemeinschaft*
6. The primary value systems of the parties need not be integrated.	6. Parties have a stated valuative purpose in entering into or adhering to the relationship. Values such as traditionalism, religious, and moral elements are important.

Only an internat whose administration, staff, and inmates share similar values can function as a *Gemeinschaft*. A mental hospital exhibiting such features is described by Stotland and Kobler (1965). Makarenko (1953, 1955) and Wolins (1974d) depict such youth communes, and Korczak (1967) explains how a *Gemeinschaft* existed in the Warsaw ghetto. However, unless determined formal efforts are made to preclude it, every internat will drift toward *Gemeinschaft*. (As Polsky, 1962, has shown, the ideology that prevails may be that of inmates and not of staff—this provides some explanation of why such drift is often stymied.)

The direction a *Gemeinschaft* will pursue is a function of the ideal values held freely by its members. These values will be converted to operating norms (Kunkel, 1970) that actuate behavior. A unified valuative ideal provides the overall vision of a Reclaiming setting, and from it develops an operational unifying theme that governs sanctions for inmate and staff behavior. To approximate the ideal values is a goal for members of a *Gemeinschaft*; each member strives to realize those values as fully as his Mastery allows.

Only an internat that enhances such participation will be effective in Reclaiming. Whether the origin of an internat's integrated value system is scientific, political, religious, or charismatic, it provides a basis for ranking behaviors. A culture develops —whether of the inmates, of the staff, or common to both— that contains symbolic and actual behavioral contingencies. Rewarding and punishing objects and events, rewarded and punished actions, are defined within this value context. A consistent value system endows the internat's Activity with an aura of wholeness, propriety, and even predestination. Herein may lie some dangers: A monolithic community that is fairly isolated may become self-destructive (see Krause and others, 1978; Lawson, 1972).

6

Maintaining the Identity of Resident and Setting

Overview

Reclaiming the inmate connotes changing one or more dimensions of Mastery. To Reclaim its inmates, an internat must be able to realign its goals, modify its adaptation to the outside world, and adjust the integration of its internal components. The successful internat must be flexible enough to modify its shape, size, and even location, yet it must also be stable enough to present a consistent identity to both external and internal constituencies. The internat must conserve itself as a physical, psychological, social, and valuative entity that imbues loyalty and fulfills expectations.

Critical to an internat's conservation is the identification and acknowledgment of its particularity. Each internat has its own spirit, its own sense of mission, which differentiates it from all others of its genre. Only by emphasizing its individuality can an internat acquire the loyalty of staff and of inmates, and create a distinct niche in its societal milieu. Such particularity is a function of events; past and present activities and their pacing define the particularity of a setting. For example, the rapid pace of the emergency rooms of county hospitals differs enormously from that of old-age homes, monasteries, or back wards of mental hospitals. Similarly internat staff, regularly crossing the boundary from the outside, notice differences between external temporal pacing, rhythms, and schedules and temporal values within the internat.

If the pace and content of an internat's Activity are internally consistent and reflect the expectations of residents, staff, and relevant outsiders, the identity of the internat is clear to all participants. For example, staff and patients in a twenty-four hour emergency room largely ignore outside time. Staff and patients tend to their affairs without regard to the rhythm of work, sleep, and meals conventional in the community. Such a setting is beneficent because the patients' needs govern the schedules of all other participants. In a prison, in contrast, the time of others is imposed on inmates, leaving large spaces between events. Time for prisoners moves slowly, although for the parole board it may move rapidly enough.

Physical space, like time perspectives, may also act to conserve or confuse. A hospital built in the shape of a cross (cruciform design) provides the faithful with continuity, a sense of recognition and belonging. The massive walls of a prison, small barred windows, and high fence transmit their intended message. Stable and long lasting, the physical plant may affirm the views of one era and contradict those of another. It may remind inmates and former inmates of the glory or privation of the past, of their special attributes or their similarity with those in the surrounding community. Big, congregate houses connote difference. Cottages near the village or interspersed with it symbolize similarity. Similarly, a converted mansion in an exclusive residential district sends its favorable message about the novitiate priests, boarding school students, or former criminals within it. The physical plant informs inmates, the staff, and the community; its message may be consistent with or contrary to an internat's purposes.

Like its physical plant, the internat's social structure has both functional and symbolic purposes. Symbolically, it affirms and conserves the existing social order. Training its leaders, containing its deviants, proclaiming its virtues, the internat is a tool and a reflection of society. Elitist internats may even be expected to present models of proper deportment for those outside.

In this sense, the internat is an embodiment of a value system applied to the behavior of its members. Hospitals are the epitome of a rationalistic, scientific approach to physical health and illness. They also represent the belief that deviance of any kind is the province of professionals, who should ideally be objective, detached, and analytical. Religious internats, in contrast, are governed by an ideology based on transcendent faith. Both hospital and monastery are standard bearers for beliefs and values supported by society. Beliefs, in turn, govern Activity, because they provide criteria for ordering behavior so as to conserve the internat and the society that has created it.

Building an Identity

Wheeler (1969) describes continuity, the forces which push toward persistence, as opposed to innovation and change. All systems of relationship must, by their very nature, be conservative or they would not persist. The family is perhaps the most conservative system. Members must of necessity share a link with the past and certain hopes and aspirations for the future. A common genetic heritage, a common social and psychological past, and shared experiences of the present inevitably produce a sense of identity. Lifton (1975, 1979), in her studies of adopted children's search for their natural parents, shows the extent to which people's past seems to them a part of their present life. Why else would adults search for childhood origins that were surrendered psychologically, socially, and legally many years before?

The attributes that conserve and identify also separate. In all internats a bond is created among members. Visible or not, this bond, often expressed in behavior as well as feelings, differentiates the internat from the surrounding society. Regardless of the qualities of the internat environment, be they humane or inimical to human survival, constructive or destructive, a sense of internal unity pervades. Members, both residents and staff, care recipients and caretakers, watched and watchers, feel themselves different, separate from others. The degree of separation depends on the functions of the internat, its past history, and the attributes of its participants. The monastery will be more conservative than the local community hospital. But even in a community hospital, the past influences present behavior. Despite rapid technological changes in medicine, the hospital's history—its physical plant, social relationships, customs, and the like—affects its present.

As internats help inmates improve their Mastery, they intend also to strengthen inmates' sense of their own identities. A strong self-identity implies "a feeling of being at home in one's body, a sense of 'knowing where one is going' and an inner assuredness of anticipated recognition from those who have it" (Erikson, 1968, p. 165). But some internats weaken inmates' self-identity; they generate a sense of failure, of worthlessness, of purposelessness and disjointedness (Erikson, 1968, p. 174). The identity of a person or of an internat persists from the past into the present, effecting current behavior, reinforcing itself, and yielding a reasonably predictable future. Responsive to the internat's identity, members know they must behave as expected or they will be rejected. Sometimes members' behavior will be understandable only in its internat context; for example, initiation ceremonies, during which the novice's identity is first defined as related to the organization's identity. Identity not only dictates initiation behaviors, but also determines their connotation. For example, abusive fraternity rites are viewed by many as merely college pranks, while the same rites in a prison would not be dismissed as pranks.

The identity of all internats is, to some extent, determined by their social otherness; internats are designed to do what normal community life cannot do or fails to do. The allusion to failure as a component of an internat's identity depends on the type of population it admits and the tasks it performs. The least failure-laden identity is shared by internats intended for training purposes followed by internats for healing and for socialization.

Training internats are distinct from internats for socialization because technical skill is the primary objective of the former. Their achievements can be counted, measured, and laid before a skeptical public in the form of statistical tables. The specificity of technical skills to be acquired is matched by the limited, clearly designated, and acceptable social outcome of training. A niche is readily available to the individual who departs a training internat that can predict at the time of entry the duration of residence and skills to be acquired. A member of such an internat has a defined curriculum and can anticipate recognition upon its completion. The curriculum is intended to produce a progressive ladder of competence resulting ultimately in a small distinction between the expert teacher and the pupil. Two types of continuity result from such an arrangement. The veteran inmate not only continues the inmate culture but returns to the same environment as an alumnus and joins the cadre of instructors—a phenomenon most unlikely in other internat types.

The identity of healing internats is in some measure a function of history. Until recently, the hospital was largely the lot of the poor, who went to the hospital for lack of a bed in which to die and were accepted out of charity or as subjects for medical instruction. The indigency of patients promoted gross distinctions between care recipients and caretakers. Distinctions persist today as the intentions of contemporary hospitals include enhancing professionals' technical proficiency and providing administrative convenience to staff. Hospitals serve well the professionals who share in an experts' culture and are the masters of their internat's identity. The hospital inmate, in contrast, resides there for a relatively brief period and can maintain the sense of personal identity he brings in from the outside. If the period of hospital care becomes extended, however, the inmate's self-identity weakens as he is deprived of contact with the external cultural matrix and not admitted fully to the hospital's internal culture.

Failure is a larger component of the identity of socializing internats. Their task is to accept individuals who have been defined as bad or misbehaving and to change the complexion of their behavior. But the socializing internat has no defined curriculum for change; it offers no more than a strong, concentrated form of the learning activities that the inmate's family, school, and other community socializing agents have already offered. Because the inmate has failed to learn from those agents, often neither the inmate nor his family, social workers, or therapists really believe that the new approach will be more effective than the previous methods. In particular, the inmate is likely to distrust the internat's ability to help him since it offers the same procedures that have already failed him or that he has failed at. Indeed, inmates are surrounded by other inmates—evidence of the internat's failure to help.

Too, part of the socializing internat's identity derives from its function as a storage unit for outcasts, people who are sent there because their community no longer wishes to tolerate their presence. Individuals—both staff and inmates—who enter such internats with a sense of purpose and an interest to help are horrified. A young volunteer describes her first experience in a nursing home: "FORGET IT! I AM NEVER GOING BACK! . . . That was written last night, just after I returned from my first night at the *** home. What is really bad is that instead of coming up with a crusader wish to help the nursing home problem, I came out last night vowing to commit suicide before I get old" (Townsend, 1971, p. 55).

Every inmate of an internat is viewed and views himself through the identity of the internat. The internat's identity is a conservative feature that determines the worth of the internat and its inmates. Like a family, an internat has a consistent identity, a "logical regularity and predictability of certain repetitious events" (Boszormenyi-Nagy and Spark, 1973, p. 1). Such is a boy's perception of his public school: "It is a school that's secure; it allows me to educate myself and be educated. I like its traditions and I've had relations as well as a brother and father here. You're always part of the school; even when you've left you're still welcomed back any time at free expense for any length. The masters live in and one can always come and see them—it's really a second home" (quoted by Lambert with Millham, 1968, p. 364).

The internat's identity may be so strong and may transfer itself to the individual so powerfully that released inmates may be unable to extinguish it. Edgerton (1967) describes a woman who spent eighteen years in a hospital and required four years on the outside to become aware that she had been released. Such persistence of identity is even more apparent while a person is still in the internat. Braly (1976, p. 191), an inmate at San Quentin, describes the situation of a Captain Dad, a guard who at one time committed a brave act and was rewarded with a rapid promotion. His heroic deed "happened twenty years before . . . and during this time admin [administration] had sometimes been hard pressed to find something Captain Dad could handle which wasn't inconsistent with his dignity." In the small universe of San Quentin prison, Captain Dad's identity as a hero, once established, continued to be maintained for decades.

Identity—an individual's or an internat's—is just such a persistence of unique behavior, activity, values, and the like. Describing a mental hospital, Stanton and Schwartz (1954) note: "If you ask people the purpose of the hospital . . . what they usually speak of are the special or unique purposes, those which they feel distinguish the particular hospital from others. . . . These purposes are usually the first that occur to the staff and the articulate patients as the sole purposes of the hospital" (pp. 44-45). Such uniqueness—specialness of ideas, premises, propositions, fundamental philosophy—may be derived from many sources.

An internat's uniqueness may be the legacy of a charismatic leader, a part of a glorious history, or a fraction of a

promising and exciting future. Father Flanagan's Boys Town
lived off his charismatic legacy long after his death. Korczak's
spirit is still embodied in the buildings of the Warsaw orphanage
from which the Nazis evacuated him in the 1940s. Menninger's
name still activates and molds the identity of the Menninger
Foundation. These leaders' charisma has been converted to leg-
end that informs present behavior.

Similarly, an internat's tradition and history are part of
its present. A boy from an English public school mentions the
importance of history and tradition to him: "I love its rather
traditional public school architecture, its uniform, its near vicin-
ity to the Abbey which unconsciously adds to the atmosphere.
Its faith which makes us at least have *one* thing in common,
though not all of us . . ." (quoted by Lambert with Millham,
1968, p. 363).

This sense of specialness contributes to the internat's life,
and changes in this specialness may cause the internat to collapse. When the specialness of a hospital described by Stotland
and Kobler (1965) was destroyed by therapists who did not
subscribe to Menninger's philosophy, the hospital collapsed because it had lost the particular "configuration of parts and relationships . . . maintained in a self-maintaining and repairing system" (Laszlo, 1972, p. 37). While internats require interchange
with their environment in order to survive, such settings also
have a sense of boundary, inner cohesion, and continuity that
must be maintained in the face of stress. To the individual inmate an internat offers membership and participation. "I don't
belong like this anywhere else," says an eighteen-year-old public school boy (Lambert with Millham, 1968, p. 364; italics
added).

Some of the behavior generated by an internat's identity
will not necessarily make sense to the outside observer but inevitably makes sense to those involved in it. Inmates and staff
intuitively comprehend the internat's identity, and their loyalty
to its persistence affects their behavior. For outsiders to understand why the Capo served the order of a concentration camp
or why the "trusty" maintains his own prison, they must consider
the inmates' identification with the internat and their loyalty to

its persistence, particularly in view of the possibility of a worse order of things. The motives for loyalty to an internat are diverse, as Boszormenyi-Nagy and Spark (1973, p. 39) point out: "Members of a group may behave loyally out of external coercion, conscious recognition of interest in membership, consciously recognized feelings of obligation, and unconsciously binding obligations to the law." Once an inmate or staff member identifies with an internat, his behavior will be influenced, perhaps even prescribed, by that person's image of the internat.

Among other historical forces, an internat's identity is also determined by the legacy that all patients, wards, and staff members leave for those following. They bequeath to newcomers messages about whether one can learn, progress, and develop within the internat. Persons who leave the internat also shape its identity by their subsequent actions. Their subsequent laudable behavior reflects positively on the internat, while unacceptable behavior contributes to the internat's negative reputation.

Time and Identity

The formation of an identity both for the setting and the person is a function of the flow of events in time. In internats time may have both continuous and disjunctive qualities (Wheeler, 1966). At West Point, for example, tradition, the style of buildings, and the upperclassmen provide continuity. Yet each class is also a separate entity, and a new pattern of activity begins each year as new members enter the flow of events that represent the internat.

This flow of Activity has no specific value other than that which residents of an internat and its observers attribute to it. The higher the frequency of positively evaluated activities, the more likely the internat's identity will be a positive one. It is exactly this identity which makes it desirable for some internats to emphasize their continuity and others to emphasize their disjunctiveness. Continuity is an asset to a reputable rest home or a prominent public school and a liability to a notorious prison or a scandal-ridden psychiatric hospital. In this respect, time may be an ally or an enemy to the internat's identity. Similarly, time is the enemy of a prisoner at San Quentin because he evaluates the flow of events negatively. However, the plebe at West Point views time positively because it carries the promise of knowledge, prestige, and recognition.

Within any social system, time is not merely an objective, physical phenomenon but rather the perceived frequency of and limiting factor for Activity. The pace appropriate to an infant nursery may be unnecessarily, even annoyingly rapid for a home for the aged or bedridden. Time is not a uniform quantity that flows at the same speed in both places. In internats, as in relativity physics, "time had always been considered to be the same for everyone; that is to say, time passed at the same rate for every person or object in the universe. Like a large, slow-flowing river whose current is the same for all points along its banks, time was considered as a uniformly flowing thing which passed at the same rate for everyone. [Einstein's] Special Theory showed that this was not true. It showed that time flowed at *different* rates for two observers moving relative to each other" (Coleman, 1954, p. 62).

Linear objective time does govern many activities in internats. Cadets spend four years at West Point and their program is further subdivided into annual intervals. Unless subjects of an indeterminate sentence, prisoners are sentenced for specific periods, and most patients enter hospitals anticipating a short, fixed stay. In many ways, residents and staff are expected to use objective time like any normal individual functioning in the outside world; schedules are derived from work, studies, and other activities. However, in the internat, as the boundaries between these activities become less distinct, the necessity for keeping in time with the outside world is lessened, and the possibility develops for specifically constructed "ancillary timetables" (Markson, 1973, p. 39).

Normal individuals, given open lines of communication and a reasonable sense of reality, regularly and necessarily shift from one time frame to another, from personal time to objective time. Inmates of internats, however, are often deprived of both communication and a sense of reality. Their personal situation or Mastery may be such that they cannot switch from personal time to objective time. A senile eighty-year-old in a nursing home may be involved in thoughts, dreams, fantasies, and a sense of self-identity that date back to adolescence. Unable to distinguish personal memories from the actual present, such a resident has a different time frame than others in the internat or the outside community.

Internats, too, function in both objective time and personal time. Thoughts, dreams, and fantasies may be the lot of social entities as well as individuals. Statues of old soldiers, hymns of bygone years, legends, old buildings and their inscriptions—all are emblems of the idiosyncratic time that is part of today's West Point. Unlike objective time, personal time can move back and forth in an instant. A healthy internat, like a healthy person, given reasonable communication with the outside world, will integrate its own past into its present without confusing the two or regressing into the past.

Because internats have strong boundaries that isolate inmates and define their routines and schedules, they profoundly affect the personal time of residents, particularly those with low Mastery. "The patients have four walls to look at all day; and three meals and three doses of medication to quiet them down; and three shifts to note coming on and going off" (Townsend, 1971, p. 195). The internat's time becomes the relevant time for inmates, while outside time is blurred. Detachment is, however, only partial since staff shifts are related to external work schedules; holidays are on the same day in the internat and out; sunrises and sunsets are at the same time. But the pace is different. In elitist settings events usually move more rapidly than on the outside; there are always interesting events and activities. In prisons, in contrast, time seems to pass more slowly as boredom and frustration take their toll.

In slow time settings, inmates with low Mastery succumb to apathy and despair. "The hospital has one circular corridor and the patients that can, go around and around all day, their posey belts [restraints to prevent self-injury] substituting for the chains of a supposedly more primitive time. I have known old ladies of eighty and some years to sit in the same wheel chairs from 9:00 in the morning until 8:00 at night without being taken to the bathroom" (Townsend, 1971, p. 194).

Inmates with higher Mastery may feel that anything appears better than the blanket of dullness: "Each Monday describes every Friday. Holidays in prison are only another mark of passing time and for many they are the most difficult days. Most of the outrages that provide such lurid passages in the folklore of our prisons are inspired by boredom. Some grow so weary of this grinding sameness they will drink wood alcohol even though they are aware this potent toxin may blind or kill them. Others fight with knives to the death and the survivor will remark, 'It was just something to do' " (Braly, 1976, p. 182).

Conflicts between individuals that are caused by different time frames are most evident in settings highly oriented to productivity. For example, patients and staff in internats specializing in physical rehabilitation are supposed to be very conscious of time, and a rapid flow of events appears to be in order. Yet, as Calkins (1970) found, patients who are old or chronically ill or mentally incapacitated have a slow inner time, which may frustrate the staff. Furthermore, since staff know that patients require varying amounts of time to make progress, they do not set time limits, leaving patients confused. While staff members or society believe that a patient is moving rapidly toward recovery, the patient may have a different image: that he is on a "treadmill, where movement occurs although nothing happens" (Calkins, 1970, p. 490).

In such situations, inmates often lose track of time: "Fred was released on leave [from an internat for the retarded] in 1945, three years after he entered the hospital. But in Fred's recollection of the elapsed time . . . 'I was only there a year and a half. I went there about 1941 and it was about 1943 when I came out. I was discharged in 1943, but it might have been 1942—I know it was either 1941 or 1942—I was only there a year and half. Hell, you guys know more about when I went in than I do' " (Edgerton, 1967, p. 43). One function of Reclaiming internats for the disturbed is to bring an inmate's internal time into closer proximity with external time. Fred's confusion may not have mattered much when he was in the internat, which tolerates time elasticity. But this disparity seriously affects his capacity to function outside because he cannot integrate successfully the personal, internat, and societal time frames. Fred's *personal time* is a function of the frequency of activity as he perceives it. Since Fred's hospital stay was punctuated by few activities, his perception of the amount of time he spent there is shorter than the objective duration of his stay.

Figure 1 depicts the intersection of three distinct time frames within an internat, an intersection that yields seven subsets.

Figure 1. Intersection of Society's, Inmate's, and Internat's Time Frames

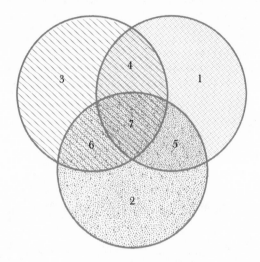

1. Society's time is the perception of time by society that disregards (or is oblivious to) the internat; for example, the fiscal year, the opening hours of stores, and train schedules.
2. An inmate's personal time is his private perception of time irrespective of society and the internat; for example, personal reminiscences, fantasies, and longings for past or future.
3. An internat's internal time is the scheduling that governs the internat's routines, regardless of both society's and inmates' time perception; for example, schedules of activities or vacation made solely for the convenience of the internat or its staff.
4. An internat's social time is that aspect of the internat's

schedule that respects society's time but disregards inmates'
time; for example, visiting hours arranged according to the
railroad schedule or reduced activities on national holidays.

5. An inmate's social time is that aspect of his time perception
that is consonant with society's time but disregards the internat's internal time; for example, an inmate's effort to
schedule his day in a manner similar to that of a nine-to-
five office worker.

6. An inmate's internat time is that aspect of his time perception that is consonant with the internat's internal time but
disregards society's time; for example, an inmate's ritualistic behavior that is guided solely by the internat's schedule
of bells or buzzers.

7. The consonant perception of time by society, inmate, and
internat is exemplified by the observation of a national
holiday in accord with the inmate's Mastery and the internat's ideology.

This seventh subset, the intersection of inmate, internat,
and societal time perspectives, constitutes the internat's identity. Figure 2 shows the time structure of an internat with a
high level of integration within both the setting and the com-

Figure 2. Illustrative Time Structure of an Internat for
Integrated Reclaiming

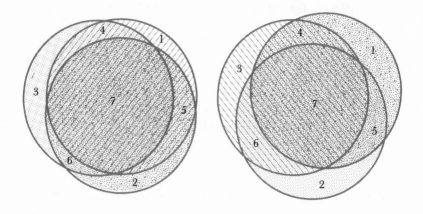

munity. The substantial overlap of the time subsets forms a clear identity for the internat. In contrast, Figure 3 shows a

Figure 3. Illustrative Time Structure of a Non-Reclaiming Internat

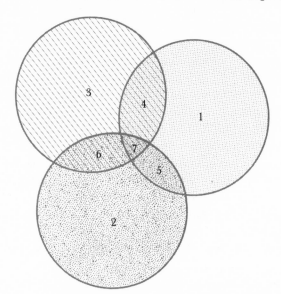

small overlap, which results in a confused identity for the internat and its inmates. The small overlap is symptomatic of internal conflict.

To achieve consistency with societal time, the inmate and internat must develop some manner for labeling or marking and for filling time. Work, organized play, study, and social encounters organize and mark time outside the internat. Clock-regulated and setting-specific, activities divide the flow of time into units. Work nine-to-five on weekdays, church on Sundays, the opera or bridge club on Wednesdays—all serve as points of temporal orientation. Multiplicity and dissimilarity make them recognizable as signs of small and different units within the flow of time.

In contrast, many internats provide few means of sectioning and differentiating time. Braly (1976, p. 181) describes the problem and points to some time-marking mechanisms: "The hardest part of serving time is the predictability. Each day moves like every other. You *know* nothing different can happen. You focus on tiny events, a movie scheduled weeks ahead, your reclass. [reclassification], your parole hearing, things far in the future, and slowly, smooth day by day, draw them to you. There will be no glad surprise, no spontaneous holiday, and a month from now, six months, a year, you will be just where you are, doing just what you're doing, except you'll be older." Confined to an environment of limited activity and not free to produce many events on his own, Braly marked off time in undifferentiated chunks, hanging on to small events in a large, uniform void. This gross, uncalibrated yardstick will serve him badly in the more precisely apportioned outside world.

To mark time, a resident may also use personal achievement as confirmed by others, changes in the internat, and external intrusions. Time may, thus, be marked by the day an inmate first got out of bed and walked, or the number of days elapsed between the hearing and granting of parole, or the last time the resident visited home. Changes in the internat also provide time markers: inmates remember when a new inmate first came to the ward or when a particular staff member left. Although such markers may be used by inmates at elitist institutions, they are more likely to be employed by the prisoner than the West Point cadet. A cadet's time frame is both more rapid and more closely related to objective time so that an internat marker is neither necessary nor sufficient for him.

Intrusions that mark time include visits by relatives, favored television programs, and appointments with external specialists who come at regularly scheduled intervals. Since these events define time, they acquire much significance. The postponement or cancellation of an expected event disturbs the inmates' time frame. In the external world or in an active internat, substitution is feasible and probable, but impoverished environments offer few alternatives. Little can replace the cancelled visit or even the television program missed because the set is broken. The infrequency of events amplifies the meaning of each simple event.

The inability to mark and manage time is a characteristic

and symbol of low Mastery. In extreme conditions, when an inmate can no longer perceive of time as marked by events, the burden of undifferentiated time torments inmates. A volunteer in a nursing home for the aged illustrates the effect of undifferentiated personal time on patients' identity: "One day is no different from the rest and even the sane patients don't know what day it is when you ask them, although some have calendars to mark off the days like the days off sentences to which they have been forced to serve. I have had patients ask me why God doesn't let them die" (Townsend, 1971, p. 195).

Passing time, waiting, doing time, making time, filling time, and, perhaps most appropriately, killing time are activities people in internats undertake in order to survive (Calkins, 1970). Since an internat's identity is, in a sense, the composite of individual responses to their physical and psychosocial surroundings, the approach most inmates take to time expresses the uniqueness of the setting and highlights its internal contradictions. Let us consider each of these approaches to time.

Passing time requires a total submission of the resident's personal time to the internat's inner time. Internat routine becomes the resident's schedule. Action and anticipation are expressed in time markers derived from the internat's tradition or its operational needs. Doctor's rounds and breakfast, lights out and changes of the guard are used as reference points in the inmate's personal life; inmates are thus detached from the outer society and from their own selves. An internat with a large contingent of members (including the care recipients and their caretakers) who are passing time functions smoothly and to no purpose other than its own survival. Residents and staff have a pattern of time management suited to a well-run human warehouse.

Waiting, though similar to passing time, is more constructive and is a behavior often appropriate in the outside world. Waiting implies an objective, but one not immediately within grasp, and connotes an awareness of social and of objective time. One waits by a clock that has intrapersonal as well as societal increments. Thus waiting is oriented to reality and has a purposiveness that passing time does not. Waiting by a person or

by an internat is constrained by society's time. Prisoners who
object to the indeterminate sentence favor waiting over passing
time. A patient's inquiry "Doctor, when may I go home?" is an
attempt to convert passing time to waiting time.

Doing time is related to passing time but with a distinction best illustrated by a veteran prisoner's admonition to a new
inmate: "Do your own time." Prisoners are detached from societal time and are expected to fully accept internat time, but
they may seek to maintain their individual identity by the
stratagem of operating within personal time. An inmate may re-
construct the past—many political prisoners write memoirs—or
plan the future, as Gandhi did when imprisoned.

Inmates who do their own time ignore the internat's temporal structure, and their independence threatens the internat's
integration. Their detachment implies a disregard for the Reclaiming objectives or abilities of the internat, announcing to
society that it is wasting its resources. By their focus on future
activity and past beliefs, such residents dispute the judgment of
a society that remanded them to an internat. By shaping their
personal lives into a cocoon around themselves, those who do
their own time impede integration. An internat filled with inmates doing their own time is a study in diversity without
unity, unless the internat possesses a common ideology and
communal activity that sustains individual isolation, such as a
monastery does.

Making time is the internat's objective for inmates. Inmates are to convert societal and personal time into internat
time, and do so to further the objectives of all three. A West
Point cadet who studies late at night, a hospital patient who
spends extra time in physical therapy exercises, a prisoner who
is working at a difficult trade—all are making time. Making time
reflects an awareness that time is Activity, while the other uses
of time appear to disregard such connotation. It also demands
some subordination of personal and of internat time to a superordinate goal that both inmate and internat accept. Usually this
goal is public and valued by society, therefore providing the inmate and the internat with leverage in their negotiations with

society for acceptance and increased resources. Inmates who make time are considered well adapted to the internat, and their behavior contributes to the internat's integration.

Because making time is a style of time management that bridges the societal, personal, and internat time frames, it is considered laudable. Residents who make time place heavy demands on the internat's flexibility in responding to their progress and effort. One response is for the internat to set a time limit for accomplishing a particular task. Hobbs (1974, p. 334), for example, defines time limits as an ally in the treatment of disturbed children. When "a newly admitted child asks 'How long do kids stay here?' [and] he is told 'about two years,' he settles down to do what is expected of him. . . . Before we admitted the first child, we set six months as the expected . . . period of stay."

Filling time is a subversion of making time. An inmate who is filling time appears to be structuring time for Reclaiming but actually has no concern for outcome. He has a pattern of deliberate Activity but has neither the personal future orientation of the inmate doing time nor the coordinated personal-societal orientation of the resident making time. Filling time is an inmate's attempt to produce the largest number of pleasurable events. Since this objective is divergent from Reclaiming, time-filling transactions are usually considered devious by internat staff. Yet an internat serving short-term or terminal clients may deliberately resort to filling inmates' time with television or other light diversion.

Killing time is the deliberate subversion of internat operations in order to provide some event that will make time seem to pass more quickly; any event will do. An internat insensitive to inmates' needs for activities will be plagued by incidents such as inmates' turning on the sprinkler system in the dormitory, going over the fence for the night, fighting, or throwing food in the dining room. An internat with a substantial number of residents who are killing time is in constant turmoil. Such residents vitiate the process of time making, impede waiting, attract to themselves the more self-confident time fillers, further isolate those who are bent on doing time, and make bland, innocuous, and vacuous time passing painfully unpleasant. The last of these results may be the only virtue of a time-killing orientation.

Each of the approaches to the use of time is probably found in every internat. The internat's identity results from the composite. Time passing with considerable waiting, time filling, and time killing define the boring, dangerous, purposeless prison. Time passing alone is characteristic of many internats that serve as warehouses, the better of which may include some time filling. A functionally organized internat with socially approved (and probably achieved) goals will have time making with some waiting but with little filling or time killing.

Conservation and Physical Surroundings

Many who argue in favor of internat care, particularly for children and youth, point to the stability of these settings to support their claims. Some of this stability is purely physical. Unlike behavioral events that produce confusing time frames, the buildings, grounds, and other components of the physical environment carry with them a sense of permanence. Etonian "boys," returning from years of service to the empire, often came to admire the old chapel, the aged trees, the familiar buildings and be reassured by them as well. In the internat's world of rapidly changing treatment ideologies, directors, social workers, physicians, nurses, and jailers, often only location and plant provide continuity.

The stability and solidity of the physical surroundings are an asset and a liability. Considerable permanence is reassuring, but it is also distinctive and inflexible. To be functionally conservative, internats, although distinctive physical entities, must not impinge upon or destroy the physical and sociocultural environment they inhabit. In colonial Philadelphia, conservation was thought to be best achieved by locating the jail in the center of town (Rothman, 1971). Later planners of internats, Kirkbride (1854) among them, thought otherwise. While Kirkbride's decisions on pastoral location were motivated by requirements of the therapy he espoused, Pennsylvania citizens were probably also pleased to see the internat, with its unusual buildings and residents, moved out of town.

The physical structure of an internat, by virtue of its distinct character, is planned with a singleness of purpose. Even the most fortunate internat, which fits into the existing environment, is subject to obsolescence as changes occur around it. Nothing seems as permanent as the plant of an internat nor, comparatively, as transient as the matrix within which it operates. The Bronx Developmental Center for mentally retarded was obsolete both as to location (originally noncontroversial, thus desirable) and size by the time the contractors handed its keys to the state of New York (Ivins, 1977). Shifts in the ideology of care outpaced the speed of construction. Less dramatic, though equally disconcerting for the adaptation of both residents and organization, are population movements, attitudinal changes, and variations in treatment fashions, all of which are likely to leave an internat orphaned of the very surroundings required for Reclaiming. Buildings and grounds represent and promote conservation but preclude flexibility.

Physical plant may be a burden or an opportunity (Rosenblatt, 1970), but it is never insignificant. Invariably built to last, costly, and immovable, buildings fix ideas in stone, glass, or concrete, imposing them on the present and conserving them for the future. Current inhabitants of Johns Hopkins, designed to the best thinking of the Civil War era, may still partake of its glory and suffer from its rigidities. Superintendents of West Point may take pride in the ancient ivy-covered halls but also find them hard to heat. The director of Pleasantville Cottage School, a childrens' internat, may recount with pride that it was among the first schools built on the cottage rather than congregate model. But the cottages are too large, the segregation by sex they imply is no longer customary, the staff quarters they provide are no longer suitable, and maintenance costs are exorbitant.

Whatever their origin, whether designed for or altered to present use, internat plants must provide for several conservation functions. Most notable are those concerning physical health and safety. Fire doors, marked exits, extinguishers, and sprinklers are the most visible conservation symbols of internat buildings. Bars on windows protect the disturbed and contain the disturbing; guardrails are placed on beds of the confused or feeble; automatic water shut-offs and large signs are provided for the disoriented. Health and safety specialists have produced, in most internats, masterpieces of physical conservation. Many safeguards are indeed helpful, protecting inmates from injury and public officials from liability.

However, as we noted in Chapter Five, safeguards that preclude all risks may also inhibit inmates' development of increased Mastery. Physical plant must respond to inmates' physical skills, offering both compensations for low Mastery and opportunities for development. It must provide for alternative ways of relating to the environment by residents who have severe physical disabilities. The architectural literature is understandably replete with cautions that elderly internat residents, for example, "are forced to cope with a decreasingly sensitive sensory apparatus" (DeLong, 1970, pp. 69-70) or that "brain-damaged older people [cannot] locate themselves in time, space, or with reference to other people [and that] multiple sensory channels [should] be used" (DeLong, 1970, p. 82). Thus all sensory functions and their limitations are relevant to location and design, as are the social, psychological, and value implications of a plant. To have a conservative function buildings must be responsive to the capabilities of those who will use them.

Range, docility, social interaction, and observability must be considered in planning the physical environment. The inmates' ability to explore and use their environment may be reduced by psychological limitations such as low intelligence, phobias, or aversions; by physical injury or deterioration; by law or social custom, as in the case of prisoners; or by value considerations requiring withdrawal, as is true for inhabitants of religious asylums.

If we follow Simon (1954, p. 399) in assuming that people learn to meet their needs by repeated trials adjusted by satisfaction and error experience, we see that low competence necessarily limits attempts and learning. For example, the income level of blacks in Chicago has been shown to restrict the location of hospitals they use (Earickson, 1970). If Simon's model is correct, then the larger the range of trials resulting from higher Mastery, the greater the possible variation of trials and, in turn, the better the ultimate fit. The object of internats is to keep this range as broad as possible and expand it as the inmate progresses. Space must, therefore, be so designed that it permits optimal functioning in the face of temporarily limited and progressively changing ability.

To offer an appropriate range is particularly difficult with regard to those populations whose movement is restricted by social, as contrasted with physical or valuative, constraints. In the case of the last, range reduction may be acceptable because it is self-imposed by deliberate decision. Restrictions due to physical limitations are amenable to objective review and are likely to yield agreement between the care recipient and caretaker to modify the environment as the inmate's physical health improves. Social constraints, in contrast, are imposed by fiat on social delinquents and some mentally ill persons. Consensus between inmate and staff is unlikely, and objective review is difficult.

Environmental docility is a corollary of range constriction. Lawton (1974) holds that a positive correlation exists between the extent of incapacity and the influence of physical environmental factors. Mastery thus governs not only an inmate's access to structures that will meet his needs but also the degree of impact the plant has on him. The lower the inmate's Mastery, the more significant is the plant, since his opportunities for escape and modification are fewer.

Range is broad and docility low in the normal human environment of the familial home, surrounded by its neighborhood and town or city. This environment offers opportunities for sociofugal (people-dispersing) and sociopetal (people-gathering) activities (Osmond, 1959). Individuals may choose when they wish isolation and privacy, intimacy, or open social interaction. Internats of the past used sociofugal arrangements to isolate certain inmates; the physically contagious were confined or banished to a leprosarium or other colony. Moral transgressors were isolated in the belief that religious salvation is best achieved in solitude.

Recent thinking about internat care tends to emphasize sociopetal activities. Osmond (1959), for example, experimented with physical arrangements that gave mental hospital patients considerable opportunity to converse and interact. His plan, based on learning theory, posits that inmate modeling and reinforcement will produce the behavior goals of the internat. From such a perspective, people-changing internats should all be sociopetal, but stabilizing, maintaining facilities, like terminal care nursing homes or even ordinary old-age homes, should not. This, in fact, is a suggestion posed by Lipman (1968) following the disengagement theory of Cumming and Henry (1961), which holds that aging persons gradually withdraw from social interaction. Reduced sociability was characteristic of residents of Victoria Plaza, an apartment complex for older people described by Carp (1970). Planners of this residence provided the usual lobby, which also served as entrance to the building, but "some residents regretted the necessity to walk through the lobby . . . because this exposed them to the view and speculation of . . . the 'lobby sitters' " (p. 179).

While planned social isolation may seem a custodial activity inappropriate to Reclaiming, it performs a positive conservative function for individuals who need or want to reduce sensory stimulation. In his design for an internat for severely retarded, nonambulatory, handicapped individuals, Sokoloff (1975, p. 20a) specifies that "the interior of the house should be simple. It should be easy for residents to orient themselves. Territories should be well defined. . . . Color should be used to identify, separate, and distinguish, rather than to excite." Such simplicity is not intended to promote progressive disengagement, but rather it is a means for the retarded to gradually integrate themselves into a more demanding environment.

Sociofugal and sociopetal considerations also enter the planning of hospitals for physically ill. Historically, the tendency has been primarily sociofugal—to enhance privacy. Such design is embodied in the Roman *valetudinarium*, a military hospital, which consisted of a large hall surrounded by patient rooms (Thompson and Goldin, 1975, p. 5). However, the advantages of privacy have to be balanced against the loss of professional supervision. The sicker the patient, the more important staff surveillance is to his well-being. Florence Nightingale, planning patient care in the middle of the nineteenth century, was against private rooms on that score alone, although she was also much concerned with ventilation.

The trend toward private rooms has continued in American hospitals, abetted by sophisticated electronic surveillance systems. The relatively short stay in these types of internats and the primary, often exclusive, focus on physical competence may account for this tendency. As a consequence, the patient is isolated from the modeling and assistance that other patients can render. Rooming arrangements should be, and usually are, different in extended care units such as hemodialysis, alcohol rehabilitation programs, or chemotherapy. The continuity of care in such units leads to an increased emphasis on the psychological, social, and valuative fields, an emphasis that requires sociopetal arrangements.

A pervasive problem of internat location and design is the difficulty of balancing conservation and stimulation. This problem is particularly troublesome when the plant's design is sociofugal or the population in care has extremely low Mastery, for example, the mentally retarded. As a *New York Times* reporter observed, "One of the most searing images . . . of Willowbrook was the child sitting on the floor . . . endlessly rocking back and forth, with nothing to look at but blank walls" (Ivins, 1977). To provide visual stimulation for children, the Bronx Developmental Center has windows that come down almost to the floor. This solution, however, does not adequately address two conservation issues: safety and stimulus overload. Parents of the potential residents were concerned with physical safety —that the windows would be kicked out. A psychiatrist was troubled by the surfeit of external stimuli over which the internat would not have control.

To balance conservation against stimulation and risk, planners must accord these factors weights appropriate to the internat's population. For example, Goldsmith (1975, p. 44)

suggests that an internat for children with impaired visual perception should have a visually simple interior: "Exaggerated
perspective, continuing vistas in long corridors or mirror reflection giving a sense of infinity should be avoided." In this case,
a visually exciting physical structure poses risks to inmates' per-
ceptual stability. In contrast, the gray sameness of many internats for the retarded holds risks so low as to induce stability,
and some visual excitement might be desirable.

A more elaborate schema for relating conservation to architectural design is advanced by Good, Siegel, and Bay (1965).
They propose a risk continuum in which patients are classified
by their level of disorganization, and space is classified by its
amenability to patient manipulation. The most disorganized patients are to receive the most conservative, predictable environments, manipulated by staff. Integrated patients are to be
housed in normal living environments that afford maximum responsibility to patients and minimal staff control.

Thus the conservation features of a physical plant may be
used to calm and reassure inmates and to pace their progress
toward higher Mastery. The rate of progress, however, is totally
idiosyncratic. Residents advance or regress individually, at a rate
specific to themselves. This variability requires a flexibility in
the physical environment that its conservative emphasis may
preclude. A person who can rapidly escape a burning internat
building needs sprinklers no more than the resident of a private
home. Automatic light control may be calming and regulatory,
but it constrains a patient whose condition is improving and an-
noys the prisoner in solitary, who finds sleep difficult in a
brightly lit cell.

Preserving the Community. Pressed by communities to
move away from their centers (where land is scarce and dear)
and from residential areas (where neighbors wield powerful political opposition), many internats find themselves in rural
areas. Such a location, however, fails to conserve the residents'
ties to the urban communities from which most of them origi-
nate. Relationships can be conserved only in the cities and
towns from which inmates come and to which they are destined
to return. Nagel (1973, p. 50) recommends that institutions be

located in or close to the city and Sokoloff (1975, p. 19a) urges that "transitional training apartments [for retarded should] be built in the community [where] they will serve to help residents acquire community living skills."

The location of internats, however, is determined not only by treatment philosophies but also by political considerations. Recently, more internats have been located in towns but not in all sections of town. Inner city urban areas—whose population has little power, due to limited enfranchisement, poverty, mobility, and urban decay—are frequently the site for internat relocation. These sections of the cities soon become internat-dominated neighborhoods, "ghettoes for the mentally handicapped" (American Psychiatric Association, 1977, p. 319). The problem is further exacerbated by the simultaneous flight of normal community members from such "social service districts" (Lauber with Bangs, 1974, p. 23) due to the seeming discomfort many people exhibit relative to any form of handicap (Kleck, 1968).

An elitist internat or a high-status internat can retain the usual community and may even contribute to its growth and prosperity. Rochester, Minnesota, takes considerable pride in the Mayo Clinic, for example. A prestigious and well-heeled internat, such as West Point, is often deemed so desirable by its near neighbors that they complain about rules restricting residents' participation in the external community. The mayor of Highland Falls, New York, complained about West Point's plans to move a visitors' information center out of the town to the institution's interior. That, said the mayor, "would turn this village into a ghost town" ("Village's War with West Point," 1979).

The consequences of an internat's location for the local population and for the inmates thus depend on the assets each side has to offer. The past status and present and future orientation of inmates affects the community's reception. The Delancey Street Foundation has shown that housing criminals and addicts in a San Francisco mansion can improve the community's acceptance of its new neighbors (Hampden-Turner, 1976). However, this strategy did not work for a youth campus in the same city. Intended for mentally disturbed youth, the campus is feared, suspected, and largely rejected by the community ("Board Unit Backs Youth Campus Plan," 1978).

With the notable exceptions of elitist programs and hospitals for the physically ill, almost all internats are in one of three types of locations. Large facilities, such as county hospitals and juvenile detention facilities, are usually in urban compounds of a very specific institutional character. Some large facilities, many of which were built decades ago, are in rural areas. The bulk of small internats are now in urban settings, but "typically, the areas which become 'dumping grounds' are high density, lower income, old or decaying, and nonwhite" (Lauber with Bangs, 1974, p. 13).

The American Society of Planning Officials is convinced that neighborhood conservation requires the dispersal of internats, and it has made some specific recommendations particularly regarding rather small facilities. These officials argue that "the existing social structure of a block can usually accommodate two or three [small internats].... Hence a limit of three facilities on a block face, coupled with a limit of fifty persons residing in these facilities, would ... [conserve] the character of the area" (Lauber with Bangs, 1974, p. 24; see also Knowles and Baba, 1973). While this limitation would, undoubtedly, be an improvement over the wall-to-wall internats of some downtown areas in American cities, the concentration still seems rather heavy. It may conform to the political realities of urban planning but is far less desirable than John Maher's choice locations for Delancey Street residences.

Ownership and Conservation. All conservationist steps that administrators and staff take in the design and management of the internat's physical plant are a function of ownership. Owners are permitted to manipulate physical environments, adjusting stimuli, safeguards, and risks to suit their own requirements. Internat residents, however, do not own their space and are usually prevented from exerting any control over their physical environment. Consider, for example, the provision of a safe location for inmates' personal belongings. Korczak believed that the internat staff "has a duty to see to it that every child owns something which is not anonymous property of the institution but definitely his own and that he has a safe place to keep it. If a child puts anything in his drawer he must be sure that nobody will touch it" (1967, p. 393).

Adults, in particular highly dependent adults, have this same need. A person "is partially defined by belongings, personal space, and props such as mirrors and pictures of significant people. Some of these features may be built into institutional rooms, thus coercing administrators into enduring the extra trouble required by their presence" (Lawton, 1974, p. 65). Ownership in internats, as in the world outside, is related to status. Staff, more privileged residents, and those with greater seniority or intelligence or physical strength have the benefit of more space and greater opportunities to separate their public "front stage" from private "back stage" activities (Goffman, 1959). In a children's ward described by Pill (1967), the hierarchy of patient, nurse, and doctor is clearly embodied in spatial mobility. Patients usually have freedom of bed, toilet, ward, and lounge. Nurses may go anywhere, although "some nurses may not be allowed in the [operating] theatre" (p. 182). Physicians, it is assumed, may go anywhere.

Physical planners respect this social hierarchy by providing physicians with rooms they can close or lock, nurses with cabinets they may secure (often with an obvious jangling of keys), and ward patients with few, if any, private spaces. The question to be pondered, though, is whether planning should respect this hierarchy or attempt to change it in order to increase residents' self-reliance, self-image, and independence. For example, what are the consequences of giving residents keys to their own rooms or lockers or of giving them access to staff rooms? There is evidence that the prestigious location of an internat translates into improved status for inmates (Hampden-Turner, 1976); inmates' control of space increases their responsible behavior (Korczak, 1967); and opportunity leads to competence and greater independence (Fairweather, 1964).

Builders of medieval hospitals understood how space may be used to express society's claim to the inmate. Chapel and religious services in the cruciform hospital conserved the past and assured a future, both crucial to the healing process. Several

centuries later, Bentham's (1791) panopticon allowed a treater
to simultaneously see—and therefore help—all the residents. The
panopticon's perfectly round building with seven tiers permitted the superintendent, housed in the middle, to see into
every cell. Such total visibility, Bentham claimed, would bring
about "morals reformed—health preserved—industry invigor-
ated—instruction diffused—public burdens lightened—Economy
seated, as it were, upon a rock—the gordian knot of the Poor-
Laws not cut, but untied—all by a simple idea in Architecture"
(Bentham, [1843], 1962, vol. 4, p. 39).

Bentham's view that society owned the internat and that
its architecture was to conserve society persisted long after his
death. The Boston Prison Discipline Society announced that
"There are principles in architecture, by the observance of
which great moral changes can be more easily produced. . . .
There is such a thing as architecture adapted to morals. . . .
Those who would rehabilitate the deviant had better cultivate
this science" (cited by Rothman, 1971, pp. 83-84).

Fixed Plant and Changing Needs. Buildings are hard to
change. Often only natural disasters or accidents destroy this
legacy of the past. Planners must consider two time gaps: one is
that between plan and finished plant; the other, between start
and end of use. Although the first of these is obviously much
briefer than the second, construction may lag behind social
thought. While the Bronx Developmental Center was being constructed, for example, professionals reversed their ideas: Small
internats were suddenly thought better than big ones, and
homeyness was deemed preferable to architectural innovation.
The internat, designed to reflect the older values, clashed with
the newer ones, and professionals and clients rejected it.

Constantly changing emphases in clinical theory, internat
methods, societal values, and types of clientele demand a flexible and movable plant. Although the internat is expected to
give its residents stability, a sense of rootedness in a shifting
world, it is also expected to be able to collect its staff and traditions, dismantle its buildings (or convert them to other uses
or cash), and relocate in new forms and new settings. Within the
past century, some childcare internats have moved from city to

suburb, and back to city; they have changed in form from congregate to pavilion to cottage to city apartment.

The arguments for flexibility are many. They are based on the inadequacy of knowledge, the unpredictability of people, and the importance of site and plant in determining Activity. The object is to reduce the plant's interference with new programs and new methods of treatment. Physical plants must strike a balance between achievement and integration requirements and those of conservation and adaptation. The appropriate balance for any given internat will vary over the four modes. Thus, the disoriented aged are best served by a stable, conservative structure well integrated to reduce confusion. Adolescents hospitalized with broken legs will seek achievement and adaptation, and flexible, changing space is the most suitable for them.

Societal Conservation

An internat—this unusual, costly, enclosed, mysterious social structure, often located out of the way and further hidden from full view by its divergent buildings and access control—is also a social good. Society has charged the internat with caring for those of its members who are too violent or irrational, too weak or ambitious, too committed or irresponsible. The inmates of prisons and monasteries, military academies and mental hospitals are different from normal community members. Their aggregation and isolation serve to maintain social order and patterns. Such maintenance, however, is only part of the internat's task. Unless the internat is a deliberate tool for annihilation, like the Nazi concentration camps, or a benign resting place for the terminally ill, such as a hospice for the dying, it must also proclaim and demonstrate its loyalty to the larger society. The following examples illustrate the public expression of internal loyalty.

At one of the Leningrad boarding schools, there was a shrine for Lenin. In front of it, with periodic regularity, two internat residents relieved those standing solemnly on guard. A portrait of Lenin, some historical photographs, a few slogans about building communism were all of the components. Yet these young people treated their guard duty as an honor. Not everyone was chosen. One Pioneer, coming off duty, explained its meaning to a visitor: "It shows that we are all part of the great Soviet Union, as Lenin had prophesied. But we do more than other schools, our shrine is more interesting, our guards more serious. We are different, so we have to be better."

John Maher of the Delancey Street Foundation in San Francisco organizes some residents who go out to teach merchants how to spot shoplifters. Former criminals are now instructors in crime prevention. They show, with consummate skill derived from years of experience in "the trade," how shoplifters work and what merchants may do to foil them (Hampden-Turner, 1976).

Speaking before a chamber of commerce group, a prison warden explains costs. Prisoners are dangerous and wily. Escape is always a possibility and rehabilitation is a long, drawn-out process, mysterious and only partially effective. The prison, he contends, must have a high budget in order to isolate the dangerous and incorrigible, while working to change the others so they will become law-abiding citizens. Members of the chamber are skeptical, but they generally agree.

A Soviet boarding school is expected to convincingly promote communism. Internats for present or former criminals should extol the law-abiding life. Hospitals, while treating the ill, should promote good health. Military academies should stand not only for martial excellence but also, and perhaps much more importantly, absolute loyalty to the existing sociopolitical structure. (It should not be forgotten that revolutions are often hatched in elitist military internat settings, making them as dangerous as the Turkish Janizaries were to the Ottoman Empire of their day.)

When they perform this task of societal conservation well, internats, though housing the deviant, become models of the desired. A reasonable assignment for elitist settings, this seems an incredible expectation of prisons, mental hospitals, juvenile halls, orphanages, and similar facilities. Yet, periodically in human history these hopes are attached to the internat operation. When Hermann Gmeiner started to collect World War II orphans off the Austrian roads and streets, he intended to form an SOS Kinderdorf based on humanity, tolerance, peace, and personal achievement. Some thirty years later, and with more than 200 villages throughout the world, his movement still has the same objectives. Some critics, who shudder at the notion of a children's institution, now concede that Gmeiner may have something of a point. SOS Villages do take in problem children and they preserve a society's patterns better than do some of the turbulent environments in which the villages are located (for example, war-torn Vietnam, Korea, Bangladesh, and Lebanon).

Henrietta Szold, the founder of Youth Aliyah, succeeded in rescuing child victims of the Holocaust. Brought to Israel (then Palestine), many thousands found themselves in youth villages. Their behavior during the Israeli war of independence and other periods of stress is still often cited as a model to the society as a whole. For example, one large and very prominent village, Ben Shemen, became the principal supplier of seeds for Israeli agriculture, while also investing considerable effort in cultural and social interaction with Arab villagers in its area (Bentwich, n.d.).

At times Americans have also considered their internats as models. The eighteenth-century founders of moral treatment considered their approach to the mentally ill as not only suited for hospitals but also as an example to society of decent interpersonal behavior. Similarly, society hoped that the house of refuge would be not only a setting for misbehaving children but also a model of honesty, diligence, obedience, and other virtues for the neighboring "poorer classes" outside (Leiby, 1978; Rothman, 1971).

Given some reasonably normal inmates, the internat can offer both protection for and an example to a society under great stress. It can improve inmates' Mastery by subjecting them to its environment, which has elements worthy of emulation by those outside. In more quiescent societies or given more deviant or divergent entering populations, the internat fails in this modeling role. Instead, like the prison described by Grosser (1969, p. 9), it becomes "a service organization, supported by the community largely for the purpose of maintaining order . . . a means of safeguarding other institutions of the society."

Internats that maintain order are lauded for this conservative function, but internats that offer models to the external community are accorded far higher social status. The lowest social status is afforded internats with large aggregations of negatively perceived individuals. Such internats are places to be avoided and, if possible, ignored. Desolate rural areas and inner city slums are the preferred locations for such internats. But, inevitably, some outsiders visit the internat, open its gates, reveal its ugliness, and demand change. Dorothea Dix did this for internats containing the insane of her day, Albert Deutsch in his. All such reforming attempts are symbolic of the ambivalence society has toward the internat.

A society conserves itself by showing not only antipathy to the depraved but also care and compassion for the deprived. State visitors are shown internats for the unfortunate in order to impress upon them the goodness of a society. Citizens are reassured by nursing homes, residential settings for the severely retarded, and orphanages for these internats are a symbol of social utility, encouraging every member to trust that he will be cared for when in extreme need. The emblems of nineteenth-century internats depicted this message: a female figure compassionately tending the sick for a hospital; a mother figure cradling a child for an orphanage; and two caring males with an adoring urchin between them for the house of refuge.

Internats bear witness to society's protection of itself and its members. They show that change may, under certain conditions, be accelerated and directed, that the past is remembered and deviance is punishable. Perhaps most significantly, they proclaim the feasibility of redemption. Recent efforts to make internats socially inconspicuous are probably short-lived because internats convey a necessary message. Changing their names from State Institution for Mentally Defective to Willowbrook, and then to Bronx Developmental Center can bring only a short-term benefit, if that. Old stigma or old glory will survive changes in names. They will probably also survive relocation (see Segal and Aviram, 1978).

The propagation of an intellectual, moral, or military elite is a particularly laudable internat task. Houses at ivy league colleges, resident religious academies, military schools are all intended for this purpose. Describing the significance of English public schools, Weinberg (1967, pp. 10-11) emphasizes their role in preserving the code of constitutional behavior:

> Britain's constitution . . . is neither written down nor codified. It comprises a miscellany of legal, quasi-legal, and legislative documents which have accumulated throughout the country's long history. . . . For the last hundred years the public schools have provided a reliable social base for the stability of historic constitutional and political ideas. The public school system has functioned as a process of socialization into behavior and attitudes which help to sustain these ideas. . . . The strong humane element in the public school curriculum induces a reverence for the past, which is necessary to sustain a constitutional and political system based on historical precedent. The ritual of the public school, especially in the chapel, prepares for the ceremonial of political life. . . . The categories of unwritten rules, especially concerning "fair play" and "what is done," combine with prescribed conduct to form personalities who fit into the political roles demanded by the constitution.

For a society to destroy an internat (for example, the Bastille) or preserve it as a museum (for example, Dachau) is to make a statement of profound social significance. Both acts define the end of an era, represent society's exclamations: No more political prisoners in France! No more genocide in Germany! The USSR's current use of mental hospitals and labor camps for political prisoners is, similarly, a profound social statement, as Solzhenitsyn (1974-1978) underscores.

Internat residence is intended to be transitional, except for monastics and terminal cases. Society can comprehend internats as temporary residences for rehabilitation or reformation but not as human warehouses. Except for the specifically holy, society feels that isolation is warranted only for short periods intended to Reclaim—a social condition that neither mental hospitals with chronic patients nor prisons with "lifers" have successfully met. So long as such internats remain, in this manner a challenge to the norms of society, they will be the subject of complaints and accusations. But critics of these internats often ignore the fact that these internats do provide at least meager sustenance to some of society's least fortunate.

Whatever their social functions, internats must also survive as social entities. The institutionalization of behaviors, relationships, symbols, means of communication, affiliation, and authority is inevitable. Internats are usually dominated by those persons who have been there the longest. When staff is transient and inmates are long-term residents, the latter end up in charge. Despite superficial appearances to the contrary, long-term prisoners and veteran mental patients exert greater influence than the newly appointed warden or medical director. Since long-term inmates remain in the internat by virtue of their maladjustment, their conservative influence usually does not promote the Reclaiming objectives that their internats profess.

Conserving Values

Bentham's eighteenth-century panopticon required that the superintendent live in the center of a tiered, round prison and continually observe and be observed. Cottage mothers at an SOS Kinderdorf are expected to live with the children in a cottage. The cottage model of childcare internats, developed in the U.S. during the second decade of this century, included in its design a home for the director. John Maher lives at the Delancey Street Foundation. Such residential arrangements have symbolic and practical consequences. Staff's residence among the inmates represents their total availability, but accessibility for inmates means restriction for staff. Symbolically, the staff's voluntary surrender of options implies their commitment to the residents.

Of course, all internats have staff who are there for lack of choice. Some staff members who seek personal security become recipients of internat services and differ from inmates only because they hold keys. Other staff see internat employment in purely vocational terms, perceiving themselves as plumbers, social workers, or physicians who happen to work in an internat. In prisons or nursing homes they function as though they were fulfilling the same roles outside. Yet other staff need the income, and internat work for them is just a job or a repeated wait for paydays, holidays, and ultimate retirement. None of these people is responding to the essence of internat existence—its totality.

In order for an internat to be a Reclaiming instrument, staff must embody Reclaiming through nearly continuous, self-denying behavior. Only a commitment to human values makes such continuous "front stage" exposure tenable. Internat workers must believe that people can change, that all have an inherent right to seek self-fulfillment and to live in humane conditions, that every person, no matter how limited, has the capacity to help others. Staff members' commitment, as Trigg (1973, p. 43) notes, "must be based on beliefs which are themselves external to the system." Staff's concerns for human potential, for humane conditions, and for growth must be expressed by "a personal dedication to the actions implied by them" (Trigg, 1973, p. 44).

Commitment requires belief but not necessarily an ideology. Like ideologies, beliefs need no empirical verification. In fact, believers may shun such a verification exercise as itself nourishing the seeds of doubt and undermining commitment. Shared beliefs, when sustained and combined into systems, provide rationale and unity for internat Activity. Korczak's (1967) children's home in Warsaw and Schweitzer's (1931) hospital at Lambaréné were both infused with shared belief in the goodness and dignity of man. Neither of these philosophers of internat care could readily conceive of a staff member's leaving to seek a better-paying job. Grasping the implications of such a request, they would urge his departure.

Korczak (1967, p. xiv) expressed in terms of beliefs the children's achievement at Dom Dziecka, the internat he directed from 1912 until 1942.

> We did not give you God, because you must
> look and find Him within yourself.

We did not give you love of country because your heart and reason must dictate your own choice.

We did not give you love of Man, because love comes from forgiveness which must be discovered through effort.

We did give you one thing—a longing for a better life, a life of truth and justice which you must build for yourself.

We hope that this longing will lead you to God, to Country, and to Love.

When the Nazis took his children from the Warsaw ghetto to the Treblinka extermination camp, Korczak remained with them to the end—to calm and to perish.

Korczak was not a religious man nor a political ideologist. At no time did he question the validity of others' beliefs so long as they were fundamentally humane. He had no eschatology that predicted the human condition nor an ideological sponsorship or reference point external to his internat. Most probably, he would have subscribed to the view that "movements which have been relatively free from ideology have contributed far more to human well-being and freedom than those which apotheosized it" (Feuer, 1975, p. 191).

Though repelled by the exclusivity of ideology, Korczak understood the utility of at least two of the three attributes that Feuer posits for every ideology: a *myth,* a *unifying philosophy,* and a *chosen group.* In Feuer's discussion, a *myth* is a set of beliefs that are not necessarily proven or provable. A *philosophy* is a set of explanations, based on the myth, that serve as a basis for action. The *chosen group* is that set of people to whom the myth and philosophy apply. Although the notion of a chosen group may be hard for the humanist to accept, it is nevertheless an attribute of many successful internats. Successful internats have been founded by Father Flanagan using Catholicism, Makarenko using communism, and the religious and Marxist Zionists who developed Israeli kibbutz youth groups and children's villages. The more distant past provides examples of successful residential yeshivot and monasteries, which not only produced well-integrated members for their own communities but also served as models and caretakers for the sick, the poor, and other members of the community.

"Every ideology aims to inaugurate a *Gemeinschaft*; that is, an ideological community characterized by unity in emotion" (Feuer, 1975, p. 104). Because of such striving, ideology serves as a strong unifying force within an internat. Isolated and total, focused on inner needs, the internat based on a strong ideology may develop such impermeable boundaries that everyone on the outside is perceived as the enemy. Historically, this has been the lot of early American communards (Caplow, 1964; Gollin, 1969; Lawson, 1972), their modern imitators Synanon ("Life at Synanon Is Swinging," 1977), and, in the most extreme form, the Jonestown cult in Guyana (Kerns, 1979; Krause, 1978). Fully isolated from external ideological influences, these groups became destructive and ultimately self-annihilating.

However, the *Gemeinschaft,* strong on the inside, may include external components. Emissaries may be exchanged by the internat, and the ideology may be derived from, or shared with, an outside community. Though ideological myths tend to override reality—when belief is maintained in the face of contrary empirical evidence (Feuer, 1975, p. 105), spurious sensory experience is considerably reduced by external ties. The scope of external ties is probably the major distinction between Dederich's Synanon (Yablonsky, 1965) and its ideological descendant, Maher's Delancey Street (Hampden-Turner, 1976). Every yeshiva, Marxist boarding school, or English public school partakes of an external mind community that not only induces sustenance and reality into the internat—by insisting on certain behaviors—but also perceives in it an ideological focal point. Maher grasped that principle. Dederich never did.

Ideologically based internats are very powerful mechanisms for change. Herein lies their utility and their danger. Representing ideological purity, such internats focus on conquest of the mind (see, for example, Merton, 1949a, 1949b, on monasteries; or Makarenko, 1955, on communist youth camps). They proceed as a learning theorist would recommend: To mold their inmates, ideological internats strive for control of the "symbolic coding and central organization of modeling stimuli, their representation in memory, in verbal and imaginal codes, and [thus] their subsequent transformation from symbolic forms to motor equivalents" (Bandura, 1969, p. 127).

In such situations inmates' change seems to follow the rules posited by Watzlawick, Weakland, and Fisch (1974). First, members move within the boundaries of the group, appearing in new combinations but without qualitative modification. Second, parts of the group, or all of it, move to a new position as a result of such external influences as a belief system or an ideology.

Belief systems (and, even more fully, an ideology) contribute to the power of an internat, providing a predetermined grading of activities and arrangement of contingencies. Issues of right and wrong paramount in such settings are settled by a fixed reference. Marx, or the Church of Rome, or the Talmud, Reverend Moon or James Jones resolve all disputes. Their decision is final. An ideology that is grounded in humane principles, conditioned by extensive debate and the lessons of history, can be life-supportive. Yet danger is always imminent. Within an internat, exclusive rights to final adjudication may lead to dissolution, when members become dissidents and withdraw (see Gollin, 1969; Lawson, 1972); or they may lead to self-annihilation, as in Jonestown (Kerns, 1979; Krause, 1978).

Some internats with ascribed Reclaiming functions, such as prisons and mental hospitals, come close to self-annihilation. Enforced inactivity (Deutsch, 1948) or violent upheaval (Mitford, 1973; Wicker, 1975) are common in such facilities. Rotenberg (1978) suggests that ideological underpinnings may be responsible for this destructiveness. When deviants are damned by society as an act of faith, any collectivity of deviants is damned by definition. Any reduction of the distinction between those on the outside and "the different ones" on the inside will be strongly opposed by society (Cumming and Cumming, 1957; Segal and Aviram, 1978). The inmates themselves are aware of society's attitude toward them, and prison and mental hospital cultures, with their long-term and recidivist participants, reinforce the outside message that damnation is permanent.

Concerned caretakers of great humanity and faith have attempted to overturn this pessimistic judgment. English and American Quakers have been foremost in this task. The Pennsylvania prison system, which failed, and moral treatment, which was probably successful, are both in large part attributable to the Quakers' efforts. Imbued with humanism and an abiding faith in earthly redemption, the Quakers attempted to use their religious ideology to promote the Reclaiming of the most severely damned. Ultimately, they failed because inmates' Mastery was inadequate for full acceptance by society, which even a century later still had no status for partially Reclaimed individuals (see Fairweather and others, 1969; Segal and Aviram, 1978).

Recently, many segments of society have embraced the belief that scientific advances such as psychotropic drugs will succeed where other methods of Reclaiming have failed ("Drugs and Psychiatry," 1979). It is too early to tell whether scientific ideology will succeed, but science has freed certain individuals from lifelong residence in internats. For example, tuberculosis is no longer a stigmatizing label, and severely handicapped individuals increasingly live in the community. Yet the same social acceptance may not necessarily await the criminal and the insane (Scull, 1977). A philosophical question remains: In order for society to be good, must it reject some members and visibly confine them in outcast settings, that is, follow solely the dictates of social Reclaiming? And a second question: Can such internats reclaim their members, that is, can an internat focused solely on social Reclaiming achieve a measure of integrated Reclaiming? The answer to both questions appears to be yes.

Society can be good and its internats can promote Reclaiming if society accepts an ideology that views the rejection of a member as temporary, and if every rejected member is considered reclaimable. Such an ideology would promote growth and protect the sanctity of life and the reclaimability of all persons. Returning to Feuer's (1975) definition of an ideology as comprising a myth, a doctrine, and a notion of a chosen group, we can propose the following ideology. The myth would hold that society promises to love all its members and that members reciprocate this love by serving society. The members' well-being is proof of society's love for them, and punishment in the case of deviance will promote well-being because punishment will bring the deviant member back into society. Internats promise to change the deviant and enable him to rejoin society as a respected member.

The doctrine of the ideology would hold that society's love is contingent on its members' accepting the role of the person to be helped (but not punished). A deviant member must seek help and reject his deviant behavior or at least reconcile it to society's demands. Internats serve to help the deviant repent, change, and receive treatment. At times, internats set an example for society by teaching the deviant how to act according to societal expectations.

In this ideology, the chosen are really made up of two groups—the internat staff and the internat residents. The former are chosen by society for the Reclaiming mission; the latter are identified as being in need of Reclaiming. By acting as society's agents, the internat staff serve as both models and enforcers, uniting myth and dogma to bring deviants back to the mainstream.

7

Understanding Structure,
Interaction,
Decision Making,
and Sanctions

The complexity of internats has resulted in segmented descriptions of their functioning. Theorists and researchers have separated people from place and have described setting as though unrelated to either people or program. Beaumont and de Tocqueville ([1836] 1964) noted a segmentation in the practices of the famous nineteenth-century prisons of the Pennsylvania and Auburn systems. Deutsch (1948, 1952) made similar observations regarding the separation of patient and hospital in studying the mentally ill in the U.S. We have used analytic segmentation as a necessary precursor to synthesis. In Chapter Two we presented the personal and organizational subsystems, and we used these as heuristic tools in Chapters Three through Six. In this chapter we present an integrative model of the dynamics of internats.

Many religious builders of medieval hospitals realized that segmentation was dysfunctional (Thompson and Goldin, 1975). More recently, insightful planners and administrators of programs for the mentally ill or the criminal have reached a similar conclusion. Kirkbride (1854) and Bentham (1791), in their consideration of total systems, showed a sensitivity to persons *in* a milieu as opposed to persons *and* a milieu. The development of a systems approach to the comprehension of internats is a logical consequence of their work.

The systems model, used in several major studies (Caudill, 1958; Polsky and Claster, 1968; Stanton and Schwartz, 1954), appears to encompass and illuminate the internat phenomenon. Because the systems approach is "a highly general, content-free conceptual framework within which any number of different substantive theories of social organization can be constructed" (Olsen, 1968, p. 228), it has been applied to the study of various social organizations, ranging from families to nations. It requires attention to the totality and its components, to all aspects of individuals and the organization. Furthermore, it compels a concern for their interaction by assuming that they form "a causal network, such that each component is related to at least some others in a more or less stable way within any particular period of time" (Buckley, 1967, p. 41).

Although the systems approach requires a consideration of the interaction of components, instructively precluding a unidimensional analysis, it has led analysts to examine an endless panoply of components. History and clientele, financing and theoretical orientation, and, in some measure, pure accident determine which components are examined. However, in any internat, Activity is inevitable and is reciprocally causal among its various subsystems. Our understanding of internats is not yet sufficiently advanced to predict the power and nature of causality, but one can usually predict the general effect of an action relative to Reclaiming. For a patient, a physician's smile at his compliance with his diet is a positive consequence, while his

visiting wife's frown at his salt-free diet is a negative consequence. The patient's personal balance sheet of positive and
negative consequences will affect his behavior and progress.

Unlike a monastery on a distant mountaintop, a hospital
is a relatively open system that permits contradictory activities.
And even the monastery, or maximum security prison, cannot
totally preclude them. An internat's balancing of such contradictions determines whether inmates regard specific Activity as
positive and thus whether the internat achieves Reclaiming. But
how are we to grasp this balance? One possibility is to look at
the whole, assuming that the behavior of individuals is determined by the needs of the whole system. Another approach begins with the behavior of individuals. It is predicated on the
assumption, expressed by Churchman (1968, p. 200), that "once
individual and social behavior have been examined in detail,
then one can discover in the observation of behavior the nature
of the whole human system." The flow of social change appears
a primary focus of the former analysis, and goal-directed social
intervention typifies the latter. To synthesize the sixteen organizational subsystems introduced in Chapter Two and discussed in
Chapters Three through Six, we must use both approaches and
begin by considering an internat's resources.

Some rare internats are able to internally generate almost
all their resources. Makarenko (1953, 1955) started and operated his youth program with little if any outside resources, and
many monasteries are also self-supporting. However, internats
for severely dependent persons—that is, nursing homes, mental
hospitals, homes for the profoundly retarded—require very
heavy infusions of outside money, manpower, and information
since the inmates themselves can make only a minimal contribution. Moreover, internats with such populations often discount
whatever contributions inmates can make, preferring to assume
their total dependency. Similarly, individuals considered dangerous or otherwise severely disturbing, whether kept in the hole
or in a padded cell, are treated as a negligible source of energy.
By ignoring internal resources, internats inevitably require substantial outside investment.

Internats may derive resources from within as well as outside the system. Prison inmates may cook their own food, serve as bookkeepers in the office and as nurses in the hospital, and some may manufacture vehicle license plates for the state. Hospital patients may wash their own faces and suggest ways to improve care. Mentally ill inmates may mend clothes, mow the lawn, or tend to the dairy herd. Kirkbride (1854) considered both the cost of an internat's operation and the healing function of risk and participation, and he insisted that internats encourage inmates to make whatever contributions they could. If we compare his views with current practice we see that all nonelitist internats have become increasingly dependent on external resources.

Whatever the source of an internat's resources, some must be directed toward organizational preservation and goal achievement, the fields of conservation and achievement, respectively. History and tradition, emblems and ideology, habit and routine —these are the sources of conservation, and their sustenance requires resources. A flag must be raised each morning. A holiday must be observed. A historical plaque must be polished or even guarded and periodically adorned with flowers. Ideology must be repeated as slogan and as act. Established relationships with the outside must be maintained and reinforced to advance an internat's adaptation.

Along with these conservative tasks, internats pursue Goals. Be they overt or hidden, accepted by all of the participants or by only some of them, the effort to attain Goals requires energy. When an internat is well established and conservation is enhanced by all its constituencies, the energy requirements for conservation may be reduced and a larger investment may be made in the achievement of Goals. Similarly, when integration is high, the Goals of inmates, caretaking staff, administration, and community converge, and the investment in conservation may drop, with a corresponding rise in expenditures for achievement.

Contingencies for Action

The interdependence of the achievement, adaptation, integration, and conservation modes and the psychological, physical, social, and valuative fields in which they find expression is the epitome of a living system. Continuously and inevitably, various components in each of the modes and fields of an organization's subsystems interact and affect each other. Activity is responsive to the effects it generates, and the response to Activity in one mode or field will affect the others. Such feedback loops depend on information (Buckley, 1967, p. 82), which, in its flow, regulates the internat's dynamics. Activity is continued or modified depending on whether the feedback loop is positive or negative.

An internat's Activity is, thus, continually subject to review and adjustment. Every positive feedback loop contributes toward a continuation of the performed Activity, while a negative feedback loop functions to reduce it. Two systemic dynamics evolve from feedback-loop operation. A system with an even number of negative feedback loops tends toward continuation of Activity. One with an odd number of negative loops tends toward discontinuation (Kunkel, 1970, p. 208; Maruyama, 1963, p. 177). The former will yield a *morphogenic* system, the latter a *morphostatic* one.

Although every internat has Activity, the mere presence of Activity does not imply modification. An internat may achieve a functional balance, a systemic steady state, in which the relationships between different actions remain constant, though all modes and fields are in play. Patients, prisoners, cadets, or monks enter; staff are engaged in their appropriate activities; the system is appropriately responsive to its feedback loops—but it seems not to develop in step with society. Faced with an established constellation of positive and negative influences, this internat survives. But when confronted by new circumstances it must reform or collapse. Synanon and Delancey Street, for example, have identical populations and purported goals but, because of their different approaches to adaptation and integration, Synanon appears destined for the societal garbage heap and Delancey Street for change and survival. Kunkel (1970), following von Bertalanffy (1968), would probably ascribe the distinction between the two to Synanon's determination to remain isolated from the outside community lest that community upset the internat's morphostatic condition.

Whether society's Evaluation of an internat is ultimately positive or negative is, as we noted earlier, determined by its "capacity to survive, adapt, maintain itself, and grow, regardless of the particular function it fulfills" (Schein, 1965, p. 97). And since an internat has multiple Goals—achievement, adaptation, integration, and conservation—a multifaceted measure of its Consequences, both costs and benefits, is necessary (Goodman, Pennings, and Associates, 1977). Only in this way, can one determine if Reclaiming is taking place. Such tests of effectiveness may be applied formally and overtly or in a more informal, impressionistic manner. These tests imply that variation in Activity is related to variation in outcomes and that some internats are more successful than others. Indeed, there is substantial evidence of integrated Reclaiming internats for various populations.

An Operant Paradigm

Focusing on the individual resident (inmate or staff) of an internat, we may use an operant paradigm to conceptualize and empirically observe all units of Activity and to point out conditions of movement toward Reclaiming. Activity entails Consequences, which are perceived as reward or punishment by the staff or inmate. Activity is likely to increase if the Consequences are positive and decrease if they are negative. Like any other social system, all internats—even those with residents of the highest Mastery—require and produce some externally generated Consequences. Also, every internat generates some Consequences on its own. There may even be many positive Consequences in settings for persons of very low Mastery, such as retarded adults and children (see Skeels, 1966).

Activity does not take place in empty space. Various conditions affect the Consequences of Activity. Those conditions perceived by the resident as affecting Consequences are called *discriminative stimuli* or *setting events*. When Activity yields positive Consequences, the resident construes the setting events as positive, that is, the resident begins to associate those setting events with positive Consequences. If the Activity yields negative Consequences, the resident associates the preceding aversive setting events with negative Consequences. A morphogenic feedback loop is established. The more of the Activity, the more positive Consequences; the more positive Consequences exist, the more positive setting events the resident recognizes; the more positive setting events, the higher the probability of more of the Activity (all other things being equal). For example, a patient on the rehabilitation ward tries to walk. The nurses smile, the physicians approve, his family and other patients encourage. These favorable Consequences form a series of positive setting events, which the patient responds to by continuing to walk. This escalating morphogenic system is depicted in Figure 4.

Figure 4. Escalating Morphogenic System

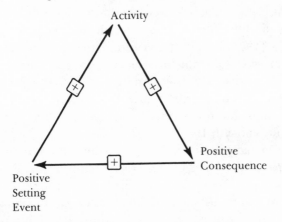

If Activity yields negative Consequences and aversive setting events, a diminishing morphogenic system is established. Figure 5 depicts such a system. In Figure 5, a plus sign between elements connected by an arrow indicates that an increase in one element effects an increase in the other and a decrease in one effects a decrease in the other. A minus sign indicates that the elements vary inversely. The arrow connecting the aversive setting event and Activity has a minus sign, indicating that the aversive setting will provoke less Activity. Such an aversive system, when sufficiently consistent, persistent, and applied to a wide range of behavior results in passivity, apathy, and ulti-

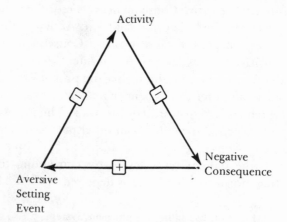

mate demise. Examples of internats that have produced such diminishing morphogenic systems include the hospitals in Spitz and Wolf's (1946) study of anaclitic depression. Similar examples are provided by nursing homes (Vladeck, 1980), mental hospitals (Deutsch, 1952) internats for the retarded (Morris, 1969), and, of course, deliberately destructive environments such as camps for prisoners of war (Segal, 1957) and labor camps (Solzhenitsyn, 1963).

Our paradigm requires two further assumptions. First, that any particular behavior cannot be reinforced and punished at the same time. Ambivalence results not from simultaneous reinforcement and punishment, but from uncertainty as to whether a given behavior will be reinforced or punished. That is, a person may hesitate to act out a certain behavior because the Consequence of the contemplated behavior is unpredictable. However, once Activity occurs it is followed either by a positive or a negative Consequence, but not by both. Second, the sum total of occurrences for a given individual is limited by his life span and, at a given moment, by his life space (Lewin, 1951). Boundaries limit the experiences a person may actually have. A prisoner at San Quentin cannot take a bus to San Francisco. Imagery, though, may go well beyond the boundaries of time and space and produce some unanticipated morphogenic consequences not evident from the relationships between Activity and Consequence.

Relative to Reclaiming, Activities may be *goal directed* or *counter-goal directed*. Internats strive to develop a system in which goal-directed Activity is consistently reinforced and counter-goal-directed Activity is punished. The kibbutz youth group described by Wolins (1974c) is an example of such a morphogenic system. When the children first entered, they indulged in various goal-directed and counter-goal-directed behavior. Kibbutz members rewarded the former and occasionally reprimanded children for the latter. At the end of several years, many of the young people qualified for membership. In some internats, however, delinquent residents are so efficient in punishing goal-directed behavior and in rewarding its opposite, that they incorporate new inmates and even staff into a counter-goal-directed morphogenic system; see, for example, the youth internat described by Polsky (1962).

Many internats do not consistently differentiate behavior as goal directed or goal opposed, and thus they cannot reinforce or punish behavior in a consistent, systematic way. This situation creates a *morphostatic* system that neither consistently promotes nor constrains Reclaiming. Though without apparent effectiveness, such internats may continue to operate at considerable economic, social, and psychic cost to the individuals involved and to their society.

Since neither internats nor societies are wholly irrational, we assume that there are discernible causes that prompt the development of morphostatic internats. Four such possible causes are: (1) confusion about goals by internat members; (2) contradictory goals among various subgroups; (3) lack of clear and consistent information about sanctions by inmates and staff; and (4) failure of policy makers and staff to comprehend or utilize a tested model of human behavior. If at least one of these four conditions is present, Activity within the internat will not predictably produce the desired changes in various elements of inmates' Mastery. Of course, even when all these constraints are absent, the variety of human conditions and imperfections of control will preclude the development of a perfect, goal-directed morphogenic internat. However, internats can reduce the likelihood of goal-directed behavior being punished or counter-goal-directed behavior being reinforced.

First, the internat must clearly specify and differentiate goal-directed Activity and counter-goal-directed Activity. Since the large number, variety, and permutations of behavior preclude a comprehensive listing of all behaviors, internats must rely on models—both inmates and staff—who illustrate acceptable goal-directed behavior for others. Second, the internat must consistently provide positive sanctions for goal-directed Activity and negative sanctions for counter-goal-directed Activity.

Internat Systems

Internats have both intrasystemic and intersystemic attributes. An example of the former is the internat's differentiation or lack of differentiation between goal-directed and counter-goal-directed behavior. An example of the latter is an internat's relative isolation from or communication with the external community. At least six ideal-type arrangements of intrasystemic and intersystemic operations are likely to occur. Five of the systems are morphostatic and will fail to generate Reclaiming or a positive Evaluation.

Undifferentiated, fully isolated internats usually cannot survive, as internal chaos soon overcomes them. Without external connections, they have no way to replenish membership or other resources. Nor is there effective internal generation, since reward and punishment ensue whether behavior is goal directed or not. Such total anarchy prevails in some transitional settings, and was to be found in certain loose communes of the 1960s. Figure 6 depicts the feedback loops of such a system.

Differentiated, fully isolated internats exist but they are rarities. Their closest approximation are remote monasteries, like Santa Katarina in the Sinai Desert, the Moravians in nineteenth-century America (Gollin, 1969), or Jonestown (Kerns, 1979; Krause, 1978). Sanctions in such an internat are unrelated to the external world, and they are clearly allocated for goal-directed or counter-goal-directed activities. All goals are internal and based on the internat's traditions. Since the internat does not adjust to external events, its system is ultimately

Figure 6. Undifferentiated, Fully Isolated Internat

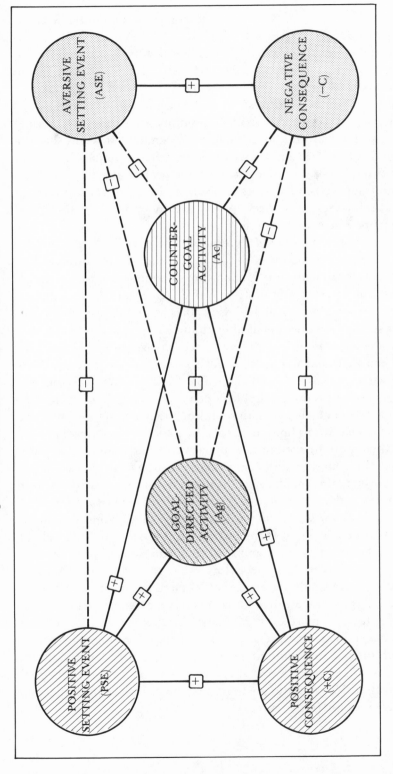

ENVIRONMENTAL
INFLUENCES

⊞ Positive feedback loop

⊟ Negative feedback loop

overtaken by them and collapses. Santa Katarina is an interesting, exceptional case. In spite of its profound, though by no
means total, isolation, it has survived for over 1,500 years as a
Greek Orthodox outpost in the Muslim world. Although its
ideological ties to the Greek community are strong, the internat
has suffered from a shortage of new members. It seems that isolated internats cannot survive. Even when internal behavior is
differentiated, the system becomes morphostatic. The phenomenon appears similar to that observed in small isolated biologi-
cal colonies, which become extinct by virtue of inbreeding.
(Figure 7 depicts this type.)

Punishment-based internats, like Devil's Island or the
Nazi extermination camps of World War II are connected to
their environment, but a condition of community acceptance is
that the internat be purely punitive (see Figure 8.) Punishment
is thus not a means of achieving goals but rather a goal in itself.
As such, punishment is used in an undifferentiated manner, thus
producing a morphostatic system. In denying a difference between right and wrong, such environments destroy not only the
inmates but also those responsible for them. Because societies
are basically rational, they will deny the existence of such internats or blame their creation and maintenance on personal and
social aberrations limited to specific periods or circumstances. It
is thus quite believable that many Germans chose not to know
that the concentration camps existed. Even some Poles living in
Oświęcim, the small town near the notorious Auschwitz, told
one of us that they did not know what was going on there.

Reward-based internats might seem to some well-intentioned people an environment proper for severely hurt individuals, but we have no example of such an internat. Such an internat would relate to the external environment, but internally
would permit only rewards; that is, the Consequences of any behavior would be positive. Such a system, in which all behavior is
acceptable, cannot survive because it lacks any criteria for confining individual expression that infringes on others or endan-
gers others. In a limited sense, Neill's (1960) Summerhill was
such an internat. Since such a system reinforces both goal-
directed and counter-goal-directed behavior, it must become
morphostatic (see Figure 9).

Figure 7. Differentiated, Fully Isolated Internat

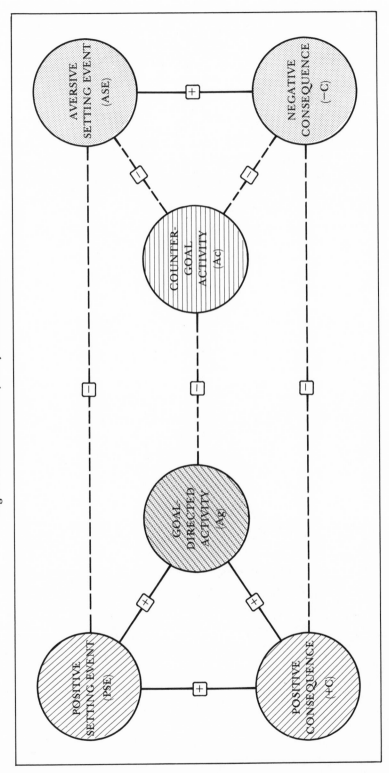

ENVIRONMENTAL
INFLUENCES

+ Positive feedback loop

− Negative feedback loop

Figure 8. Punishment-Based Internat

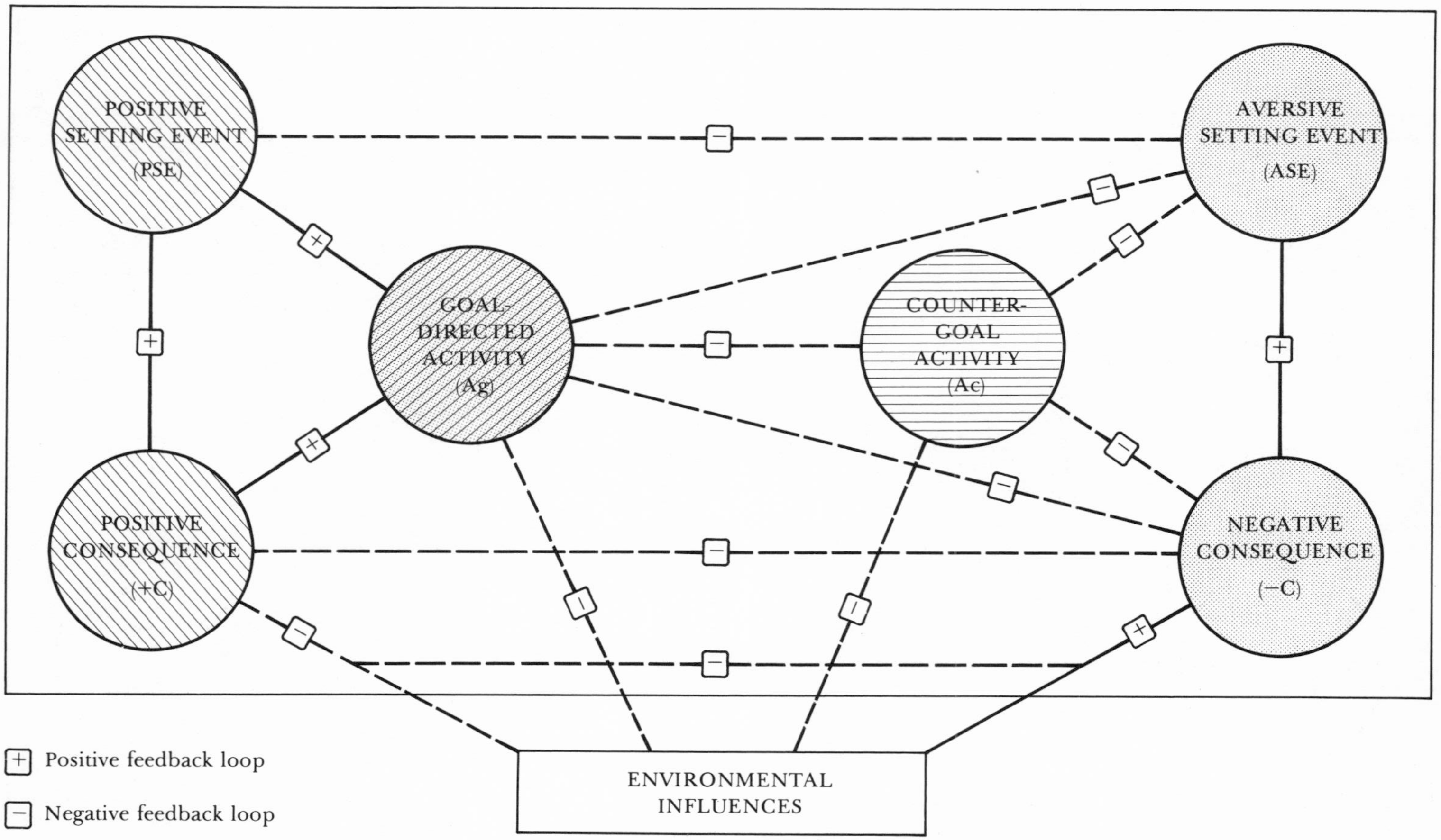

AVERSIVE SETTING EVENT (ASE)

NEGATIVE CONSEQUENCE (−C)

COUNTER-GOAL ACTIVITY (Ac)

GOAL-DIRECTED ACTIVITY (Ag)

POSITIVE SETTING EVENT (PSE)

POSITIVE CONSEQUENCE (+C)

ENVIRONMENTAL INFLUENCES

+ Positive feedback loop

− Negative feedback loop

Figure 9. Reward-Based Internat

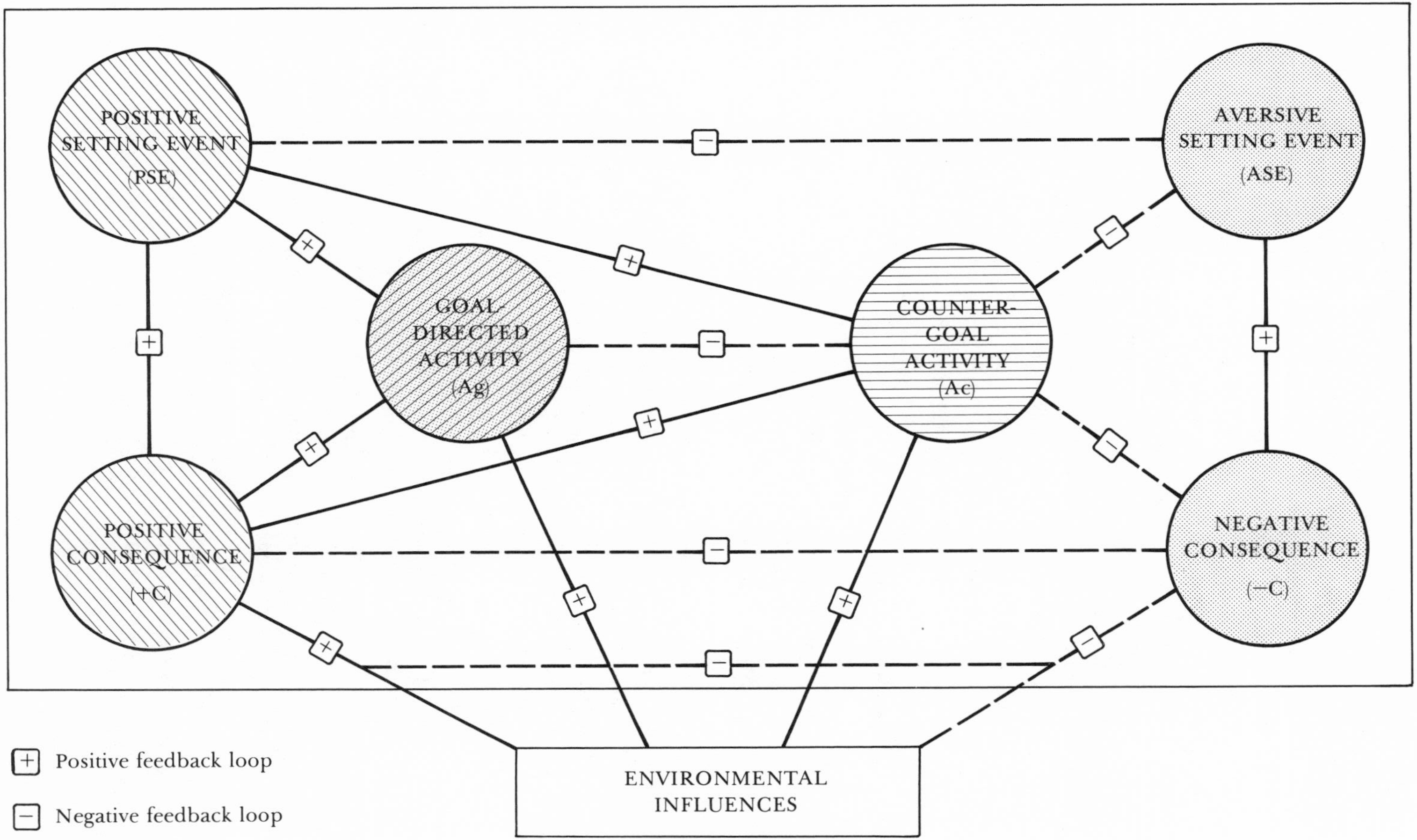

Undifferentiated punishment and reward internats are unlike the preceding two types of systems, which although dysfunctional are consistent. Internats that do not differentiate goal-directed and counter-goal-directed behavior are simply confused, using punishment and reward in a largely unpredictable way. Because these internats may have numerous and possibly contradictory goals, staff may not know what behaviors promote the attainment of goals, and inmates may define the relationship between rewards and goals differently from both the external community and staff. Internats for troublesome people —whether inmates are children or aged, criminal or insane—in a humane society tend to be of this type. Although the intentions of such internats may be laudable, lack of differentiation must lead to a morphostatic system that cannot achieve Reclaiming (see Figure 10).

Normatively appropriate reward and punishment internats include Korczak's children's home, Father Flanagan's Boys Town, a kibbutz youth group, Maxwell Jones' hospital, Delancey Street, and West Point. Their system operates on a model different from the five preceding types, and it represents the only morphogenic model consistent with theory and supported by practice (see Figure 11). Five conditions govern this model. First, the internat is an integral part of a community that has defined for it reasonable, specific goals. Second, the community and the internat both accept the propriety of rewarding and punishing Consequences. Third, a positive Consequence ensues when an inmate or staff or relevant outsider displays goal-directed behavior; a negative Consequence ensues in response to counter-goal-directed behavior. Fourth, it is intended that the discriminate use of positive and negative Consequences in a consistent, normatively appropriate manner will have ripple effects through the internat; positive Consequences will produce positive setting events, and negative Consequences will produce aversive setting events.

Fifth and finally, the effect of positive and aversive setting events should thus result in a morphogenic system that promotes the Reclaiming goals of the internat and society with increasingly more positive Consequences and fewer negative Con-

Figure 10. Undifferentiated Reward and Punishment Internat

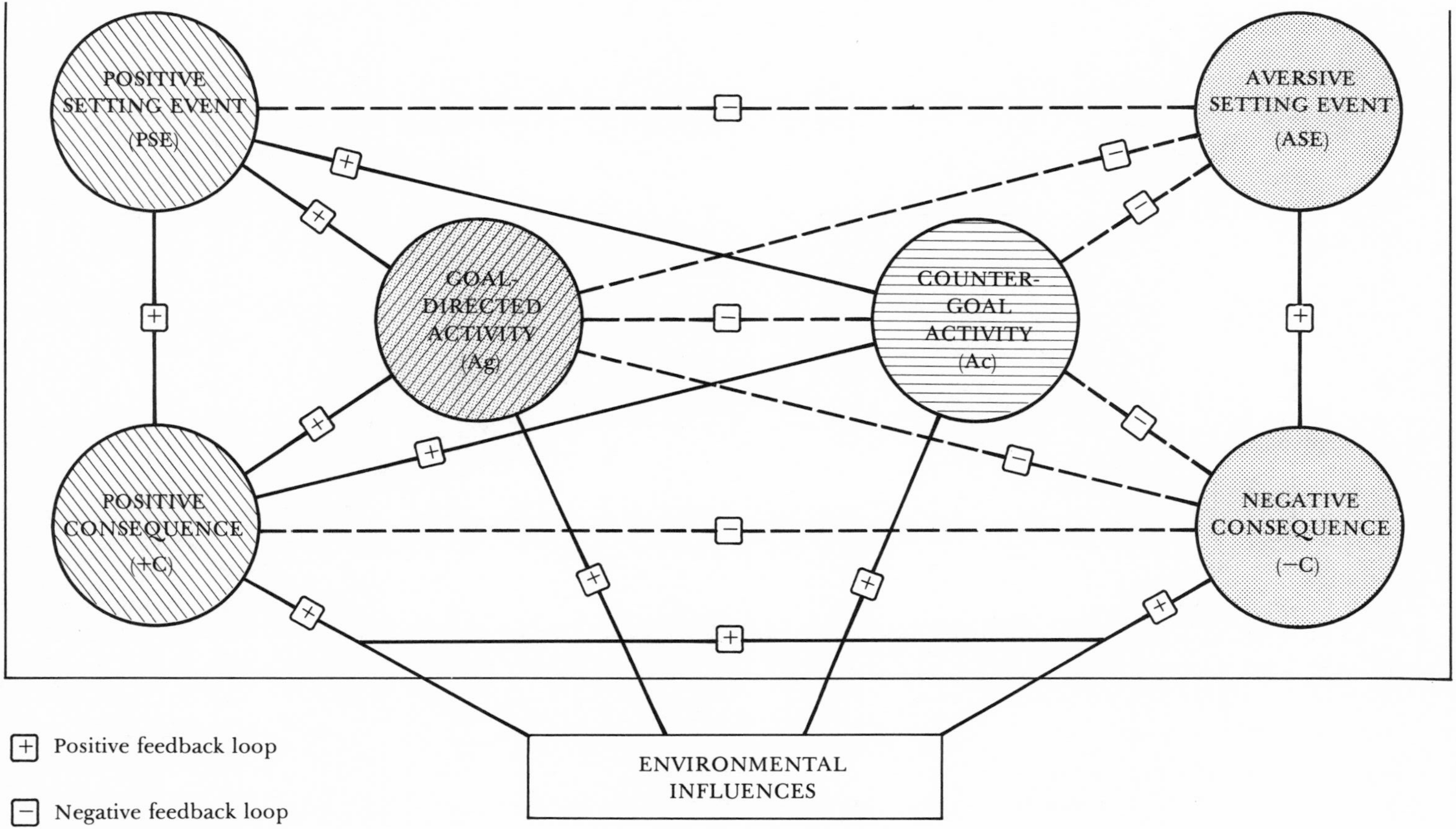

Figure 11. Normatively Appropriate Reward and Punishment Internat

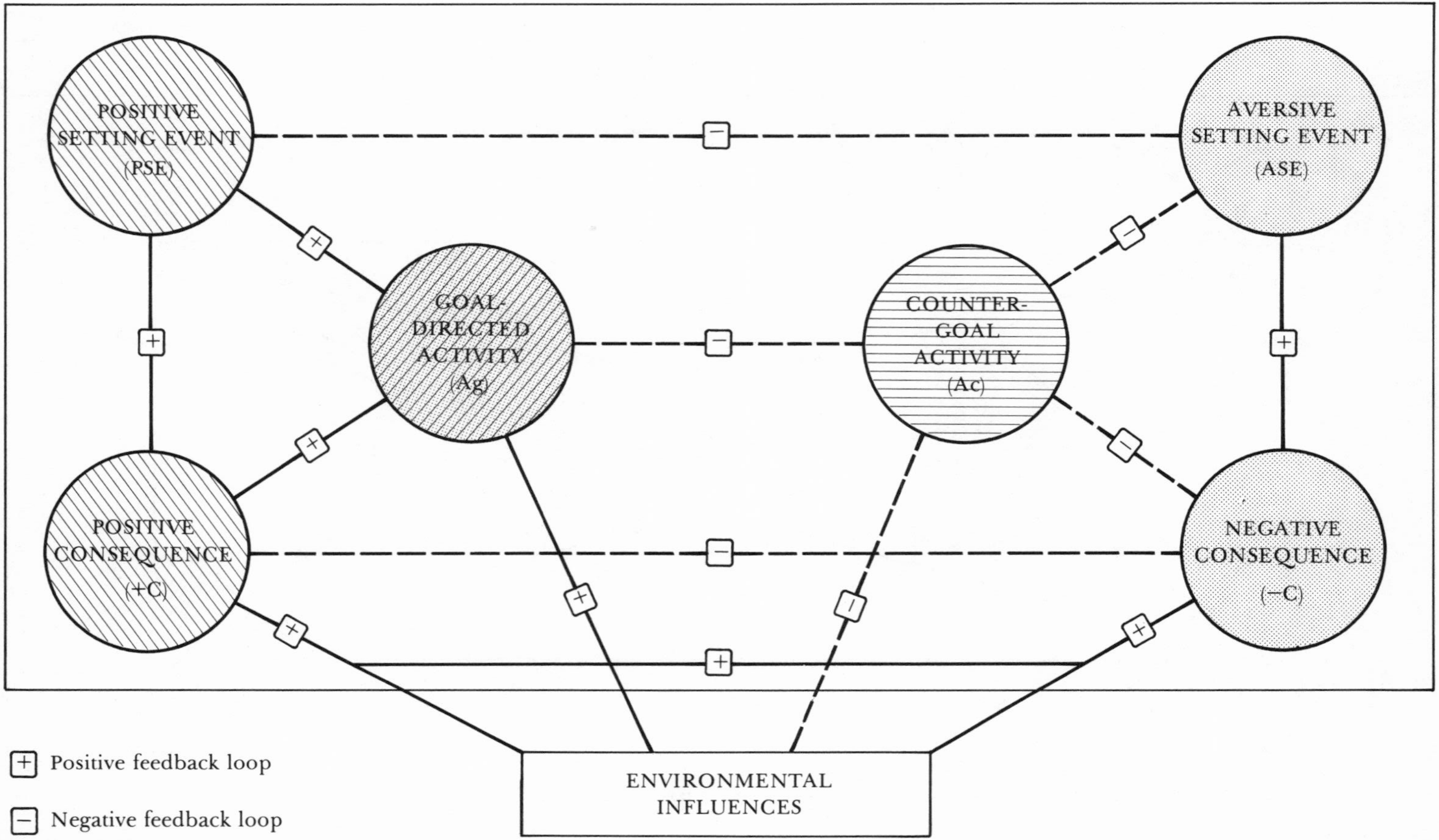

AVERSIVE
SETTING EVENT
(ASE)

NEGATIVE
CONSEQUENCE
(−C)

COUNTER-
GOAL
ACTIVITY
(Ac)

GOAL-
DIRECTED
ACTIVITY
(Ag)

POSITIVE
SETTING EVENT
(PSE)

POSITIVE
CONSEQUENCE
(+C)

ENVIRONMENTAL
INFLUENCES

+ Positive feedback loop

− Negative feedback loop

sequences. However, punishment remains available and is used to reprimand the new recruit or the veteran inmate faced with new or unfamiliar circumstances. (Figure 11 depicts these five conditions.)

Returning now to Kunkel's (1970) and Maruyama's (1963) theories about feedback loops, we recall that only loops with even numbers of negative Consequences are likely to be morphogenic. Of the six models we have presented, the first five fail to meet this condition. (They have seven, five, eleven, seven, and seven negative loops, respectively; see Figures 6 through 10.) Morphogenesis should be present only in the model depicted in Figure 11, which has six negative loops. This model requires consistent, discriminative responses that are identical to those that occur regularly in the outside community. Just as coming to work on time, doing homework, making a sale for the company are rewarded outside the internat, acts directed toward Reclaiming are rewarded in the internat. Dangerous, disturbing, or even distracting behaviors may be punished.

Many elitist internats achieve this morphogenic model. So do some internats for the ill, the poor, and the ex-convicts—those internats run by charismatic leaders or those strongly based on ideology. The question is how nonelitist internats can introduce goal-directed morphogenesis in the absence of an ideology or a charismatic leadership.

Past efforts to do such, particularly during the period when human behavior was conceived as governed by mechanistic laws, have been based on assumptions that good internats should have the characteristics of Weber's ([1925], 1947) bureaucracy or follow Taylor's (1907) principles of industrial engineering. But these models were intended to be applicable largely to systems in which people manipulated objects. They do not fully explain behavior even in their intended spheres and fall significantly short of meeting the requirements of people-changing systems.

Weberian expectations, when forcefully imposed on a people-changing organization, produce inmate dissatisfaction and invest caretakers with a bureaucratic personality (Gouldner, 1954; Merton, 1940). Mechanistic models of human behavior are undermined by human variability and individual needs. Generally, theories that posit high levels of predictability have not proven useful when work "is nonroutine and there is a good deal of uncertainty as to how to do a job" (Perrow, 1977, p. 8). Instead, Perrow (1977) recommends that "we should find out how to manipulate the reward structure, change the premises of the decision makers through finer controls on the information received and the expectations generated, search for interdepartmental conflicts that prevent better inspection procedures from being followed, and after manipulating these variables, sit back and wait for two or three months for them to take hold" (pp. 17-18).

Perrow's recommendation to control Activity through the reward structure seems appropriate advice to an internat that seeks to effectively promote Reclaiming. Likewise, his recommendation has some implications for other organizational systems. When Goals are declared and Activity is designed to meet them, appropriate organizational restructuring and rules of operation will evolve. The organizational structure will have clearly defined goal-promoting and counter-goal-directed behavior and rules that specify sanctions. Thus organizational structure will be shaped by Activity, just as Activity will develop from the organizational structure. March and Simon (1958, p. 170) even suggest that organizational structure be considered as the relatively stable aspects of Activity patterns.

Structuring Activity

We may use Perrow's (1977) concepts of reward structure, information, and interdepartmental conflicts along with Kunkel's (1970) model of Activity, Consequence, and setting event to analyze a sequence of behavior. Our example is from Brendan Behan's *Borstal Boy* (1958, p. 40). The participants are Mr. Whitbread and Mr. Holmes, officials of the internat, and Behan and Charlie, two inmates.

[1] "And 'old up your 'ead, when I speak to you."

[2] " 'Old up your 'ead, when Mr. Whit-bread speaks to you," said Mr. Holmes.

[3] I looked round at Charlie. [4] His eyes met mine and [5] he quickly lowered them to the ground.

[6] "What are you looking round at, Behan? Look at me."

[7] I looked at Mr. Whitbread.

[8] "I am looking at you," I said.

[9] "You are looking at Mr. Whitbread—what?" said Mr. Holmes.

[10] "I am looking at Mr. Whitbread."

[11] Mr. Holmes looked gravely at Mr. Whitbread, [12] drew back his open hand, and struck me on the face, [13] held me with his other hand and struck me again . . .

[14] "You are looking at Mr. Whitbread—what, Behan?"

[15] I gulped and got together my voice and tried again till I got it out. [16] "I, sir, please, sir, I am looking at you, I mean, I am looking at Mr. Whitbread, sir."

Mr. Whitbread's first act serves as a positive setting event to both Mr. Holmes and Behan and is reinforced by Mr. Holmes' behavior (2), while Behan looks at Charlie (3) who, by meeting his eye and lowering his own eyes (4, 5) probably punishes him. At the same time Behan's behavior also serves as a positive setting event for Mr Whitbread's next behavior (6), which is reinforced by Behan (7, 8). Behan's behavior now serves as a positive setting event for Mr. Holmes' behavior (9). Holmes presents Behan with an aversive response to his behavior (7, 8) and a positive setting event to provoke Behan's next move (10). Mr. Holmes, reinforced by Behan (10), now presents Behan with a series of punishments (11, 12, 13, 14) which provoke Behan's subsequent behavior (15, 16). These behaviors reinforce both Mr. Whitbread and Mr. Holmes. Some of the behaviors in this scene are also discriminative stimuli for Charlie, but Behan does not report his behavior.

Holmes and Whitbread are each reinforced three times.

Behan receives negative responses or punishments four times. Charlie may or may not be reinforced. In this situation, as in many others transpiring within non-Reclaiming internats, staff receive positive Consequences and inmates receive negative ones. Thus the situation was probably aversive to the inmates and reinforcing to the staff members. One cannot conclude from this vignette whether the staff's behavior was goal oriented or not. It is conceivable, though improbable, that the Goal of the internat was to punish inmates by making them uncomfortable. If so, the Goal was achieved in this scene. There is a very high probability that in this borstal the Goal of inmates does not correspond with the Goal of their caretakers and the administration. In short, at the very best, this is a setting for social Reclaiming.

The interaction described by Behan consists of behaviors and their positive and negative Consequences. Almost every internat uses both reward and punishment; it is the ratio of rewards and punishments that determines the climate of the internat. This ratio in itself, though, will have no effect on Reclaiming unless rewards and punishments are used in a consistent goal-directed strategy. Such consistency requires a high degree of convergence between the Goals of all participants—inmates, staff, administration, and community. In Behan's borstal convergence is poor. The English public school or the hospital for physically ill displays higher convergence such that Goals are clear and generally accepted, and goal-directed behavior is generally rewarded.

Furthermore, aside from rewards in the formal, rule-defined interaction of staff and inmates, informal structures exist for both groups. Informal structures reward only observable behavior that takes place in the presence of the relevant others, whose expectations are usually clear. Such reinforcement yields a high rate of behaviors that are strongly resistant to extinction (Buehler, Patterson, and Furniss, 1966), even when they are inconsistent with an internat's Goals. Since informal structures of internats are generally dominated by their inmates, they, and not staff, determine the balance of contingencies. At West Point, cadets usually reinforce staff and community expectations; at Sing Sing, the prisoners undermine them.

When the same behaviors serve both general goals, more proximate objectives, and specific tasks, than policy, strategy, and tactics (techniques), respectively, are aligned. Reinforcements from, and on, all levels of inmates, staff, administration and community follow a specific action. Such alignment occurs when society both embraces the goals of an internat and accepts the authority of its professional specialists in developing strategy and techniques. Community hospitals, military academies, and elitist boarding schools are examples of such internats. Activities appropriate for the achievement mode in such settings will be identical with or, at worst, consistent with the integration and conservation of the internat. The latter two, being of a strategic or tactical nature (that is, largely technical) will be adjusted for goal achievement by the authoritative professionals. Furthermore, in internats where policy, strategy, and tactics are convergent, adaptation, our fourth mode, is a natural consequence of such convergence. In effect, such fortunate internats define their own goals with full societal approval and, of course, they also set the criteria of proper policies, strategies, and tactics. The result is a high rate of Reclaiming and a positive societal Evaluation.

Mental hospitals, prisons, and similar low-status internats are not so fortunate. Outside forces are disparate, often conflicting, and expectations may contradict professionally determined internat strategies, or even techniques (tactics). For example, community groups may want criminals or the insane to be isolated during their Reclaiming. Isolation may, however, be contraindicated by theories of effective treatment. Or treatment strategies acceptable to the outside community may require a substantial component of punishment, which is inimical to many therapeutic tactics. Such divergence will confuse and demoralize staff and inmates (see McCleery, 1969).

Usually, internats can adjust to external expectations. American children's internats have changed from "orphanages" to "schools" to "residential treatment centers" within the past seventy-five years. Some still occupy the same plants and pay allegiance to old traditions. In reviewing the changes these internats have experienced, one finds that for internats, like other social institutions, the ease of change is inversely related to size of the behavioral unit: Global modifications require less effort than specific ones. Policy is easier to change than strategy, which is in turn easier to modify than tactics. Tactics and technique, being the responsibility of numerous, variously located individuals with established patterns of operation, are the most difficult aspect to change. Moreover, because the treatment components—those supposedly aimed specifically at Reclaiming—in most internats are subject to varying, often conflicting interpretation, they are inconsistently reinforced. As a result, behavior will persist even when it does not correspond to new policy or new strategy.

Coherence and consistency of expectations, from the level of Goals to that of minor technique, mark the effective internat. Activities in all four modes serve as discriminative stimuli to promote an unending spiral that culminates in Reclaiming and positive societal Evaluation. Internats such as monasteries, yeshivot, military academies, elitist boarding schools, and hospitals for the physically ill function thusly. To be sure, society's expectations of these internats are not totally consistent and invariant over time. When the call is out to abolish West Point or to integrate working-class children in the English public schools, these internats become subject to some of the conditions of contradiction and confusion that are the constant fare of non-elitist internats.

The morphostatic structures of the five types of internats presented earlier may be ascribed to societal uncertainty. When the demand is specific—"Execute the murderer" or "Heal the sick"—a morphogenic model is possible because an internat's functions are clearly specified. Of course, in a pluralistic society expectations are rarely uniform. Some oppose capital punishment; others reject medical intervention, believing in other types of cures. When no consensus exists, internats fail and calls for their abolition spread.

Yet society will always need residential settings for some of its members. We may move the inmates of mental hospitals to group residences in town, or send delinquents to group homes, or transfer the inmates of Willowbrook to the Bronx Developmental Center, or help as many of the aged as possible to live in their own homes—but we cannot do without internats altogether. Smaller, closer, more humane internats may temporarily be more acceptable to society, but their deviant residents are not. The serious and socially responsible question is how to create effective internats, not how to abolish all internats. In Chapters Eight and Nine we present our recommendations for effective policy, strategy, and tactics.

8

The Reclaiming Mission of the Internat

A town fool in one of Scholem Aleichem's stories refused to go near a hospital. "More people die there than anywhere else," he observed; "if I go near, I will die too." The argument that sick people go to the hospital to be healed did not affect the fool's conviction. Bolstered by excellent evidence, that of numerous funerals starting from the hospital's morgue, his evaluation of the hospital was understandably negative. Since we know something about comparable recovery rates for similar illnesses, inside hospitals and outside them, we are amused by the fool's conclusion. Only a fool would behave that way, we surmise. Nonetheless, is the fool totally wrong?

Suppose the hospital were a collective of persons with highly contagious illnesses and the physicians knew little of isolation techniques or other ways to reduce cross-infection. Illness would spread within the hospital, which would indeed become a source of death, as the fool believed. The high mortality rates of infants in American foundling homes at the turn of the century (Lord, 1878, p. 171) confirm the fool's assumptions. Our modern hospitals, of course, are rather effective in preventing the contagion of physical illnesses. But internats for mentally ill, criminal, or retarded populations are not successful in preventing contagion in the psychological, social, and valuative fields. Such internats, filled with outcasts who are labeled deviant, have not been able to Reclaim their inmates nor to protect inmates from iatrogenic contagion. They confirm the fool's conclusions, although society expects that such settings, like hospitals, should effect a greater improvement in a higher proportion of inmates than would occur outside.

Were internat personnel as forthright as Scholem Aleichem's fool, they would tell the community that many of their internats are settings in which inmates deteriorate rather than improve. Of late, some staff members have said so, and they have called for total deinstitutionalization. But society demands that certain persons be sent to internats for Reclaiming. Unacceptable deviants are to be treated in undesirable settings composed of others like themselves. Society expects internats to succeed in Reclaiming, yet knows that professionals' inability to control behavioral contagion precludes Reclaiming in such settings.

Caught in this paradoxical situation, inmates and staff of these internats help to perpetuate it. Rather than point to the inherent contradictions and demand a resolution, or treat the paradox as an ill-conceived, cruel hoax, they seriously attempt to do what cannot be done. Staff go about their business applying band-aids, while contagion rapidly spreads. Communities send their ailing off to internats, trying to ignore the contagion or to limit it to the periphery of a remote site. Continued failure to yield Reclaiming is the inevitable fate of such internats unless the paradox is restated or, in the words of Abelson and Rosenberg (1958), the situation is transcended. A "second-order change" must take place through redefinition of the relationships between the internat and the outside society (Watzlawick, Weakland, and Fisch, 1974).

Four kinds of internats have successfully reframed the paradox. Hospitals for the physically ill have isolated contagion; thus few patients become sicker because they are in the hospital. Further, hospitals limit their competence to purely physical phenomena, thus yielding a high rate of Reclaiming. Similarly, training internats, intended to inculcate special skills, claim expertise in their limited field. They point to narrow achievements that correspond to society's demands. Religious and other ideology-based internats have also transcended the paradox by claiming special competence at self-definition. The yeshiva and convent dictate their own terms and confront society with the choice of totally accepting or abolishing them. Finally, charismatic leaders use this same approach. Father Flanagan at Boys Town, Chuck Dederich at Synanon, A. S. Neill at Summerhill, Korczak at his Warsaw children's home—all succeeded in temporarily transcending the paradox by the force of their personality. But after Father Flanagan's death Boys Town again became subject to the paradox, and the recent disintegration of Synanon (Craib, 1979) illustrates that charisma cannot always transcend the paradox.

Generally, internats for the mentally ill, criminal, or retarded cannot limit their tasks to a few dimensions. Nor do most pursue communal ideologies or possess charismatic leaders. Faced with such internats and their activities, society may reduce the "cognitive imbalance" (Abelson and Rosenberg, 1958) in a number of ways.

Denial is one technique for averting the consequences of a paradox. Society may either deny that it expects an internat to succeed in Reclaiming or deny that the internat is a place in which people deteriorate. For example, society defines internats like the Molokai leper colony or Devil's Island as non-Reclaiming. Internats for the severely retarded and for the chronically and terminally ill are also covered by such a rationale, though not overtly. To deny that the internat may worsen rather than improve its residents, society can fill its internats with expensive staff and equipment. Some failing internats for delinquents and the disturbed have annual costs per inmate in excess of twice a factory worker's annual wages. High costs are considered a criterion of an internat's quality and society's beneficence, although they may reflect only high levels of waste.

Second, the dissonance caused by the paradox may be reduced by *bolstering*. A negative element may be viewed as tenable when assumed to yield an accepted positive result. Heart surgery may be painful, expensive, and debilitating, but it restores a patient's health. Similarly, regarding internats, it may be said that removing people from familial environments is hurtful, but the promise of improved Mastery is worth such discomfort.

Third, the society may use *differentiation* between aspects of an internat to make the internat's achievements seem more consistent with community expectations. Although some people object to the way that a military academy regiments cadets, they praise the academy for producing leadership, teaching specific skills, inculcating patriotism, and other positively perceived functions. Even the prison, isolating and degrading as it may be, has some positive aspects to commend it. Community leaders, for example, may proudly refer to the number of prisoners who completed their high school education while incarcerated.

Finally, society may use a form of *transcendence,* by defining the conflicting elements of the paradoxical situation as necessary components of a larger, superordinate whole. A community, for example, may realize that its mental hospital has its good side and bad side, but that since the community cannot exist without the internat, it should endeavor to improve it. Or society will understand that although cheating and hazing in the military academy detract from its status and effectiveness, the solution is to improve the academies rather than call for their abolition. In short, a necessary component of any well-ordered society is an ideological commitment to its internats.

Internat as Totality

Any procedure for reframing the paradox must consider the internat as a totality. The concept of a total institution as currently understood by professionals and public alike is one of content and process, uniform and predetermined, with a centralized authority for all inhabitants. Such authority, controlling all essential functions, is at times defined as necessarily pathogenic. Centralized authority is usually suspect although some such authorities escape suspicion. That parents totally control the life of their infant or that a self-sacrificing nurse tends a gravely ill person—these are accepted as proper and beneficial instances of centralized authority. Centralized authority, it appears, is deemed beneficial in caring for persons with very low Mastery.

When all dimensions of an individual's Mastery are inadequate, then all aspects of his life require total control. Persons with some Mastery are expected to require less control. A parent and a warden both have power, but the latter is expected to permit the care recipient ever-greater discretion in determining his own life. The relationship between recipient and caretaker is a function of the recipient's Mastery. A good nurse may control physical behavior, but not the social, psychological, or value expressions of a patient. A Quaker-run prison, similarly, attempted control over thought and association, but much less over physical expression.

Control over the behavior of another individual imbues the caretaker with commensurate power. Total control implies absolute power, tolerable in human interactions only in the presence of extremely low Mastery and unstinting love. Even then, such a relationship must be temporary, and the Goals of care recipients, caretakers, program managers, and outside society must be in conformity. If the inmates and staff surrender totally to the leadership, and the leadership's Goals differ vastly from society's, the result is an isolated cult that views society as the enemy, for example, Jonestown.

A much more common occurrence is that the four participating groups reach a limited consensus on Goals. Often, they will agree only on a single dimension of Mastery, leaving all other behavioral aspects unsettled and open to negotiation. The process of negotiation affects any loving relationship between care recipient and caretaker and curtails the absolute power of the centralized authority. When a boy in a correctional internat wants permission to visit his family, consent or denial is the subject of the discussion, but process is at issue far more than content. The internat's director and the boy are dealing with the manner in which consensus on Goals and Activity will be determined. Whether the boy gets to do what he wants is usually of lesser importance than the manner in which the decision is made.

The process by which negotiations are made is often more important to the internat's functioning than the content of the compromise. The use of an appropriate process to yield consensus will often lead participants to accept otherwise intolerable conditions. For example, rules concerning behavior are more acceptable to inmates and staff if they are made by group decision rather than by a central authority's fiat. When a patient, prisoner, or cadet wants to move from one room to another, the process by which permission is granted affects the inmate's subsequent behavior as much as the granting or refusal of the request.

The low Mastery of some inmates may constrain the process. In some internats inmates are not allowed to participate in decision-making processes as a punitive or precautionary measure. For example, prisons and mental hospitals, with seemingly incontrovertible logic, confine their inmates' participation in internat processes to the safety of therapeutic sessions. Inmates are encouraged to confront their emotions and fears as openly as possible, but they are not to confront internat policy. Successful internats invariably allow inmates to participate in real-world process. Korczak (1967) used a participatory self-governance structure; Fairweather and others (1969) describe ward discussion and decision groups; Maher developed a series of real-world games at Delancey Street (Hampden-Turner, 1976).

Although any specific item of content has a time-limited existence, an internat's process provides the continuing dynamic character of the setting. An internat's decision-making process determines how participants reach consensus on Goals; how the internat will define acceptable, desirable, and unacceptable behavior; and what rewards and punishments are to be used. Process determines the criteria for participation in rule making and the gradation of restriction in Activity based on Mastery.

In a well-orchestrated internat, expectations of an inmate's behavior will be appropriate to his Mastery. The internat will carefully evaluate a new inmate's Mastery, and a continuous process of evaluation and self-evaluation will lead to regular adjustments of this appraisal. If such evaluation is made by inmates, staff, and administrators—rather than by staff alone—it is likely to address all dimensions of Mastery and incorporate various perspectives. Fairweather and others (1969) found that patients were, collectively, excellent judges of one another's success on the outside. Braly (1976) believes the same to be true for prisoners. The totality of an internat allows for differential responsiveness in accord with an inmate's Mastery, that is, control over the environment may be adjusted to an inmate's needs. As noted earlier, Good, Siegel, and Bay (1965) make exactly such a proposal regarding mental patients' freedom in the use of physical space.

If behavioral expectations and Activity are to be individualized to suit each inmate's Mastery, the internat must develop processes that provide for continual reassessment of and consensus on each inmate's Mastery and of the population's range of Mastery. The internat must also develop a process for reaching consensus on Goals so that convergence among the Goals of inmates, staff, administrators, and the community is high. Any fundamental contradictions among goal makers should be overtly acknowledged and then resolved or explicitly accepted as unavoidable. The internat's process should set expectations on all dimensions of Mastery that allow for some growth-promoting risk. The internat may well find that control of certain aspects of Activity may be transferred from caretakers to care recipients, affording the latter greater responsibility and greater opportunity for growth. Finally, the internat must develop a contingency structure that provides positive feedback loops for each aspect of its consensual process.

Differential Totality

Since the inmates of an internat, like any population, are considerably varied in their Mastery, some inmates require no more control on some dimensions than the normal population outside. The internat's totality should thus be differential, applying control only to those dimensions of Mastery that require internat control. Hospitals for the physically ill provide an example of such differential control. While maintaining near-total control of physical conditions, they generally eschew intervention in the psychological, social, or valuative fields. This approach seems effective and certainly efficient for patients with appendicitis, broken legs, or pneumonia. Patients whose illnesses are of longer duration (for example, tuberculosis) or greater complexity (for example, renal malfunction) require a broader approach, and hospital control of these patients extends beyond the physical.

Instituting differential totality in other settings is considerably more difficult. For example, how does one isolate the specific areas of low Mastery of an abandoned child, an incarcerated felon, a confused octogenerian? How does one differentiate which areas should be controlled by the internat and which areas should be the responsibility of the inmate? Most internats devised for such individuals use an undifferentiated, diffused mode of intervention, usually accompanied by undifferentiated punishment and reward. A modicum of control is sought over all fields, but substantial control is attained in none. Except for the Quaker internats in the Pennsylvania system and some recent attempts at token economies, most internats have responded by assuming the general incapacity of an inmate, thus making for unfocused intervention.

The differential control used by internats that care for the physically ill provide a potentially constructive pattern for internats whose residents have low Mastery in several fields. Such hospitals require patients to relinquish medical control over certain fields but assume patient competence in nonmedical affairs. A patient is authorized to sign a document based on the assumption that he can understand it and act in his own best interest. Similarly, a patient's desire to say morning prayers is not subject to a physician's control; the patient retains authority in this matter. The internat thus acknowledges the patient's authority and Mastery in certain fields. Should the patient use a telephone by the bed to negotiate a business transaction or offer religious counseling to a distressed roommate, most hospitals will condone such behavior, having previously limited their expertise and control to the physical field.

Other internats can adopt a similar approach. Psychiatric hospitals, prisons, and internats for the aged or retarded can identify each inmate's Mastery in each field and encourage inmates to exercise their competencies to the fullest. For dimensions of Mastery on which an inmate is competent, the internat can exert only controls identical to those on the outside. For example, able inmates can work and receive full value for their effort, while being charged for the costs of maintenance. An exchange relationship is thus established, preparing the inmate for outside living without caretaker control. The internat will exert total control only over those areas in which an inmate has substantial deficiencies. This approach may require some constraints, some psychological intervention, and a good deal of social isolation. In such areas will be the profound difference between the inside and the outside, between inmate and staff, care recipient and caretaker.

Such an approach implies a model of intervention that builds on the inmate's capacity rather than his disabilities—an oft-repeated dictum of various clinical professions, especially of social work. Few internats, however, have applied this clinical dictum. Possibly, the risk believed to exist under assumptions of competence and differential totality was deemed too high. Yet, given the evidence that assumed dependency and declared incompetence promote greater dependency and greater incompetence, presumptions of capability in some fields of Mastery should govern internat programming if Reclaiming is the objective.

For example, in Meoni, an internat for delinquents (described in Wozner, 1965), totality applied to only two areas of deficiency and Activity appropriate to these areas. First, attendance at group discussions was compulsory. The object of this rule was to teach inmates that conflict resolution can and should be achieved through talk, not physical aggression. Second, all inmates were required to pay a graduated part of maintenance costs from income they derived by working outside. The purpose of this rule was to teach inmates the relationship between work (production), reward (consumption), and responsibility. Penalty for noncompliance was transfer out of this preferred setting. The internat chose to exert total control in these two areas alone because it considered these critical issues in achieving Reclaiming.

To be sure, an internat could decide to control a larger number of areas, but such expansion incurs the danger of diffused focus. Only strongly ideological settings can maintain a high degree of total authority over many aspects of inmates' life. In such internats ideology provides a single all-encompassing Goal that dictates the specifics of all behavior. For example, members of a yeshiva observe all religious commandments pertaining to prayer, Sabbath, diet, laws of personal purity, and so on. This totality can be achieved only because all actions are seen as composing a single ideological obligation. A charismatic leader may instill a similar commitment from his followers.

Internats that do not have a unifying ideological theme may seek to evaluate individual items of behavior, each in its own context and on its own merit. But such a task would be endless, for an infinite number of behaviors would require evaluation. To reduce this task, an internat may choose to deliberately ignore some aspects of behavior (possibly entire fields or modes) and concentrate attention on selected areas. In the hospital, total attention is paid to the physical field and some to the psychological. In a village acculturating young immigrants, attention is focused on the social and valuative fields. Other behaviors are treated as an undifferentiated background, receiving attention only sporadically and by virtue of their implications for the dimensions of concern. Thus an internat defines a field in which it claims specialized expertise. When an individual in the community exhibits a specific deficiency, he is addressed to the appropriate expert internat. Such specialization and differentiation do define some contemporary internats—for example, a person with a broken leg heads for the hospital—but not all.

There are four anticipated consequences of differentiation. First, specialization should lead to a limited content and process within an internat. Hospitals treating physical ailments are thus limited, but mental hospitals, jails, and orphanages are not. Second, specialization should endow the setting with expert power, the authority for promulgating its own rules of intervention in matters pertaining to the sphere of differentiated totality. The medical profession currently has such authority; nonprofessionals do not feel free to dictate hospital operations. But other internats do not have such authority and outsiders frequently express their opinions regarding internat affairs.

Third, specialization permits, even requires, innovation in the restricted areas of differentiated totality, and it is expected that knowledge and expertise will be transmitted to new members of the profession. University hospitals provide for the transmission of medical knowledge and expertise, but there are no similar institutions for prisons, orphanages, or old-age homes. Fourth, specialization narrows and deepens accountability as the internat consistently disclaims responsibility for some areas of Mastery. In those areas in which the internat claims expertise it should be accountable for outcomes, methods, and admissions. Specifically the specialized internat defines for society what it should expect as the outcome of intervention. Society then has a basis for deciding whether it wants such outcomes as compared with others. The specialized internat similarly specifies its methods of intervention, allowing society to estimate the internat's costs in all fields. Society can then compare the social, psychological, financial, and valuative costs of specific operations and decide whether anticipated benefits outweigh estimated costs. The specialized internat also specifies the characteristics of the population for whom its declared objectives are likely to be achieved. Specification of intake both reduces costs, as inappropriate inmates are not admitted for care, and also promotes the specialization of the internat.

Decisions

Internats organized on the principle of differential totality allocate decision-making responsibility to inmates and staff. Decisions in fields outside the internat's expertise are left to the full discretion of individuals, be they inmates or staff. The hospital does not care whether a patient reads the comics or financial pages, popular literature or a religious tract, while boarding school well might. Within the sphere of its concern, the internat will attempt to manage decisions by persuading or requiring inmates to undertake that Activity most likely to result in Reclaiming.

Centralized strategy and decentralized tactics appear to be most effective in promoting Reclaiming. (On strategy, see Belknap, 1956, pp. 13-54, 69-98; McCorkle and others, 1958, pp. 152-172; Sykes, 1958, pp. 3-39, 130-134; on tactics, see Burling, Lentz, and Wilson, 1956, pp. 108-124, 182-198; Stanton and Schwartz, 1954, pp. 67, 263.) Centralized strategy leads to internat unity and a clarity of purpose consistent with goals declared to the community. Decentralized tactics permit flexibility of action in specific situations, enhancing innovation, broad personal involvement, and responsibility.

Decision making in the internat concerns a variety of issues relevant to its institutional, managerial, and technical affairs. Institutional decisions pertain to goals and the policies of the internat; managerial decisions concern objectives and strategy; and technical decisions relate to tasks and tactics. All three types of decisions are influenced by constraints and contingencies of the internat's task environment and there is a considerable overlap between these three areas, but the differentiation seems to be valid for analytic purposes.

The internat must develop a decision-making process that yields institutional, managerial, and technical decisions. Thompson (1967) proposes that coherence is more likely to occur in some areas than others. Decisions, he explains, are based on beliefs about cause-effect relations and preferences regarding possible outcomes (p. 134). He posits four types of decision-making processes: computational, compromise, judgmental, and inspirational (see Chapter Three). The prevalence of computational decisions in an organization will be reflected in the coherence between strategy and tactics and, in turn, will relate to the achievement of goals. While no organization is ruled solely by a computational strategy, such a strategy usually results in high effectiveness.

In many internats, decisions are judgmental and inspirational. Except in hospitals for physical ailments, means are very seldom certain, and the objectives of some internats are general. Thus, judgments must be made regarding the approximation of objectives. If means and objectives are obscure, inspirational decisions are made. However, judgmental and inspirational decision making apply only to decisions on treatment. Administrators and inmates usually use compromise and even computational decision-making processes. Both the administration and the inmates—unlike the professional therapists—are usually subject to prescriptive rules. The dominant decision-making forces are to be found in an undeclared coalition between the administrators of the internat and the inmates.

In an ideological internat, beliefs about goals and means are relatively certain. The commitment of members and a sanction system are secured by reference to the ideology, which governs totally all Activity and decision making. When goals and means are less certain, members' commitment can be secured by their participation in decision making. Hospitals, because they operate to a considerable degree on computational decisions may rely solely on professional decisions. But prisons that do so erupt, and nursing homes so structured reduce their inmates to incompetence. Such internats must involve all members in decision making in order to assure that Activity is appropriate to an inmate's Mastery and expectations.

The Reclaiming internat must thus develop a decision-making process that addresses both the inmates' personal subsystems and the internat's organizational subsystems (see Chapter Two, Tables 1 and 2). Attention to personal and organizational subsystems must apply to all aspects of Activity. Before explaining the components of such a Reclaiming internat's subsystems, let us consider one example of such an integrated approach to personal and organizational subsystems. We will examine physical facilities and differentiate the internat as a vessel from the internat as an instrument. We use the metaphor of a vessel to describe an internat that merely contains the inmate while he is subjected to professional attention. In contrast, internats that consider organizational and personal needs, thus promoting integrated Reclaiming, function as instruments.

Vessels or Instruments

Spitz, in his classic study of infants in two internats—a nursery in a women's prison and a foundling home, attributes some of the difference in development to environmental factors. He characterizes one of these factors, the visual radius, in each internat as follows:

> In the nursery . . . trees, landscape, and sky are visible from both sides. . . . Bustling activity of mothers carrying their children, tending them, feeding them, playing with them . . . is usually present. The cubicles of the children are enclosed, but the glass panes . . . reach low enough for every child to be able at any time to observe everything going on all around. He can see into the corridor. . . . He can look out of the windows, and he can see babies . . . just by turning his head. . . .
>
> In foundling home the corridor into which the cubicles open . . . is bleak and deserted. . . . Most of the time nothing goes on to attract the babies' attention. . . . Hanging bed sheets over the foot and the side railing of each cot . . . [obstruct the view from the crib so that] the child lying in the cot is effectively screened from the world. . . . The result . . . is that each baby lies in solitary confinement . . . and . . . the only object he can see is the ceiling [Spitz, 1945, pp. 62-63].

Infants in the nursery developed at a rate similar to that of a comparison group in middle-class families, while those in the foundling home fell substantially behind within several months of birth. While Spitz describes other factors that differentiated the two settings, he attributes considerable importance to stimulus deprivation in the foundling home. Buildings, rooms, crib sheets, and windows are not merely inert objects; rather, each contributes to the instrumental nature of a setting; aspects of an internat's physical setting constitute Activity.

We earlier noted that medieval hospitals were planned so that all patients could have visual and auditory contact with religious services in the chapel. That such a clearly instrumental use of space had a religious source is not surprising. Ideological unity, posing clearly ascriptive relationships between human well-being and religious practice, required the centrality of the chapel in the treatment process. Subsequent secular internats, however, considered space as an organizational problem, and the instrumental use of space was reintroduced into internat planning only by proponents of moral treatment in the nineteenth century. When moral treatment was succeeded by other therapies, spatial planning again dictated organizational layouts that reflected "an insensitive, hygienic, well regulated hopelessness" (Osmond, 1959, p. 7). Internats again became vessels.

Why did the conception of an internat as a vessel prevail? First, while an instrumental idea of an internat naturally follows from a holistic view of the individual, the vessel concept reflects an emphasis on organization needs. Whether the holism is religious or psychodynamic in origin, the holistic view posits the interdependence of body, mind, and soul: Treat one and you change the others. Thus, the chapel-hospital is a logical application of a holistic religious ideology. In the absence of such a holistic approach to care, internats tend to ignore aspects of the inmate's needs and focus on the organization's needs.

Second, the vessel concept seems to minimize risk. By reducing interaction between the inmate and his environment, the vessel reduces unanticipated accidents. For example, it is less risky to present a ready-made model playground to a children's internat than to let the children build one.

Third, when a large proportion of the internat's environment is declared or perceived to be inert, less emotional investment is required of the staff. In the most extreme cases, even the care recipients are declared to be inert and they blend into the woodwork.

Fourth, many planners seem to assume that vessels are less costly to build and maintain than are instrumental internats because the latter must be flexible enough to match changes in inmates' needs and conditions. That this is not necessarily true is documented by the superiority of tents over hospital buildings in the recovery rates of Civil War wounded or by the effectiveness of informal inmate self-help groups as compared with formal therapy, but the assumption persists.

Finally, the vessel conception is no doubt due, in some part, to sheer inertia. Since most internats' physical and social structures are less amenable to change than the treatment theories that govern the caretakers' behavior within them, changes in physical plant must inevitably lag behind clinical theory. In the face of such discrepancies the most comfortable assumption is that the surroundings do not matter.

Although physical space and decision-making processes are related, these two aspects of internat structure may vary independently. A vessel with centralized decisions is a total organization in the manner of any well-structured bureaucracy. A vessel with broadly distributed decision power resembles a democratic bureaucracy. The first type of vessel will be oriented to social Reclaiming and is particularly functional as a storage internat. The second type can promote integrated Reclaiming since inmates' needs and intentions play a part in decisions. Such internats will function reasonably well in training or physical healing, that is, when the dimensions of Mastery to be affected are both specific and narrow.

Instrumental internats with centralized decision structures are exemplified by internats headed by charismatic and omnipotent leaders. (Ungraced by the leader's omniscience, they become total vessels.) Instrumental internats with widely distributed power are organizations oriented to integrated Reclaiming and show particular competence in socialization, mental healing, and conservation. In the absence of charismatic leadership, only differential totality, that is, a distribution of decision-making power relative to Mastery, can achieve Reclaiming.

Reclaiming Organization Subsystems

The Reclaiming internat addresses both personal and organization needs. Table 3 shows the sixteen Reclaiming organization subsystems. These subsystems follow the fields and modes described in Chapter Two (see Tables 1 and 2).

The subsystems shown in Table 3 are, of course, ideal types. To realize the goals in each of the subsystems, an internat must plan appropriate Activity. A well-intentioned, charismatic,

Table 3. Reclaiming Organization Subsystems

Field / Mode	Psychological–Behavioral	Physical	Societal	Cultural–Valuative
Expressive	Striving of internat to attain its members' potential; to enable them to take initiative, make decisions to advance personal growth, be industrious, retain their individuality, be active, attempt to change environment to meet their needs, enjoy achievement and productivity. Internat experiments and changes to meet its members' needs.	Autonomy of internat to allocate resources and physical means according to internal criteria, thus enabling members to develop and safeguard their physical well-being, to exercise their motor skills, practice control over their physical environment, learn and use various instruments, express acquisitiveness, know their environment and master it.	Prestige and influence of internat in general community enhances its members' standing in society, their relative progress on social ladder, and their personal advancement in both internat and general society.	Achievements with respect to general system of values to which internat is committed; facilitation of members' belonging to a cultured and value-conscious society, their appreciation of the arts, internalization of values, and striving for external expression of values.
Adaptive	Interaction of internat's members with environment; ability of members to shape and use recreational facilities; interaction of professionals with their external counterparts; interaction of inmates and outsiders; ability of members to plan their future post-internat environment; degree of similarity between internat and external environments, preparation for post-internat life.	Reciprocal adaptation of the internat and surroundings as physical entities; opportunity for members to produce useful things, to use tools and equipment; to dress appropriately, use eating utensils properly, keep their persons and surroundings clean; to maintain their health and normal sexual functioning.	Reciprocal relationship between internat and other social institutions facilitates members' participation in various social systems, enables them to derive satisfaction from social activity, and aids their adjustment to new social environments.	Reciprocal adaptation of internat's and society's values through interaction between members' values and society's cultural, scientific, and artistic activities.
Integrative	Organization of internat's various components such that members can practice problem-solving, experience novel situations, exercise and learn skills, assume gradually increasing responsibility and independence. Internat balances various intervention techniques and different goals to achieve relative consensus among staff and consistent internal policy.	Balanced, harmonious, internally compatible organization of internat's physical components; appropriateness of buildings to grounds, furnishings to buildings and members; physical environment facilitates members' well-being, health, physical ability and allows for illness and organic dysfunction.	Organization of roles such that members can adapt and experiment with variety of roles; preparation for fitting into various social settings; members learn to gain social acceptance by conformity without sacrifice of individuality, and to carry out various formal tasks and meet social expectations in order to gain sense of belonging.	Balance and compatibility among members' values and belief systems facilitates moral behavior in accord with values accepted by society, development of personal value systems, behavior appropriate to those systems, and pride in cultural heritage.
Conservative	Dominant belief system based on human rights, enabling members to build a positive self-image, to exercise their beliefs, express their opinions, use their potential, demonstrate their skills, plan for the future, retain their individuality.	Stable financial endowment and material properties provide security and enable members to live and manage their environment according to their genetic constitution and physical predisposition.	Preservation of enduring social characteristics of internat as a social institution gives residents a sense of membership in human society while they reside in internat; members identify with persistent human values and are guided by models in larger, external society.	Commitment to identity-forming ideology with ties to respected past and behavioral implications for present and future.

and benevolent autocrat like Korczak, Father Flanagan, or John Maher seems to *naturally* attend to the requirements of each of the subsystems without formal procedures. Such sensitive leaders communicate with inmates, staff, administrators, and community such that all these participants' Goals determine Activity. Through informal means, such leaders estimate Mastery, calculate Consequences, and involve everyone in the decision process. Conflicting views are entertained, each is more or less explicitly weighed, a course of Activity is plotted. "Games" at Delancey Street (Hampden-Turner, 1976) are an elaborate and forceful illustration of this process. Korczak's children's self-government, wall newspapers, and court are another (see Korczak, 1967, pp. 378-462). It should be noted that both Maher and Korczak were targets of complaints by care recipients and were even accused of failing to fully adhere to the professed mission of their settings.

Decision Making and Differentiation. An internat that is conceived of as a vessel cannot adequately realize the goals of the Reclaiming organization's subsystems. Caudill's (1958) description of the organizational dilemmas confronted by a mental hospital illustrate this contention. Concerned with the efficient operation of the vessel, the staff of this setting focuses only on the conflicting opinions of staff. Though staff views may, conceivably, reflect those of patients, the latter are not considered a party to the conflict. The patient is an object, not a reactive subject.

> The question of the values of the various role groups certainly is involved in the confusion often felt by senior physicians or residents between the administrative and therapeutic aspects of their roles. . . . Such problems raise the procedural issue of the advisability of the separation between administrative and the therapeutic responsibilities in the work of a psychiatric hospital. . . . [T]he very process of separation creates its own problems as it increases the likelihood that disagreement will develop between administrator and therapist, both of whom exercise control over the patient. . . . [T]his

is not just a problem for the psychiatric hospital or general hospital, but is inherent in a situation whenever there are dual lines of authority. Such a situation can arise in military organizations between line and staff control, or it can occur in universities between the faculty members who do the teaching and the administrators who care for the physical upkeep and financial condition of the institution [Caudill, 1958, p. 83].

A bureaucratic conception of decision making cannot create an instrumental internat that fulfills the needs of the Reclaiming organization subsystems. Such a setting may achieve its official purposes of "protecting the public and . . . meeting the minimal needs of patients" (Stanton and Schwartz, 1954, p. 404), but it will fail in its self-declared objectives of "meeting the more highly cultivated needs of patients and in bringing about lasting improvement in mental disorder" (p. 404). In short, such an internat will achieve social Reclaiming but not integrated Reclaiming.

Although Stanton and Schwartz attribute the failure of the mental hospital to the fact that it "has not been planned systematically on the basis of current knowledge of the nature of mental disorder" (p. 404), they ultimately come forth with a more telling deficiency: "More generally, the hospital suffered conspicuous inadequacies in its organization of decision making; the whole subject was rarely discussed and then was usually treated in a most unrealistic way" (p. 405). These authors then point out that "correction of organizational defects can safely be achieved only on the basis of detailed information concerning the participation of patients and its relation to illness and recovery" (p. 405). They indicate that an effective instrument must involve all participants in its decision process in order to permit the expression of all views and their amalgamation into Activity. Residents or staff can improve their Mastery only through the exercise of their ability to choose.

Ability to Choose. Choice in a socially interactive system is determined by level of Mastery in each field. The ulcer patient (but not the seminarian) may decide what book to read, and the seminarian (but not the ulcer patient) may decide what food to eat. When they enter particular internats, the patient and seminarian agree to surrender the right to choose in specific matters. What is always at issue is whether, by choice or compulsion, the inmate yields too much control to the internat. This is the fundamental charge against total internats, and it is also their Achilles' heel. Critics contend that most inmates are subject to internat control in areas of Mastery in which they suffer from no greater deficiencies than the public at large.

Criticism is usually not addressed to areas of physical care, but to matters of self-actualization, or an internat's control in matters psychological, social, and valuative. Internats are seen as depriving their inmates of the natural right to self-determination, thus undermining a decision-making process crucial to effective Reclaiming. Such criticism is particularly widespread in open, individualistic societies, in which constraints on internat residents' right to choose are viewed as directly contradictory to the expressed values and practices of the external society.

Residents of internats are no different from anyone else with regard to the desire to choose and a healthy sense of their own self-interest. It is not reasonable to assume *qualitative* differences between people in internats for the elite and those in prisons, psychiatric hospitals, and other such settings. These populations undoubtedly differ in their Mastery on some dimensions, but the differences are *quantitative*. The physically weak do have some muscles; persons with a low IQ do have some intelligence; persons with low self-control do have some will power (Thoresen and Mahoney, 1974). When responsibility for decision making is based on an individual's capacity, all internat residents can be allowed to participate, to choose. Some inmates will have more to contribute on particular subjects because they have greater capacity for judgment. For example, violent prisoners are perfectly capable of judging the quality of food or the comfort of cells but perhaps not the composition of work groups or seating arrangements in the dining hall.

Boundaries of Acceptable Decisions. Decisions are not made in a vacuum but in the context of a belief system that dictates what is valued and how much. However practical, pragmatic, and evidence-oriented a decision, it is always *evaluated* according to the values of the decision maker. Free choice is always curtailed by what one believes to be true and right. Of course, individuals do not always choose what is right, but when a choice is made that is not right, guilt or shame is the consequence.

An internat's ideology defines values for its members. It is a belief system to which reclaimed members adhere and which prescribes the value goals for the as yet unreclaimed. If the internat's ideology is a refined version of an ideology prevalent in society, the internat will function as an agent of change within society and will meet with accolades (West Point, a prep school). If the values of a socializing internat such as a prison diverge from society's ideology, society will condemn the internat as a failure. Similarly, if an internat's ideology is similar to society's, but society regards it as subversive (for example, most mental hospitals), the internat will be judged a failure.

This is the great paradox: an internat cannot do much about unattainable social expectations; therefore, society must modify its expectations or abolish such internats. Abolition is unlikely, since internats are widely used in many societies—but the paradox must be solved. A possible solution, as we suggested earlier, is to conceive of the internat as a differential totality. This conception would modify an internat's characteristics and facilitate change in society's attitudes. The internat would declare its primary areas of concern and expertise, the dimensions of Mastery on which its inmates are markedly different from members of outside society. In such areas the internat's control and authority would be total, and society would evaluate the internat solely on its efforts in those selected areas.

To propose maximal participation in decision making by all members of an internat begs the question of formal versus informal structures. Of course there will be a large informal flow of communication under the formal surface. In this respect, the prison and mental hospital are no different from West Point or the monastery. All social settings have covert structures, just as all behaviors have some latent functions. In full-participation Reclaiming internats, a considerable measure of convergence occurs between the formal and informal structures as all participants contribute to decision making and debate proposals with reference to Reclaiming. Public discussion and compromise are essential to a sensitive and purposive Reclaiming internat.

Decision Making to Favor Reclaiming

In the open process of decision making, within a context of specified goals, participants' behavior depends on their attitudes toward Reclaiming. Three types of dispositions have been observed in various settings. For example, Almond (1971) identified three types of patients in a short-term therapeutic milieu: the "preconverts," who entered the internat possessing values similar to those of staff; the "unit converts," who during their residence in the unit adopted values similar to those held by staff; and "rejectors and renegers," whose values were and remained discrepant with those held by the staff. Since caretakers may also be preconverts, unit converts, or rejectors, we prefer to group them with the care recipients in our three characterizations of individuals' attitudes toward Reclaiming.

We designate as *Opponents* those staff and inmates whose ideas oppose the Reclaiming effort. Ideology, professional training, personal preference, or lack of capacity (low Mastery) may cause individuals to adopt this position. *Fanatics* are those inmates or staff who believe in Reclaiming, but their ideas do not tolerate any flexibility in implementing the Reclaiming process. Fanatics include the full convert who assumes a holier-than-thou attitude and the zealous staff member who cannot comprehend the need for moderate risk taking and flexibility. *Universal Reclaimers* also believe in Reclaiming, but their ideas incorporate a tolerance for compromise and setbacks. They are willing to take risks, make allowance for individuals' different levels of Mastery, and are able and willing to see Reclaiming as a gradual process.

The mix of Opponents, Fanatics, and Universal Reclaimers varies among different types of internats. Just as the hospital for physical illness and the prison have different Reclaiming tasks, so, too, do Opponents or Fanatics in these internats display different behavior. For each subsystem in each type of setting certain attitudes and actions are a mark of opposition or fanaticism.

During open discussions of the internat's functioning, some Opponents and Fanatics will be frustrated; some staff will leave, and some inmates will escape or withdraw into themselves. However, the identification of Opponents and Fanatics has its utility. These individuals provide rallying points for like-minded staff and inmates, and foils for discussion of Reclaiming policies and Goals. The open expression of all positions is useful. Some individuals will cross over to another camp, and inconsistencies in an individual's position will naturally be challenged.

With reference to the Reclaiming objectives of an internat, the functions of Opponents, Fanatics, and Universal Reclaimers will differ considerably among the sixteen subsystems. Fanatics, for example, reinforce the ideological base of a setting, affirm its objectives, and symbolize its stance to the outside; however, they also interfere with integration through their exaggerated demands on other members. Opponents serve as the brakes of an internat; they challenge others' headlong rush toward Reclaiming and provide support for members who are skeptical of Reclaiming and members new to the internat. Universal Reclaimers provide constructive balance in each subsystem. The most effective balance in each subsystem depends on the Reclaiming objectives of that subsystem. In the following review of the sixteen Reclaiming organization subsystems, we propose a rationale for the allocation of decision-making power among Opponents, Fanatics, and Universal Reclaimers that seems most conducive to the internat's effective functioning.

Psychological-Behavioral Field. The expressive mode of the psychological-behavioral field is the subsystem for defining the specific goals and strategies of the internat. If the internat is to yield Reclaiming, then its goals and strategies must be in the hands of the Universal Reclaimers. They identify with the Reclaiming goals of the internat and are also able to consider resistance to them by Opponents and Fanatics; the former resist Reclaiming ideas, and the latter, blind to the conservative needs of people, demand change at any cost. Although the inclusion of these two groups in the decision-making process presents some risk, nevertheless, they should participate to a limited extent. The Fanatics pose the greater problem as they may formulate unachievable goals and select unacceptable techniques. Opponents strive to distort or displace Reclaiming goals and techniques, but since the internat exists to change Opponents, Reclaiming functions must be addressed to them. In this subsystem, thus, most decision-making power should be allocated to Universal Reclaimers, some to Opponents, the least to Fanatics.

The adaptive mode of this field concerns the internat's reciprocal relationship with the task environment. As the Opponents' prior, outside environment shaped and controlled their behavior, substantial continuation of such contacts may merely reinforce their opposition. Thus much of the interaction with the outside should be reserved for the Universal Reclaimers, although Fanatics can also be useful as their orthodox viewpoints stimulate environmental involvement. Their fanatic demands can be counterbalanced by the community and by Universal Reclaimers' influence. Recommended allocation of decision-making power: Most power to Universal Reclaimers, some to Fanatics, least to Opponents.

The integrative mode of this field concerns the balance among the various Reclaiming activities within the internat. At issue are such questions as: Who is to be rewarded or punished and how? What educational, therapeutic, and training methods are to be used and with whom? Who does what and where? Who learns what and how much? Universal Reclaimers should share power equally with Opponents, who represent the views of new entrants and the uncommitted. Fanatics should have little power in these decisions lest their fervent demands impair the graduality of process essential to Reclaiming.

The conservative mode of this field concerns the processes of identity formation within the internat. The ideas and actions of internat residents crystallize its identity. Fanatics, in their zeal, epitomize the Reclaiming position the internat represents. They should share power equally with the Universal Reclaimers. The Fanatics' zeal does not pose a problem here because their fervency will inevitably be attenuated as the internat's ideally projected identity is realized in practice. Opponents should have very limited power since they seek to introduce identity messages contrary to Reclaiming.

Physical Field. The expressive mode of the physical field concerns the internat's control and autonomy over physical resources. The allocation and organization of physical resources determine the matrix of the internat's Activity. Control over physical resources also has symbolic meaning, which transcends practical consequences. All members should have considerable decision-making power in this area. Fanatics, Opponents, and Universal Reclaimers should have nearly equal power; the last should be able to prevent deliberately overzealous or counterproductive decisions.

The adaptive mode in this field concerns the similarity of the internat's physical environment to the outside. The physical environment is a very visible and powerful aspect of internat living. An environment that is either too elaborate or too demeaning, stark, or simple can seriously impede Reclaiming. Each member needs a comfortable environment appropriate to his experience, identity, present Mastery, and future goals. In this subsystem, equal decision-making power should be granted to Opponents, Fanatics, and Universal Reclaimers.

The integrative mode of this field concerns the integration of the internat's physical components. Often legitimate complaints against an internat focus on the physical inconveniences it unnecessarily imposes. Since such deficiencies are most likely to be identified by Opponents, their views in this area deserve careful consideration, and they should have considerable power. Fanatics, though, should be granted little power since their extreme libertarian or restrictive views can be counterproductive. Universal Reclaimers should play the role of negotiators or mediators with a decisive voice.

The conservative mode of this field concerns the physical foundation of the internat and its members, and thus this subsystem has major implications for the internat's long-term policies and plans. Opponents can influence the process in a manner detrimental to the internat's future development. However, it is important to permit expression by all members concerning personal foundations: the space they find congenial, the diet they are used to, the environment that gives them a sense of belonging, and so on. Decision-making power should be allocated such that Opponents have little power and Fanatics and Universal Reclaimers have equal power.

Social Field. The expressive mode of the social field concerns the prestige of the internat. Issues concerning internat prestige should be in the hands of the Fanatics and Universal Reclaimers, with the latter counterbalancing the extremism of the former. Opponents should have minimal power because their involvement is likely to undermine an internat's efforts to gain or maintain prestige; Opponents' contributions will be more subversive than constructive.

The adaptive mode of this field concerns the interaction between the internat and external social institutions. The delicate relationships between the internat as a unit and its social environment are easily subject to deterioration. Given the paradoxical position of the internat in society, these sensitive linkages should be in the hands of the Universal Reclaimers, those reliable, moderate, but firm believers in Reclaiming. Very little power should be given to Fanatics and Opponents.

The integrative mode of this field concerns the balance among the various social roles in the internat. This subsystem constitutes the arena in which the Reclaiming effort is fought out and real life issues are addressed. Universal Reclaimers and Opponents should have equal power. Opponents must experience here a sense of importance, of being taken into account. Fanatics, though useful, should have less influence lest they antagonize the Opponents to such an extent that the balance provided by the Universal Reclaimers is jeopardized.

The conservative mode of this field concerns the enduring social characteristics of the internat. Activities in this subsystem provide the major opportunity for caretakers to show Opponents that the internat really cares about them. By treating Opponents as members rather than as social outcasts, caretakers demonstrate to the Opponents the Reclaiming functions of the internat as defined by social norms. Fanatics pose a danger here as they may insist that the internat strive toward an ideal type that is beyond the capability of most care recipients or the actual wishes of outside society. Thus, in this subsystem equal power should be granted to Opponents and Universal Reclaimers and little power to Fanatics.

Cultural-Valuative Field. The expressive mode of the cultural-valuative field concerns the value-consistency of the internat. Commitment to the internat's values is represented by the Universal Reclaimers. They stand for values expected to be dominant at the conclusion of the Reclaiming process, and they should have the most power in this subsystem. Fanatics represent an orientation to ideal values that, if pursued with zeal, can be more dangerous than useful. Opponents, who represent an unacceptable value orientation, should have the least power.

The adaptive mode of this field concerns the interaction between the internat's and the environment's values. The concern in this subsystem is the accord between actions (behavior) and a given value set, not with the selection of values. All members should be involved. Fanatics and Opponents should have equal power, but less than the Universal Reclaimers.

The integrative mode of this field concerns the integration of the internat's belief systems; it is the ideological battleground. Here decisions are made regarding the everyday manifestations of contrasting belief systems. Does the internat have routines that contradict its Reclaiming ideology? Are members deprived of their human dignity by techniques that are intended to Reclaim them? Fanatics' views may tend to stress stripping more than shaping, and Opponents will promote ideological positions that counter Reclaiming. In this area, most power should be given to Universal Reclaimers, with some balanced power given to Fanatics and Opponents.

The conservative mode of this field concerns the internat's ideology. Fanatics necessarily press for the ideology of an internat and express it in its clearest, even though extreme, form. Opponents will detract from ideological clarity, yet their challenge must be heard. Thus equal power should be granted to Fanatics and Universal Reclaimers, little power to Opponents.

Constraints. The allocation of decision-making power

among Opponents, Fanatics, and Universal Reclaimers requires that a distinction be drawn between participation in the *process* and decision-making *power*. Participation may include full access to all councils with right of comment, the election of representatives, or vicarious experience through observation. A Reclaiming internat should seek maximal participation in one of these forms for all members. However, the allocation of power should be limited by Mastery. In evaluating Mastery, administrators and staff must remember that limitations in one dimension do not imply diminished capacity in others. The tendency to generalize a specific handicap to an overall disability is common outside of internats. Although this assumption of general incapacity may be based on kind intentions, such misconceptions exaggerate the true limitations imposed by many handicaps (Gliedman and Roth, 1980).

Redistribution of power may appear to endanger the internat that is filled with Opponents or Fanatics. If, however, a balance can be struck by the Universal Reclaimers, the open decision process will bring positive results. Only the distribution of power, at least over some issues, to all or most members, mitigates the undifferentiated totality of a system. Of course, not all members have the ability to make personally and socially constructive decisions on all issues. This is true of individuals in internats and of individuals outside. But in the external community most issues are not under centralized control, while within internats they usually are. To function effectively an internat must become a differential totality, which requires a selective narrowing of total central control. Decision power must be distributed to individuals (inmates and staff) and their subgroups in accordance with their Mastery and their identification with Reclaiming.

The example of the U.S. Constitution provides an appropriate analogy. The framers of the Constitution constructed a system of checks and balances that allowed expression of opposing and fanatical views; even the most antagonistic and bizarre views could be entertained. Free speech and, ultimately, universal franchise were intended to place expression and decision making in the hands of all. Universalists saw to it, though, that moderated behavior expectations prevailed—those suited to the normal citizen with the usual foibles and capabilities. The new land was no utopia nor was it so intended.

Similarly, internats must be built on a base of human imperfection; indeed, their task is specifically to improve the Mastery of their imperfect inmates. A decision-making structure that allows Opponents and Fanatics to be heard, but grants the Universal Reclaimers control will best promote Reclaiming. Because goals and means for achieving Reclaiming are often uncertain, those most affected by an internat's Activity are probably also the most appropriate judges of Activity.

In this context some observations of Nobel laureate Herbert Simon (lecture at the University of California, Berkeley, February 1, 1980) are helpful. In social designs there are no ultimate, final goals, for these would imply a final time horizon we do not possess. Desirable goals for social institutions, thus, are those that best fulfill four conditions: (1) They maximize the number of alternatives for both the person and the organization; neither anarchy nor tyranny are desirable; (2) They do not require irreversible commitments, so that the inevitable human error may be rectified; (3) They deepen knowledge and increase the capacity of both persons and organizations for new experiences; and (4) They allow individuals to enjoy participating in the design and achievement of goals. As Hobbs (1974, p. 339) has phrased it: Internat members "should know joy."

In participating in the formulation of their internat's functioning, members will be constrained by inadequate and even erroneous conceptual formulations and skill insufficient for assessing consequences. Thus, some would argue that participatory decision making within an internat conceived as a differential totality is inadequate to promote Reclaiming because of the lack of clarity about the specific levels of Mastery that constitute Reclaiming and the operational procedures for assessing them. Defining the desired Mastery and the methods for achieving it must be the long-term objectives of professionals if internat care is to yield Reclaiming with greater consistency. This task cannot be overshadowed by concerns about organizational control or procedures. Organizational rigidity must surely not infringe needlessly on the limited joy of an internat's often luckless inhabitants.

9

Revitalizing Residential Settings: Concepts for Action

An internat is a confined, reasonably comprehensible entity. Like the family, its bonds are a bit more substantial than those of other social institutions and are more internally focused. Distinctions of physical plant and social constraints on entrance and departure make the internat a reasonably predictable, manipulable entity that, despite external infringements, controls its own destiny to a considerable degree. Fanatics, Opponents, and Universal Reclaimers enter, may be retained, or changed, or discharged.

Although a good deal of recent literature emphasizes the interpenetration of internat and community, the internat is intended as an organization whose orientation is inward. Internats are designed to segregate people from the community in order to achieve greater control over them and over the forces that affect them. Outsiders may perceive such control as negative (for example, a prison's restrictions on inmates' mobility) or as positive (for example, a hospital's reduction of infection). But control is inevitably the underlying rationale for internats as such, no matter what their populations or specific goals may be.

Control is necessary to effect deliberate, premeditated changes in inmates' Mastery. Control in itself is not oppressive unless it is used solely to warehouse people whom no other social environment will have. Warehouses are oppressive not because they achieve overwhelming control over inmates but rather because they lack humane and purposeful ends for which the controls are a means.

Control

An internat is defined by its Activity, and the object of internat manipulation is the inmate's behavior. Having control of the hospitalized patient, the physician and nurse may determine whether he lies in bed or goes to physiotherapy, takes one medication or another, has visitors or not. Like their patients, the professionals within the hospital are also somewhat controlled by the internat, by rules, expectations of colleagues, orders from superiors.

Thus the primary task of an internat is to provide Activity that elicits the desired behaviors from staff and inmates. Bentham believed that the panopticon's inmates would behave as desired because they could be observed from the superintendent's centrally located house. Modern behaviorists assume that the most effective control of behavior lies in the manipulation of rewards and reinforcements. While such an approach (as, for example, in a token economy of Ayllon and Azrin, 1968) rests primarily on rewards, it is a close relative of the punitive setting in which behavior is controlled by strong prohibitions and aversive sanctions. But in the most effective internats, change is induced neither through formal observation by presumably omniscient or omnipotent staff nor through the dispensation of rewards by staff. Rather, all residents, be they care recipients or caretakers, serve as models and reward bearers. Whether their relationship is formalized or not, *all* members of an internat determine one another's behavior.

Behavior reflects Goals, responds to Consequences, and is directly contingent upon Mastery. Thus, manipulation of Goals, Consequences, and Mastery will affect behavior. A proper mix of Opponents, Fanatics, and Universal Reclaimers will move the internat to adopt appropriate Activity. Although their behavior is partly a function of Activity itself, it is also, in large measure, a result of manipulated Goals, Mastery, and Consequences. Let us consider how the internat can control each of these components to yield Activity that is most appropriate to Reclaiming.

In open voluntary systems in which Goals are well articulated, consensus about Goals and determination of Activity are markedly simplified. For example, if the clinical staff and administrators of a hospital announce that their internat exists to serve the physically ill, the community will either acquiesce to this intention and support their work, or move for the closing of that internat. Members of the community will come to the hospital with problems of physical health. Those who desire other objectives, whether cures for neurosis or vocational training, will stay away. Errors of misplacement can be rapidly remedied, as patients and staff with inappropriate Goals will leave. The internat's clear enunciation of its Goals should reduce goal divergence among its members since, supposedly, staff and patients with only certain types of Mastery and Goals will enter the internat. Goal convergence should effect high consensus on Activity, positive Consequences (including a low ratio of costs to benefits), effective Reclaiming, and positive societal Evaluation.

Such, indeed, would be the case were total convergence on Goals possible. However, even within a hospital for physical ailments—the internat with perhaps the most clearly and consistently articulated Goals—all kinds of positional and personal discrepancies prevent total convergence. As we noted in Chapter Three, the community wants costs held down; the clinical staff wants maximum benefits and interesting cases; some patients want the best treatment regardless of cost, while others are malingerers and not interested in the most efficient care. Goal divergence results despite the screening process.

Furthermore, even among persons who share the same Goals, personal differences in Mastery will yield different behaviors and responses to Activity. Whether the patient is young or old, employed or unemployed, active on the outside and eager to get well and leave, or passive and happy for the few days of pleasant environment and workmen's compensation payments, will influence his behavior. New admissions, postoperative patients, and patients awaiting immediate discharge all have different medical routines, emotional responses, and psychological needs. Thus while Goal convergence and clarity are desirable, some divergence is present even in the medical hospital. Such divergence can, however, be reduced through members' participation in a differential totality.

The broader the range of inmates' levels of Mastery, the more diverse the inmates' Goals may be, and the more difficult the internat's task in devising appropriate Activity. For example, a crippled child with a protracted heart ailment and an aged woman with renal malfunction both have physical disabilities, but their behavior and response to Activity will differ. The difference will, in part, be due to the differences in Goals attributed to, and accepted by, them. The child's Goal in the expressive mode of the physical field should entail a progressive increase in capabilities, while the aged's Goal is to slow the rate of decreasing functioning. A second Goal of the aged may be a quiet, accepted, dignified death or the tubes, wires, and machinery of new life-support systems.

If an internat's concerns extend over several fields of Mastery, convergence on Goals becomes even less likely. To be sure, highly ideologized settings achieve a considerable degree of convergence, but at a cost entailing the surrender of many personal prerogatives. There is more convergence in the yeshiva and the monastery than in the correctional training school or state prison, not only because people enter the former voluntarily but also because they can leave voluntarily if the internat does not meet their needs. Internats that do not have an ideological base must seek other means by which to narrow the fields of Mastery to which they attend. Such narrowing must be based on a clear definition of purpose that results from a negotiated consensus among the internat's members and the community.

Internats can also affect their inmates' behavior by manipulating the Consequences of Activity. For example, many Soviet families sent their children to the *shkoly internaty* (boarding schools) because the schools provided excellent living conditions, an attractive benefit. (The costs of such schools, however, to the government became so high that Khrushchev's dream of placing millions of children in these settings faded along with him.) Behavior may also be bought more directly, as it is in token economies or the more ancient tokenism of the trusty system in prisons and jails.

More interesting, and more ubiquitous, is the manipulation of an inmate's behavior through the promise of positive benefits. If the anticipated benefit of unpleasant Activity has a high probability (or even certainty) of achieving a desired Goal, then the inmate may be induced to undertake the Activity. For example, if prisoners are told that good behavior, as defined by staff and administrators, leads to a reduced sentence, then the incidence of good behavior will rise, other things being equal. Of course, all other things are usually *not* equal. Fanatics aim to pursue the formal internat Goals at all costs, while Opponents have an agenda of their own. The responsibility of the professional caretakers is to explain how Activity is related to Goals. By producing evidence of such linkage, the staff of internats underscore the utility and legitimacy of some behaviors while denying others. Also, by causally relating certain Activity to Mastery and to Goals, the staff can determine who belongs in their internat and who does not, who can be helped and who cannot.

The selection of those who can and need to be helped is not always made by the caretakers. Prisons do not decide who their inmates may be, neither do most mental hospitals or inter-

nats for the severely retarded. This selection is usually made for
the internats by the community. While it would seem reasonable that each internat set the Mastery criteria for admission
and discharge, only certain settings are accorded this privilege.
Physicians who participate in a hospital for physical ailments
decide who will be admitted as a patient. Directors and faculty
decide who will be accepted in boarding schools. But internats
for mentally ill, retarded, and criminal populations have inmates
thrust upon them.

By selecting its membership, an internat can manipulate
Activity. The behavior of the newly admitted athlete or scholar
will tend to enhance the athletic or scholarly Activity of the
boarding school. But the behavior of the accomplished con
artist will interrupt the prison's planned Activity. The task of an
internat is to capitalize on behavior of the first type and to divert,
change, or counteract behavior of the second. In this process
the internat uses Goals and Consequences, as previously discussed, but most effectively it may use the Mastery characteristics of all the residents. Models, rewards, and a ubiquitous emphasis on integrated Reclaiming come from them. Since residents,
with their varied attributes of Mastery, give meaning to Consequences and determine the direction of Goals, the Mastery of
residents determines not only their own behavior but that of all
others nearby. Control of Mastery is, therefore, control of Activity, and since Activity yields higher Mastery, the internat can
thus by controlling Mastery yield improved Mastery. Consider
the following example.

A local boarding school and a training school both admit
adolescents. The boarding school selects those who agree with
its Goals, say, scholarship, athletics, and culture. Adolescents
who do not accept the set of formal and informal Goals are not
admitted, or if admitted are quickly dismissed. Those who excel
are retained and lauded. Universal Reclaimers are encouraged, and convertible Fanatics and Opponents are retained. But
any student who neither exhibits nor strives for acceptable behavior is ejected.

At the training school nearby the reverse takes place. Although the staff, administrators, and community indeed have

selected certain Goals and behaviors as ultimately desirable, the inmates are admitted because they do *not* exhibit those behaviors. Unable to control the admission of inmates, the training school must resort to promoting constructive behavior through selection of staff and the changing of both staff and inmates. In this manner, the training school attempts to encourage the same positive spiral of Mastery and Activity that yields success in the boarding school. But the correctional setting is quickly stymied. Regularly filled with inmate Opponents, some inert staff and a few Fanatics, it does not have enough Universal Reclaimers to provide models for good behavior or balance in the decision-making process. Whenever an inmate does improve his Mastery, adopt the internat's Goals, and become a model for others, the community expects the internat to discharge that inmate as reclaimed. Thus the internat retains Opponents, probably discourages all but the most ardent Fanatics, and simply overwhelms the Universal Reclaimers.

Lacking control over the Mastery of its inmate population, an internat can turn its attention to the quality and quantity of staff and to therapies for changing inmates. Internats hope that larger numbers of better-trained professionals and auxiliary personnel will positively affect Activity, that an increased ratio of staff to inmates will yield more desirable behavior. But even the highest staff-inmate ratios cannot guarantee Reclaiming. If the majority of inmates are Opponents, they model and reinforce counter-goal-directed behavior. And, as in Polsky's (1962) *Cottage Six,* they may win over inmate newcomers and even staff.

Although internats provide a variety of therapeutic interventions intended to change inmates, such efforts are, in large measure, vitiated by the daily exigencies of internat life. Only clinical intervention that is swift, drastic, and fully dependent on staff (for example, in medical hospitals) seems to modify the behavior and subsequently the Mastery of inmates. In all other cases, clinical intervention can be no more than an auxiliary device, subordinate to Activity generated by the Mastery attributes of the internat's members. Only internats that control the admission and discharge of inmates—thus controlling the Mastery and Goals of their population—can fully realize the sixteen Reclaiming organization subsystems presented in Chapter Eight.

Instrumental Issues

Discussions among Opponents, Fanatics, and Universal Reclaimers always pertain to the instrumental quality of their internat. A number of issues must be settled in order to decide who will be admitted to the internat, what they will do, and why they will do it. In this section we present several of the most important issues that confront members of an instrumental internat.

Continuity is the first issue on the agenda of an existing internat. Both successful and failing internats build on their past. Physical plant and location, society's attitude toward the internat, and the internat's traditions encourage the internat to continue being what it has been. Actions of the past are repeated in the present, although their outcomes may not be those desired or intended. Yet internats do have some choices. Buildings can be abandoned. Inmates can be dispersed. New instruments can be created. If the internal Opponents or external critics are strong enough, the internat may be compelled to change or close. An old plant may continue to be functional—despite its negative associations—if population and uses are substantially changed. Or if the plant and its location are the basic problem, an internat can move the same population to another setting.

Deinstitutionalization as a movement may not have improved the lot of previously incarcerated mental patients, but it did have the salutary effect of disrupting the continuity of a failed system. Discontinuity may be achieved in yet another way—through cohort control. West Point admits a class once a year. Any entering Opponents may be converted or ejected before the next class arrives, while the extremism of Fanatics is usually tempered by reality factors. Thus, each fall the academy is ready for the challenge of newcomers. The newcomers are a large enough group that, although they are weak and confronting a new situation, they nevertheless can affect the system as they subject existing arrangements to a critical review. In contrast, many internats receive care recipients and caretakers sporadically and individually. These individuals are absorbed into the ongoing operations, and their effect on the setting's continuity is insignificant. If an internat is full of Opponents, they inevitably win over the newcomers.

Both continuity and discontinuity are important in internat care. While a Reclaiming setting is intended to be as continuous as possible, unless the internat is fundamentally a warehousing facility Goals are best served by a deliberately induced discontinuity in the life of the care recipients—and possibly also the caretakers. To encourage new behavioral patterns, the internat must engage in the discontinuities of unfreezing, moving, and freezing.

A second issue for internats derives from their status as surrogate families. Most internats are intended to return their inmates to family units. Since inmates are sent to internats because their needs cannot be met by their families, internats must in many ways be unlike families. Neither West Point nor San Quentin can achieve their Goals by modeling themselves on family structures. Yet, new inmates' initial adaptation to the internat and discharged inmates' adaptation to society seem to require that the internat not be too dissimilar to a family setting. Expectedly, most internats are confused about how closely their structure and values should resemble those of a family. How familylike should the internat be? How much contact should inmates have with their family? How much change should the family undergo while their member is in care?

In making decisions about its similarity to a family and its relationship with inmates' actual families, an internat must consider the consequences of the community's perception of the internat. If internats are perceived as similar in competency to a good family, then society is unlikely to view the benefits of internats as justification for their high costs. Society's cost-benefit comparison and, therefore, its Evaluation will always be unfavorable to internats. Settings whose primary functions are in the psychological, social, or value fields suffer most from such comparisons with families, particularly if the internat's de-

fined objectives are both broad and vague. Residential treatment centers, correctional schools, particularly those for the
young, receive the most criticism. Hospitals for physical ailments and training facilities for technical skills are perceived to
offer something families cannot and thus are rarely criticized on
this score. Hospitals and skill-instructing programs should serve
as a model for other internats in this respect. By clearly defining
narrowly specific and measurable objectives along particular dimensions of Mastery, internats can influence society to perceive
them as distinctive people-changing environments not as expensive surrogate families.

Because internats, except those for the terminally ill and
monastics, are transitional settings, they often emphasize their
resemblance to a family at the beginning and end of an inmate's
residence to ease adaptation. For example, some internats allow
entering inmates substantial contact with their own families to
reduce the shock of transition. However, the shock of the dissimilar setting may be a most effective unfreezing mechanism.
Thus some internats consider the new entrant's adaptation more
important than the continuity of the entrant's contact with his
family or the external community.

Contact with his family can promote or impede modification of the care recipient's Mastery, depending on whether family members are Opponents, Fanatics, or Universal Reclaimers.
If the inmate's family identifies with, or can be converted to accept, the internat's Goals, family contact is an obvious asset as
it will reinforce goal-directed behavior. A family that rewards
the inmate for goal-directed behavior with praise, encouragement, celebrations, or gifts becomes a partner in Reclaiming. To
do so, the family must understand its role in relationship to the
internat's tasks and comprehend what constitutes a purposive
reward. Many (perhaps most) families of care recipients cannot
function in such a disciplined manner. Filled with guilt or uncertainty, their attitude may be indiscriminately approbatory or
punitive. Neither the internat nor the inmate can be expected to
succeed in the face of such behavior by the family.

Thus, the question arises how much the internat should
attempt to change an inmate's family. The only reasonable an-

swer appears to be: No more than is necessary for the benefit of the inmate in regard to the specific dimensions of Mastery the internat has chosen for differential, yet total attention. Teaching the family about their adolescent's brain condition or his psychosis is appropriate in this context, but a concern for their housing is most likely not. All interactions with the family must be focused on the inmate. Any diffusion of effort will obscure the internat's objectives and competence, and lead inevitably to failure.

Although an inmate is ultimately to rejoin his family, the internat's social structure should not be determined by this intention. Internats cannot and should not attempt to resemble families simply because a return to familial life awaits discharged inmates. Indeed, even the cottage with cottage-mother and cottage-father is a device to foster peer relationships not to mimic parent-child relationships. Most internats cannot, in any event, realize a familylike structure. Their power lies in peer models and the positive influences that peers can exert. To provide necessary family models during the latter stages of the inmate's residence, once the inmate's Mastery is adequate to address adaptation to the outside society, the internat can open itself to bilateral familial contacts.

A third issue is *dependency,* the extent of an individual's reliance on a nurturer as contrasted with self-reliance. The internat seeks to increase its inmates' self-reliance during their residence. Upon a new inmate's arrival, many internats use a stripping process to initially sever some or most of the inmate's ties to the outside, thus redirecting the inmate's orientation to the intrainternat environment. Cutting hair and changing clothes, along with an initial quarantine, be it physical or social, are symbols of a new beginning. If the object of such actions is change, then, despite their unpleasantness and shock effect, they have utility. Except in internats for terminal inmates, stripping serves to create in the new inmate a high level of initial dependency that reduces his power to oppose the internat's efforts to change him.

Of course, some inmates find it simpler to surrender to dependency than to emerge from it. To encourage inmates to become more self-sufficient, internats must offer them a ladder of expectations and opportunities. In an internat filled exclusively with dependent inmates, such a ladder will have no users and thus no utility. But an internat that involves all its members in decisions about its operations encourages inmates to develop expectations of increasingly self-reliant behavior. The overly dependent person who may have been treated as childlike, can slowly ascend the internat's ladder of expectations for him and begin to develop expectations for himself. Peer modeling, group pressure, and group expectations will contribute to the inmate's increasing self-reliance and sense of social responsibility. The acceptance of living by rules and responsibly participating in the creation of rules are both signs of self-reliance and social responsibility. When Opponents, Fanatics, and Universal Reclaimers meet, argue, and decide, all members are expected to and have the opportunity to make their own rules in interaction with others. They become part of a self-governing society, and they tend to accept and enforce the rules they themselves have agreed on.

Yet even this sense of group responsibility, which leads to collaborative rule making, is most likely an insufficient basis for an inmate to maintain independent behavior in the outside world, where he is subject to conflicting pressures. Inmates must internalize their personal growth as they test it with ever-decreasing reinforcement. Home leave, vacations from the internat, and open interactions with the outside offer the inmate the opportunity to affirm the rightness of the behavior he has learned in the internat prior to his departure from the internat. Each step in such a progression toward competence can be accomplished in a social context that provides models and rewards with minimal risks.

The need to provide *models* of the desired behavior is the single most-ignored issue in failing internats. Society, in its haste to isolate the negatively deviant, has opted to aggregate such deviants in internats. Once inmates improve, society's concern for their independence and the cost of keeping them in care compels their release from the internat. Inevitably, prisons, psychiatric hospitals, and similar internats become a refined, care-

fully selected collectivity of those whose behavior is unacceptable. These inmates then become the models for the newcomer
and the primary source of reinforcement for behaviors he exhibits. Staff, while conceivably consequential, are usually too
different from inmates for the latter to perceive them as meaningful models. Should a staff member suggest to inmates that
they model themselves on him, inmates will understandably ask
what the staff member understands about being like them.
Clearly, the only people who are really like an inmate are other
inmates.

Even more consequentially, inmates are always present,
unlike staff who stay in their offices, go home in the evenings,
or disappear for lengthy vacations. Always nearby with a smile
or frown, words of approval or rejection, small but consistent
acts of reward or punishment, inmates constantly provide one
another with responses that reinforce their own values. Just as
West Point upperclassmen set the tone of their internat, so do
long-term inmates at Sing Sing. The process is the same, but the
social desirability of the two outcomes distinguishes them as
does the fact that West Point staff and inmates reinforce one
another, while Sing Sing staff and inmates do not. Staff efforts
cannot overcome the numerous Opponents. West Point is able
to retain inmates who model desired behavior and are in a position to reinforce it, the upperclassmen. Sing Sing, in contrast,
discharges inmates who would provide positive models for newcomers.

If Reclaiming internats are to succeed, they must be able
to retain inmates who can provide positive models; they must
retain inmates who are Universal Reclaimers. This proposition
may, at first, sound heretical as it suggests that internats retain
inmates who seem ready to return to productive lives in the
community. But such inmates can also lead productive lives in
the internat. By extending their residence for a period, they can
further refine their own skills as well as serve as a model to
other inmates. During this final period of residence, an inmate
would assume those caretaker functions that maximally challenge and strengthen his Mastery. Indeed, to retain within the
internat an inmate who could possibly make it outside is pro-

fessionally defensible and morally tolerable only if the opportunities provided assure continued, maximal utilization of the
inmate's current Mastery. In this way, the inmate continues to
develop and grow, while his presence adds strength to the voice
of the Universal Reclaimers and reduces the dichotomy between
caretaker and care recipient, a dichotomy that, as we have seen,
impairs Reclaiming.

Consider the following three examples of internats that
use a procedure similar to our recommendation. A Yugoslav
home for children and adolescents, located in the center of a
large city, provides care for abandoned, neglected, and disturbed children as well as housing for college students and ap-
prentices who were formerly care recipients and now serve as
caretakers. This internat also houses high school students who
are still receiving care but also have caretaker functions with the
younger children. Our second example is a home for the aged in
Great Britain. The internat houses couples who reside in semi-
sheltered units, some single individuals who live in a hotellike
residence, and some debilitated persons who live in an integrated medical facility. Residents move back and forth in these
several subsettings with the more able helping out other inmates, and the home's chapel is open to the nearby community
for its celebrations.

Our third example is a large, old American internat for
the retarded. Over the years, a suburban community developed
around the internat, and the once-isolated internat adapted to
this change. Some buildings are still used for inmates but others
have been converted into a vocational school and a shopping
mall. The more capable inmates study and work in these places,
though they still reside within the internat with the less advanced inmates. Others live in several cottages on the grounds
that are similar to houses nearby. They work as staff in the internat, receiving regular salaries while learning the rudiments of
caring for people.

Risk attends such an approach as it does all other aspects
of Reclaiming, and risk is another major issue in decision making. It is clear, that in order for an inmate to move from total
dependency even to rule-directed behavior, both he and the sys-

tem must take chances. In the outside world, people are presumed able to calculate the consequences of their behavior to themselves and to others in order to minimize risk. Even there, danger signs are posted over manholes, caution with fire is advised near explosives, and the like. Within internats the issue of risk is complicated by the presumption of inmates' incompetence or malevolence. Are not these the very reasons that inmates are in internats? But to foster independence and development, the good internat, like the good parent, must take chances and must encourage care recipients and caretakers to take some risks.

Risks range from the inconsequential to the foolhardy. Individuals differ in their abilities to discriminate and judge. Who is to decide how much risk this inmate can constructively assume at a given time under given circumstances? As Fairweather and others (1969) have found, peers may be the best judges, in particular when they must also live with the consequences of their judgments. When should a young delinquent with a record of car thefts be permitted to drive the internat car? When should a disoriented old man go into town alone? When should the substantially retarded girls in this group move into an independent household nearby? If risks are assumed too early, disaster may ensue. But if risks are delayed too long, inmates' growth will be stunted. Controlled risk is, obviously, preferable to stagnation.

Risk taking also improves the internat's overall social system; as inmates test and verify their competence, their successes will encourage them to contribute more to the social system. Thus both individuals and the group benefit from evaluating risks and taking risks. Furthermore, the risks assumed by more capable inmates provide goals for the less capable. As in other decision-making discussions, Fanatics may be overly zealous, and Opponents overly pessimistic. Universal Reclaimers will attempt to measure each situation and each person to determine which risks will encourage the development of Mastery.

Bureaucratic prerequisites affect decisions about risk, just as they impinge on definitions of competence and the presence of competent inmate models. Administrative duties are easiest if care recipients are relegated to the status of incompetent, dependent objects who require minimal variability. Such an internat performs simple routinized operations: intake, service, discharge. Patients are fed; roofs are repaired; telephones are answered. But such an internat will not succeed in Reclaiming anyone. Only variability creates a ladder of models, behavioral expectations, and performance that is the essence of Reclaiming. Only participatory decision making permits inmates to become subjects and then instruments of their own change.

Certainly organizations must maintain a measure of routine, and some standardization is unavoidable. Accounts must be kept, bills paid, plant maintained. Admissions and discharges ebb and flow with the school year, court calendar, or meetings of the parole board. The basic question is how to maintain a bureaucracy with a human face, more than that, with a caring heart. Apparently, this can be achieved only through dispersed involvement in and responsibility for decisions. As an inmate's competence increases, his control over his surroundings must similarly increase. The inmate must be regarded as a producer of change, not as a product. Internats that view inmates as products or objects to be created or serviced by an assembly line of professionals and staff cannot but fail in Reclaiming, although their organizational operation may be efficient.

Thus control in Reclaiming organizations must be broadly distributed. The dispersion of authority may place a strain on the bureaucracy, but it is an essential component of Reclaiming. The allocation of control must be consonant with Mastery. As the inmate progresses toward greater competence and from dependency to independence and social responsibility, he should acquire greater authority over his own behavior and then over the behavior of others. As the inmate's control increases, caretakers and administrators must relinquish their control.

Among the most common complaints in many internats are complaints by inmates regarding control over personal possessions, private space, and personal routines. Any Reclaiming internat must grant control in this area to the inmate, to the extent he can assume control. With this authority the inmate must be given the responsibility for the social consequences of his exercise of his rights. An inmate must be told that greater self-authority entails increased concern with the common good, that as he is able to decide more for himself, he must also do more for himself and for others who may be less able. Thus care recipients learn to be independent and giving, and not just dependent and consuming. In the process, care recipients improve their Mastery, and the internat can generate energy rather than merely consume resources.

Energy and resources are another issue for internat decision making. Most internats consume large amounts of external energy and resources; some operate on a continuous deficit, dependent on government funding or private contribution. They assume that their residents are capable only of consumption, and legal constraints, insurance requirements, objections from organized labor, and tradition all reinforce this assumption. Thus twenty disturbed adolescents at a residential treatment center who are full of unspent energy and a terrible need to learn, to do, and to show competence find themselves served by a cook, a gardener, a laundryman, and other staff. The internat organizes recreation for them, but does not allow them to engage in real work, which would help them learn skills, gain self-confidence and self-respect.

Consider the benefits that would accrue to individual inmates, staff, administrators, the internat's organizational subsystems, and the community if those disturbed adolescents were allowed to use their energy constructively. Peers and staff would decide when an inmate could assume caretaking responsibilities within the internat or go out and help in the nearby nursing home or childcare center. If inmates are not allowed to apply their energy to constructive, meaningful work, their accumulated surplus energy will be vented in behavior that is truly harmful. Prison riots are not only a means for expressing grievance. They also provide inmates with something to do—a kind of staggered, gruesome Olympiad of the correctional system. Inmates—of prisons and other internats—have, after all, only three ways to use their energy: in self-reclaiming and socially useful activity, in rioting and other destructiveness, and in self-cancelling withdrawal. Reasonably healthy persons use their

energies—and that of their internat—either for growth or de-
struction. Their choices will be determined by the opportunities
the internat affords them.

To develop and maintain a setting that provides for Reclaiming, internats that control their structure should require
their professionals to perform three tasks: population control,
risk assessment, and symptomatic intervention. Internats whose
professionals do not or cannot control these tasks will be severely impaired in their Reclaiming functions. Population control is
essential to produce and maintain a reasonable ladder of models
and reinforcements for desired behavior. A balance between
more competent, better adjusted, more stabilized inmates and
those in need of more assistance is conducive to easier and more
effective intervention. Professionals should decide who enters,
who leaves, and where each stays, considering not only the
needs of an individual inmate but of the setting as a whole. To
fill an internat with the most debilitated aged, the most violent
criminals, or the most retarded adolescents is destructive. Such
places offer no internal evidence of hope for inmates and not a
shred of reciprocity between them and staff.

Second, professionals must perform risk assessment, an
essential and delicate task. While peers may be good at render-
ing judgments, professional insight and authority are necessary
to moderate such judgments and to confer upon decisions the
requisite status. Since Mastery and operational circumstances
are ever-changing, the professionals involved in risk assessment
must maintain close contact with the care recipients and the internat realities. They must also be willing to assume risks, since
continuous error on the side of safety will stifle growth and lead
to stagnation and atrophy.

Third, symptomatic intervention by professionals is required in order to rapidly enhance some specific capabilities of
care recipients or reduce handicaps that impede their progress.
Inmates can benefit from an internat setting only if they remain
there; thus professionals must address any condition that threatens to prematurely terminate an inmate's residence. Physically
violent inmates must learn self-control. Those with unusual
characteristics must develop ways to fend off ridicule or avoid
ostracism. It is the role of professionals to address such prob-

lems sympathetically and expeditiously. Inmates also need professionals to instruct them in skills—whether sports, gardening, math, or debating—that will enhance their participation in internat life.

Only a *unifying theme,* evolved from the interaction of Fanatics and Opponents and promoted by the Universal Reclaimers, can give coherence to the internat in its many tasks. Who should be the models? What should be the reinforcements? What risks should be taken? How should energy be invested? All such questions must be answered within some kind of ideological framework. Ideology motivated the society to open the internat and must motivate the participants to play their respective roles.

An ideology need not be political or religious. Indeed some ideologies that found their most profound expression in internats were neither political nor religious. Moral treatment of the mentally ill and the methodologies of the Pennsylvania and Auburn prisons of the nineteenth century, though rooted in Quakerism, were ideologies of care. As total systems of thought, they provided answers to all of the significant questions that internats pose: What to build? Where to build it? Who should be admitted? What should they do? Similarly, a scientific ideology —the germ theory of disease—informs the modern hospital for physical ailments.

An ideology can provide orderly, coherent, meaningful answers within an internat, just as it does in society itself. But the balance between Opponents, Fanatics, and Universal Reclaimers is different in the internat than in society. Internats are the social receptacles for Fanatics and Opponents, while society is the domain of Universal Reclaimers. To be successful settings for Reclaiming, internats must also be guided by Universal Reclaimers. Until internats are so constituted their success rate must, regrettably, be far lower than necessary.

An Optimistic View

Operating under constraints—confused or conflicting Goals and little consensus on Activity—internats, especially those for deprived, disturbed, and disturbing populations, have often been evaluated negatively. Periodic drives to close internats have been based on the premise that, by and large, these facilities fail to meet the expectations of their sponsoring societies. Yet proponents of deinstitutionalization at times ignore two significant facts: Internats always remain part of the social landscape, serving both elites and deprived, disturbed, and disturbing populations; and some settings are successful in achieving integrated Reclaiming for a significant proportion of their inhabitants. Closing of internats, then, is neither feasible nor efficacious. A more reasonable and more socially responsible approach is to modify and improve internats.

The experiences of successful internats for various populations, the ideas of their creative leaders, and the contributions of social and behavioral science suggest the direction such improvement must take. Moral treatment and milieu therapy, the work of such personages as Korczak and Jones, and such behavioral research and data as those generated by learning theory yield the components of a concept we have designated integrated Reclaiming. This label, like that of any well-formulated concept, designates an idea in the mind and a set of operational definitions. Our concept of integrated Reclaiming is based on the idea that an internat is an instrument in which all Activity is coordinated for achieving the specified Goals. The operational definition of such an internat is along the ten dimensions (issues) discussed earlier in this chapter. A successful internat, one which meets the requirements of integrated Reclaiming, is one that has positively resolved these operational issues. First and foremost, a successful internat is guided by a clear, consistent, and broadly accepted ideology, whether of a scientific, religious, or political nature. Second, in pursuit of its integrated Reclaiming Goals such an internat accumulates support from both internal and external forces. This support guides the internat's decisions regarding work with families, selection of inmates and their retention, role definitions of both inmates and staff, and the intervention functions of professionals. Third, such an internat employs risk and inmate energy as instruments in the Reclaiming process.

Can an integrated Reclaiming internat be created? Of

course, since each of the internat leaders to whom this book is dedicated has created an internat of this kind. Children and adults, the mentally ill and criminals, war orphans and emigres have all been helped in these programs. Others can also be Reclaimed as the intuitive insights of Korczak and Schweitzer, Gmeiner and Kirkbride, Jones and Pestalozzi are realized in operational definitions and put to use for the benefit of both internats' inmates and their societies. What distinguishes all the successful internat founders is their ability to build integrated Reclaiming settings despite the numerous societal impediments we have discussed. Unfortunately, most internats simply fail to overcome the societal obstacles. If a society indeed aims to achieve integrated Reclaiming in its internats, society must change its impeding expectations. Inevitably an internat, like any social creation, mirrors its creator—the society to which the internat belongs.

References

Abelson, R. P., and Rosenberg, M. J. "Symbolic Psychologic: A Model of Attitudinal Cognition." *Behavioral Science*, 1958, *3*, 1-13.

Advisory Council on Child Care. *Community Homes Design Guide*. London: Her Majesty's Stationery Office, 1971.

Aichhorn, A. *Wayward Youth*. New York: Viking Press, 1935.

Allerhand, M. E., and others. *Adaptation and Adaptability: The Bellefaire Follow-Up Study*. New York: Child Welfare League of America, 1966.

Almond, R. "The Therapeutic Community." *Scientific American*, 1971, *224*, 34-42.

Almond, R., Keniston, K., and Boltax, S. "Patient Value Change in Milieu Therapy." *Archives of General Psychiatry,* 1969, *20,* 339-351.

American Hospital Association. *Hospital Accreditation References.* (Rev. ed.) Chicago: American Hospital Association, 1961.

American Hospital Association. *Hospital Statistics.* Chicago: American Hospital Association, 1977.

American Psychiatric Association. "Legal Issues in State Mental Health Care: Proposals for Change. Zoning for Community Residences." *Mental Disability Law Reporter,* September-December 1977, pp. 315-325.

Astrachan, B., Harrow, M., and Flynn, H. "The Experimental Introduction of Values into a Psychiatric Setting." *Comprehensive Psychiatry,* 1969, *10* (3), 181-189.

Ayllon, T., and Azrin, N. H. *The Token Economy. A Motivational System for Therapy and Rehabilitation.* New York: Appleton-Century-Crofts, 1968.

Bach, G. R., and Wyden, P. *The Intimate Enemy: How to Fight Fair in Love and Marriage.* New York: Morrow, 1969.

Bachrach, L. L. *Deinstitutionalization: An Analytical Review and Sociological Perspective.* Rockville, Md.: National Institute of Mental Health, 1976.

"Back in Prison: An Innocent Man Gives Up." *San Francisco Chronicle,* October 29, 1977, p. 30.

Bagdikian, B. H. *The Shame of the Prisons.* New York: Pocket Books, 1972.

Bagehot, W. *Physics and Politics.* London: K. Paul, Trench, and Trübner, 1906.

Bakal, Y. (Ed.). *Closing Correctional Institutions.* Lexington, Mass.: Heath, 1973.

Bamford, T. W. *Rise of the Public Schools.* London: Nelson, 1967.

Bandura, A. *Principles of Behavior Modification.* New York: Holt, Rinehart and Winston, 1969.

Barker, R. G. *Ecological Psychology.* Stanford, Calif.: Stanford University Press, 1968.

Barton, R. *Institutional Neurosis.* Bristol, England: Wright, 1959.

Bateman, J. F., and Dunham, H. W. "The State Mental Hospital as a Specialized Community Experience." *American Journal of Psychiatry*, 1948, *105*, 445-448.

Beaumont, G., and de Tocqueville, A. *On the Penitentiary System in the United States and Its Application in France.* (F. Lieber, Trans.) Carbondale, Ill.: Southern Illinois University Press, 1964. (Originally published 1836.)

Beers, C. W. *A Mind That Found Itself: An Autobiography.* New York: Doubleday, 1925. (Originally published 1908.)

Behan, B. *Borstal Boy.* London: Hutchinson, 1958.

Belcher, J. C. "Background Reviews of Patients and the Therapeutic Community." *Journal of Health and Human Behavior*, 1965, *6* (1), 27-35.

Belknap, I. *The Human Problems of a State Mental Hospital.* New York: McGraw-Hill, 1956.

Bentham, J. *An Introduction to the Principles of Morals and Legislation.* Oxford: Clarendon Press, 1907. (Originally published 1789.)

Bentham, J. *Panopticon: Or the Inspection House.* London: Payne, 1791.

Bentham, J. *The Works of Jeremy Bentham.* (11 Vols.) New York: Russell and Russell, 1962. (Originally published 1838-1843.)

Bentwich, N. *Ben-Shemen: A Children's Village.* Israel: Études Pédagogiques, Fédération Internationale des Communautés d'Enfants, n.d.

Bettelheim, B. *Love Is Not Enough: The Treatment of Emotionally Disturbed Children.* New York: Free Press, 1950.

Bettelheim, B. *The Informed Heart.* New York: Free Press, 1960.

Bettelheim, B., and Sylvester, E. "A Therapeutic Milieu." *American Journal of Orthopsychiatry*, 1948, *18*, 191-206.

Beuf, A. H. *Biting of the Bracelet: A Study of Children in Hospitals.* Philadelphia: University of Pennsylvania Press, 1979.

Bloch, S., and Reddaway, P. *Russia's Political Hospitals: The Abuse of Psychiatry in the Soviet Union.* London: Gollancz, 1978.

Bloom, B. S. *Stability and Change in Human Characteristics.* New York: Wiley, 1964.

"Board Unit Backs Youth Campus Plan." *San Francisco Chronicle,* March 1, 1978, p. 9.

Bockoven, S. J. *Moral Treatment in American Psychiatry.* New York: Springer, 1963.

Boszormenyi-Nagy, I., and Spark, G. M. *Invisible Loyalties.* New York: Harper & Row, 1973.

Braly, M. *False Starts: A Memoir of San Quentin and Other Prisons.* Boston: Little, Brown, 1976.

Bronfenbrenner, U. "Developmental Research and Public Policy." In J. M. Romanyshyn (Ed.), *Social Science and Social Welfare.* New York: Council on Social Work Education, 1974.

Buckley, W. *Sociology and Modern Systems Theory.* Engelwood Cliffs, N.J.: Prentice-Hall, 1967.

Buehler, R. E., Patterson, G. R., and Furniss, J. U. "The Reinforcement of Behavior in Institutional Settings." *Behaviour Research and Therapy,* 1966, *4* (3), 157-167.

Burling, T. L., Lentz, E., and Wilson, R. N. *The Give and Take in Hospitals: A Study of Human Organization in Hospitals.* New York: Putnam's, 1956.

Calkins, K. "Time: Perspectives, Marking, and Styles of Usage." *Social Problems,* 1970, *17* (4), 487-501.

Caplan, R. B., with Caplan, G. *Psychiatry and the Community in Nineteenth-Century America: The Recurring Concern with the Environment in the Prevention and Treatment of Mental Disorder.* New York: Basic Books, 1969.

Caplow, T. *Principles of Organization.* New York: Harcourt Brace Jovanovich, 1964.

Carlebach, J. "Some Aspects of Residential Child Care and the Role of the *Madrich.*" In M. Wolins and M. Gottesmann (Eds.), *Group Care: An Israeli Approach.* New York: Gordon and Breach, 1971.

Carp, F. M. "The Elderly and Levels of Adaptation to Changed Surroundings." In L. A. Pastalan and D. H. Carson (Eds.), *Spatial Behavior of Older People.* Ann Arbor: Institute of Gerontology, University of Michigan–Wayne State University, 1970.

Carter, R. M., Glaser, D., and Wilkins, L. T. (Eds.). *Correctional Institutions.* Philadelphia: Lippincott, 1972.

Caudill, W. *The Psychiatric Hospital as a Small Society.* Cambridge, Mass.: Harvard University Press, 1958.

Caudill, W., and others. "Social Structure and Interaction Process on a Psychiatric Ward." *American Journal of Orthopsychiatry*, 1952, *22*, 319-334.

Child Welfare League of America. *Standards for Services of Child Welfare Institutions.* New York: Child Welfare League of America, 1963.

Churchman, C. W. *The Systems Approach.* New York: Delacorte Press, 1968.

Clemmer, D. *The Prison Community.* Boston: Christopher, 1940.

Cohen, H. L., and Filipczak, J. *A New Learning Environment: A Case for Learning.* San Francisco: Jossey-Bass, 1971.

Coleman, J. A. *Relativity for the Layman.* New York: William-Frederick, 1954.

Conley, R. W. *The Economics of Mental Retardation.* Baltimore: Johns Hopkins University Press, 1973.

Cooper, D. G. *The Death of the Family.* New York: Pantheon, 1971.

Corsini, R. J. *Methods of Group Psychotherapy.* New York: McGraw-Hill, 1957.

Craib, R. "Synanon Accused of Misusing Funds." *San Francisco Chronicle*, December 4, 1979, p. 16.

Cressey, D. R. (Ed.). *The Prison: Studies in Institutional Organization and Change.* New York: Holt, Rinehart and Winston, 1961.

Cressey, D. R. "Contradictory Directives in Complex Organizations: The Case of the Prison." In L. E. Hazelrigg (Ed.), *Prison Within Society.* New York: Doubleday, 1969.

Cumming, E., and Cumming, J. *Closed Ranks.* Cambridge, Mass.: Harvard University Press, 1957.

Cumming, E., and Henry, W. E. *Growing Old: The Process of Disengagement.* New York: Basic Books, 1961.

Cumming, J., and Cumming, E. *Ego and Milieu: Theory and Practice of Environmental Therapy.* New York: Atherton Press, 1962.

Darin-Drabkin, H. *The Other Society.* New York: Harcourt Brace Jovanovich, 1962.

DeLong, A. J. "The Micro-Spatial Structure of the Older Person: Some Implications of Planning the Social and Spatial Environment." In L. A. Pastalan and D. H. Carson (Eds.),

Spatial Behavior of Older People. Ann Arbor: Institute of Gerontology, University of Michigan–Wayne State University, 1970.

Deutsch, A. *The Shame of the States.* New York: Harcourt Brace Jovanovich, 1948.

Deutsch, A. *The Mentally Ill in America: A History of Their Care and Treatment from Colonial Times.* (2nd ed.) New York: Columbia University Press, 1952.

Devereux, A. "The Social Structure of a Schizophrenic Ward and Its Therapeutic Fitness." *Journal of Clinical Psychopathology,* 1944, *6,* 231-265.

Dix, D. L. *Remarks on Prisons and Prison Discipline in the United States.* Boston: Munroe and Francis, 1845.

"Drugs and Psychiatry: A New Era." *Newsweek,* November 12, 1979, pp. 98-104.

Durkheim, E. *Suicide.* (J. A. Spaulding and G. Simpson, Trans.) New York: Free Press, 1951. (Originally published 1897.)

Earickson, R. *The Spatial Behavior of Hospital Patients.* Research Paper No. 124. Chicago: Department of Geography, University of Chicago, 1970.

Edgerton, R. B. *The Cloak of Competence: Stigma in the Lives of the Mentally Retarded.* Berkeley: University of California Press, 1967.

Ellis, J., and Moore, R. *School for Soldiers: West Point and the Profession of Arms.* New York: Oxford University Press, 1974.

Erikson, E. H. *Identity: Youth and Crisis.* New York: Norton, 1968.

Etzioni, A. "The Organizational Structure of 'Closed' Educational Institutions in Israel." *Harvard Educational Review,* 1957, *27* (2), 107-126.

Etzioni, A. "Deinstitutionalization . . . A Vastly Oversold, Good Idea." *Columbia Forum,* Spring 1978, pp. 14-17.

Fairweather, G. W. (Ed.). *Social Psychology in Treating Mental Illness: An Experimental Approach.* New York: Wiley, 1964.

Fairweather, G. W., and others. *Community Life for the Mentally Ill: An Alternative to Institutional Care.* Chicago: Aldine, 1969.

Feldman, S. (Ed.). *Cognitive Consistency: Motivational Antece-*

dents and Behavioral Consequents. New York: Academic Press, 1966.

Ferguson, T., and MacPhail, A. N. *Hospital and Community.* London: Oxford University Press, 1954.

Festinger, L. *A Theory of Cognitive Dissonance.* Stanford, Calif.: Stanford University Press, 1963.

Festinger, L., Schachter, S., and Back, K. *Social Pressures in Informal Groups.* New York: Harper & Row, 1950.

Feuer, L. S. *Ideology and the Ideologists.* Oxford: Blackwell, 1975.

Folks, H. "The Care of Delinquent Children." In *Proceedings of the National Conference of Charities and Correction, 1891.* Boston: Press of George H. Ellis, 1891.

Folks, H. "Why Should Dependent Children Be Reared in Families Rather Than in Institutions?" *Charities Review,* 1896, *5,* 140-145.

Foucault, M. *The Birth of the Clinic: An Archaeology of Human Perception.* (A. M. Sheridan Smith, Trans.) New York: Vintage Books, 1975.

Foucault, M. *Discipline and Punish: The Birth of the Prison.* (A. Sheridan, Trans.) New York: Vintage Books, 1979.

Foy, F. A. (Ed.). *1980 Catholic Almanac.* Huntington, Ind.: Our Sunday Visitor, 1979.

French, J. R., and Raven, B. "The Bases of Social Power." In D. Cartwright and A. Zander (Eds.), *Group Dynamics.* New York: Harper & Row, 1960.

Freud, A., and Burlingham, D. *War and Children.* New York: International Universities Press, 1943.

Friedman, E. P. "Spatial Proximity and Social Interaction in a Home for the Aged." *Journal of Gerontology,* 1966, *21,* 566-570.

Fuchs, E., and Havighurst, R. J. *To Live on This Earth: American Indian Education.* New York: Doubleday, 1972.

Furgurson, E. B. *Westmoreland: The Inevitable General.* Boston: Little, Brown, 1968.

Galloway, K. B., and Johnson, R. B., Jr. *West Point: America's Power Fraternity.* New York: Simon & Schuster, 1973.

Garabedian, P. A. "Social Roles and Processes of Socialization in the Prison Community." *Social Problems,* 1963, *11,* 139-152.

Gerson, M. *Family, Women, and Socialization in the Kibbutz.* Lexington, Mass.: Lexington Books, 1980.

Giallombardo, R. *Society of Women: A Study of a Women's Prison.* New York: Wiley, 1966.

Gil, D. "Institutions for Children." In A. L. Schorr (Ed.), *Children and Decent People.* New York: Basic Books, 1974.

Glaser, D. *The Effectiveness of a Prison and Parole System.* Indianapolis: Bobbs-Merrill, 1964.

Glazer, N. "Should Judges Administer Social Services?" *The Public Interest,* 1978, *50,* 60-84.

Gliedman, J. "The Wheelchair Rebellion." *Psychology Today,* August 1979, pp. 59-64, 99, 101.

Gliedman, J., and Roth, W. *The Unexpected Minority: Handicapped Children in America.* New York: Harcourt Brace Jovanovich, 1980.

Gmeiner, H. *The SOS Children's Villages.* Innsbruck: SOS-Kinderdorf-Verlag, 1971.

Goffman, E. *Presentation of Self in Everyday Life.* New York: Doubleday, 1959.

Goffman, E. *Asylums: Essays on the Social Situations of Mental Patients and Other Inmates.* New York: Doubleday, 1961.

Goldenberg, P. "Masterwork or Nightmare?" *New York Times,* May 3, 1977, pp. 43, 46.

Goldsmith, B. "Designing for Physically Handicapped Children—Are You on the Right Level, Mr. Architect?" In J. Loring and G. Burn (Eds.), *Integration of Handicapped Children in Society.* London: Routledge & Kegan Paul, 1975.

Gollin, G. L. "Family Surrogates in Colonial America: The Moravian Experiment." *Journal of Marriage and the Family,* 1969, *31* (4), 650-658.

Good, L. R., Siegel, S. M., and Bay, A. P. (Eds.). *Therapy by Design: Implications of Architecture for Human Behavior.* Springfield, Ill.: Thomas, 1965.

Goodman, P. S., Pennings, J. M., and Associates. *New Perspectives on Organizational Effectiveness.* San Francisco: Jossey-Bass, 1977.

Gouldner, A. W. *Patterns of Industrial Bureaucracy.* New York: Free Press, 1954.

Grosser, G. H. "External Setting and Internal Relations of the Prison." In R. A. Cloward and others (Eds.), *Theoretical Studies in Social Organization of the Prison.* Pamphlet No. 15. New York: Social Science Research Council, 1960.

Grosser, G. H. "External Setting and Internal Relations of the Prison." In L. E. Hazelrigg (Ed.), *Prison Within Society.* New York: Doubleday, 1969.

Gubrium, J. F. *Living and Dying at Murray Manor.* New York: St. Martin's Press, 1975.

Hage, J., and Aiken, M. *Social Change in Complex Organizations.* New York: Random House, 1970.

Haley, J. *The Power Tactics of Jesus Christ and Other Essays.* New York: Avon Books, 1971.

Hall, E. T. *The Hidden Dimension.* New York: Doubleday, 1966.

Hampden-Turner, C. *Sane Asylum.* San Francisco: San Francisco Book Co., 1976.

Hazelrigg, L. E. (Ed.). *Prison Within Society.* New York: Doubleday, 1969.

Hebb, D. O. *The Organization of Behavior.* New York: Science Editions, 1961.

Hillery, G. A., Jr. *Communal Organizations.* Chicago: University of Chicago Press, 1968.

Hobbs, N. "Helping Disturbed Children: Psychological and Ecological Strategies." In M. Wolins (Ed.), *Successful Group Care: Explorations in the Powerful Environment.* Chicago: Aldine, 1974.

Hobhouse, M. A., and Brockway, A. F. (Eds.). *English Prisons Today: Being the Report of the Prison System Enquiry Committee.* London: Longman, 1922.

Hollingshead, A. B., and Redlich, F. C. *Social Class and Mental Illness: A Community Study.* New York: Wiley, 1958.

Homme, L., and others. *How to Use Contingency Contracting in the Classroom.* Champaign, Ill.: Research Press, 1970.

Hopkins, B. L. "The First Twenty Years Are the Hardest." In R. Ulrich, T. Stachnik, and J. Mabry (Eds.), *Control of Human Behavior: From Cure to Prevention.* Vol. 2. Glenview, Ill.: Scott, Foresman, 1970.

Hopkirk, H. W. *Institutions Serving Children.* New York: Russell Sage Foundation, 1944.

Horn, W., and Born, E. *The Plan of St. Gall.* Berkeley: University of California Press, 1980.

Hunter, R., and Macalpine, I. *Three Hundred Years of Psychiatry, 1535-1860: A History Presented in Selected English Texts.* New York: Oxford University Press, 1963.

Irwin, J., and Cressey, D. R. "Thieves, Convicts, and the Inmate Culture." In H. S. Becker (Ed.), *The Other Side.* New York: Free Press, 1964.

Ivins, M. "New Center for Retarded Opposed as 'Obsolete.' " *New York Times,* May 3, 1977, pp. 43, 46.

Jahoda, M. "Notes on Work." In R. Lowenstein and others (Eds.), *Psychoanalysis: A General Psychology.* New York: International Universities Press, 1966.

Janov, A. *The Primal Scream: Primal Therapy: The Cure for Neurosis.* New York: Putnam, 1970.

Johnson, E. H. "Prison Industry." In R. M. Carter, D. Glaser, and L. T. Wilkins (Eds.), *Correctional Institutions.* Philadelphia: Lippincott, 1972.

Johnson, F. M. "Court Decisions and the Social Services." *Social Work,* 1975, *20* (5), 343-347.

Joint Commission on Mental Illness and Health. *Action for Mental Health: Final Report of the Joint Commission.* New York: Basic Books, 1961.

Jones, M. *The Therapeutic Community.* New York: Basic Books, 1953.

Kerns, P., with Wead, D. *People's Temple, People's Tomb.* Plainfield, N.J.: Logos International, 1979.

Kirkbride, T. S. *On the Construction, Organization, and General Arrangements of Hospitals for the Insane.* Philadelphia: Lindsey and Blakiston, 1854. (2nd ed., London: Lippincott, 1880.)

Kleck, R. "Physical Stigma and Non-Verbal Cues Emitted in Face-to-Face Interaction." *Human Relations,* 1968, *21* (1), 19-28.

Kleemeier, R. W. (Ed.). *Aging and Leisure.* New York: Oxford University Press, 1961.

Kleinfeld, S. "Declaring Independence in Berkeley." *Psychology Today,* August 1979, pp. 67-78.

Knowles, E. S., and Baba, R. K. *The Social Impact of Group Homes: A Study of Residential Service Programs in Residen-*

tial Areas. Green Bay, Wisc.: Green Bay City Planning Commission, 1973.

Korczak, J. *Selected Works of Janusz Korczak.* Warsaw, Poland: Scientific Publications Foreign Cooperation Center of the Central Institute for Scientific, Technical, and Economic Information, 1967.

Krantz, S., and others. *Model Rules and Regulations on Prisoners' Rights and Responsibilities.* St. Paul, Minn.: West, 1977.

Krause, C. A., and others. *Guyana Massacre: The Eyewitness Account.* New York: Berkeley, 1978.

Kunkel, J. H. *Society and Economic Growth: A Behavioral Perspective of Social Change.* New York: Oxford University Press, 1970.

Lambert, R., with Millham, S. *The Hothouse Society.* London: Weidenfeld and Nicolson, 1968.

Lambert, R., Bullock, R., and Millham, S. *A Manual to the Sociology of the School.* London: Weidenfeld and Nicolson, 1970.

Lander, L. "The Mental Health Con Game." *Health/PAC Bulletin,* July/August 1975, *65,* 1-24.

Laszlo, E. *The Systems View of the World: The Natural Philosophy of the New Developments in the Sciences.* New York: Braziller, 1972.

Lauber, D., with Bangs, F. S., Jr. *Zoning for Family and Group Care Facilities.* Report No. 300. Chicago: American Society of Planning Officials, Planning Advisory Service, 1974.

Lawson, D. *Brothers and Sisters All Over This Land: America's First Communes.* New York: Praeger, 1972.

Lawton, M. P. "The Human Being and the Institutional Building." In J. Lang and others (Eds.), *Designing for Human Behavior: Architecture and the Behavioral Sciences.* Stroudsburg, Pa.: Dowden, Hutchinson & Ross, 1974.

Leiby, J. *A History of Social Welfare and Social Work in the United States.* New York: Columbia University Press, 1978.

Lennard, H. L., and Bernstein, A. *Patterns in Human Interaction: An Introduction to Clinical Sociology.* San Francisco: Jossey-Bass, 1969.

Leonard, C. T. "Debate on Placing-Out Children." In *Proceedings of the National Conference on Charities and Correction, 1881.* Boston: Williams, 1881.

Lewin, K. *Field Theory in Social Science.* New York: Harper & Row, 1951.

"Life at Synanon Is Swinging." *Time,* December 26, 1977, p. 18.

Lifton, B. J. *Twice Born: Memoirs of an Adopted Daughter.* New York: McGraw-Hill, 1975.

Lifton, B. J. *Lost and Found: The Adoption Experience.* New York: Dial Press, 1979.

Lindheim, R., Glaser, H. H., and Coffin, C. *Changing Hospital Environments for Children.* Cambridge, Mass.: Harvard University Press, 1972.

Lindsley, D. R. "Geriatric Behavioral Prosthetics." In R. Kastenbaum (Ed.), *New Thoughts in Old Age.* New York: Springer, 1964.

Linton, T. E. "The Educateur Model: A Theoretical Monograph." *Journal of Special Education,* 1971, *5* (2) (entire issue).

Lipman, A. "A Socio-Architectural View of Life in Three Homes for Old People." *Gerontologia Clinica,* 1968, *10,* 88-101.

London, P. *Behavioral Control.* New York: Harper & Row, 1969.

Lord, H. W. "Dependent and Delinquent Children, with Special Reference to Girls." In *Proceedings of the Fifth Annual Conference of Charities.* Boston: Williams, 1878.

Luft, H. S. "HMOs, Competition, Cost Containment, and NHI." Unpublished paper presented at the American Enterprise Institute conference on "National Health Insurance: What Now, What Later, What Never?" Washington, D.C., October 4-5, 1979.

McCleery, R. "Correctional Administration and Political Change." In L. E. Hazelrigg (Ed.), *Prison Within Society.* New York: Doubleday, 1969.

McCorkle, L. W., and Korn, R. "Resocialization Within Walls." *Annals of the American Academy of Political Science,* 1954, *293,* 88-98.

McCorkle, L. W., and others. *The Highfield Story.* New York: Holt, Rinehart and Winston, 1958.

Main, T. F. "The Hospital as a Therapeutic Institution." *Bulletin of the Menninger Clinic,* 1946, *10,* 66-70.

Makarenko, A. S. *Learning to Live.* Moscow: Foreign Languages Publishing House, 1953.

Makarenko, A. S. *The Road to Life: An Epic of Education.* (3 vols.) Moscow: Foreign Languages Publishing House, 1955.

Manard, B. B., Kart, C. S., and Van Gils, D. W. L. *Old-Age Institutions.* Lexington, Mass.: Heath, 1975.

Manocchio, A. J., and Dunn, J. *The Time Game: Two Views of a Prison.* Beverly Hills, Calif.: Sage, 1970.

March, J. G., and Simon, H. A. *Organizations.* New York: Wiley, 1958.

Markson, E. W. "Readjustment to Time in Old Age: A Life Cycle Approach." *Psychiatry,* 1973, *36* (1), 37-48.

Marshall, H. E. *Dorothea Dix—Forgotten Samaritan.* Chapel Hill: University of North Carolina Press, 1937.

Maruyama, M. "The Second Cybernetics: Deviation-Amplifying Mutual Causal Processes." *American Scientist,* 1963, *51,* 164-179.

Mayer, M. F., Richman, L. H., and Balcerzak, E. A. *Residential Group Care for Dependent, Neglected and Emotionally Disturbed Children in the United States and Canada.* New York: Child Welfare League of America, 1977.

Medvedev, Z., and Medvedev, R. A. *A Question of Madness.* New York: Knopf, 1971.

Merton, R. K. "Bureaucracy, Structure and Personality." *Journal of Social Forces,* 1940, *18,* 560-568.

Merton, R. K. *Social Theory and Social Structure.* (Rev. ed.) New York: Free Press, 1957.

Merton, T. *Elected Silence.* London: Hollis and Carter, 1949a.

Merton, T. *The Waters of Siloe.* New York: Harcourt Brace Jovanovich, 1949b.

Mill, J. S. *On Liberty.* Chicago: Regnery, 1955. (Originally published 1859.)

Miller, D. *Growth to Freedom: The Psychological Treatment of Delinquent Youth.* London: Tavistock, 1964.

"Minimal Wage: 'Sheltered' Workshops Restrict Pay of the Handicapped to as Little as 10 Cents an Hour." *Wall Street Journal,* October 17, 1979, pp. 1, 24.

Mitford, J. *Kind and Usual Punishment: The Prison Business.* New York: Knopf, 1973.

Moos, R. H. *Evaluating Treatment Environments: A Social Ecological Approach.* New York: Wiley, 1974.

Morris, P. *Put Away.* New York: Atherton Press, 1969.

Morris, T., and Morris, P. *Pentonville: A Sociological Study of an English Prison.* London: Routledge & Kegan Paul, 1963.

Mumford, L. *Faith for Living.* New York: Harcourt Brace Jovanovich, 1940.

Munk, M. "The Residential Yeshiva." In M. Wolins and M. Gottesmann (Eds.), *Group Care: An Israeli Approach.* New York: Gordon & Breach, 1971.

Murphy, L. B. *Growing Up in Garden Court.* New York: Child Welfare League of America, 1974.

Nagel, W. C. *The New Red Barn: A Critical Look at the Modern American Prison.* New York: Walker, 1973.

Neill, A. S. *Summerhill: A Radical Approach to Child Rearing.* New York: Hart, 1960.

Noble, J. H. "Limits of Cost-Benefit Analysis as a Guide to Priority-Setting in Rehabilitation." *Evaluation Quarterly,* 1977, *1,* 347-380.

North, F. A., Jr., Wilkinson, P., and Oliver, T. K. "Regional Planning of Hospital Facilities for Children." *American Journal of Diseases of Children,* 1977, *131,* 400-404.

Olsen, M. *The Process of Social Organization.* New York: Holt, Rinehart and Winston, 1968.

O'Neill, H. "*Wilder* v. *Sugarman*: The Crisis in Child Care." *New York Affairs,* 1974, *1* (4), 38-47.

Osmond, H. *Psychiatric Architecture.* Washington, D.C.: American Psychiatric Association, 1959.

Oursler, F., and Oursler, W. *Father Flanagan of Boys Town.* New York: Doubleday, 1949.

Owen, J. K. *Modern Concepts of Hospital Administration.* Philadelphia: Saunders, 1962.

Palazzoli, M. S., and others. *Paradox and Counterparadox.* (E. V. Burt, Trans.) New York: Aronson, 1978.

Pappenfort, D. M., and Kilpatrick, M. D. *A Census of Children's Residential Institutions in the United States, Puerto Rico, and the Virgin Islands: 1966.* Chicago: School of Social Service Administration, University of Chicago, 1970.

Parsons, T. *The Social System.* New York: Free Press, 1951.

Parsons, T. *The Structure of Social Action.* New York: Free Press, 1968.

Pastalan, L. A., and Carson, D. H. (Eds.). *Spatial Behavior of Older People.* Ann Arbor: Institute of Gerontology, University of Michigan-Wayne State University, 1970.

Patterson, G. R. *Families: Applications of Social Learning to Family Life.* Champaign, Ill.: Research Press, 1971.

Perrow, C. H. "The Short and Glorious History of Organizational Theory." In H. L. Tosi and W. C. Hamner (Eds.), *Organizational Behavior of Management: A Contingency Approach.* (Rev. ed.) Chicago: St. Clair, 1977.

Pestalozzi, J. H. *How Gertrude Teaches Her Children: An Attempt to Help Mothers to Teach Their Own Children and an Account of the Method.* (L. E. Holland and F. C. Turner, Trans.) Syracuse, N.Y.: Bardeen, 1915. (Originally published 1801.)

Piliavin, I. "Conflict Between Cottage Parents and Caseworkers." *Social Service Review,* 1963, *37,* 17-25.

Pill, R. "Space and Social Structure in Two Children's Wards." *Sociological Review,* 1967, *15,* 179-192.

Polsky, H. W. *Cottage Six: The Social System of Delinquent Boys in Residential Treatment.* New York: Russell Sage Foundation, 1962.

Polsky, H. W., and Claster, D. S., with Goldberg, C. *The Dynamics of Residential Treatment.* Chapel Hill: University of North Carolina Press, 1968.

Porter, L., and Lawler, E. "Properties of Organization Structure in Relation to Job Attitudes and Job Behavior." *Psychological Bulletin,* 1965, *64,* 23-51.

Porter Sargent. *The Handbook of Private Schools.* Boston: Porter Sargent, 1975, 1977.

President's Commission on Law Enforcement and Administration of Justice. "State Correctional Institutions for Adults." In R. M. Carter, D. Glaser, and L. T. Wilkins (Eds.), *Correctional Institutions.* Philadelphia: Lippincott, 1972.

President's Committee on Mental Retardation. *Residential Services for the Mentally Retarded: An Action Policy Proposal.* Washington, D.C.: U.S. Government Printing Office, 1970.

Prime Minister's Committee for Problem Children and Youth. *Report on the Internat Care System for Young People Who*

Reside Away from Their Families. Jerusalem: Prime Minister's Committee, 1972. (In Hebrew.)

"Prison Growth Continues Record Pace." *San Francisco Chronicle,* May 12, 1980, p. 9.

"Prisons." *Encyclopaedia Londinensis.* Vol. 21. London: J. Adlard, 1826.

Public Schools Commission. *First Report.* London: Her Majesty's Stationery Office, 1968.

Reding, G. R. Letter in *Psychiatric News,* May 1, 1974, p. 7.

Redl, F., and Wineman, D. *Children Who Hate.* New York: Free Press, 1951.

Reynolds, Q. *I, Willie Sutton.* New York: Farrar, Strauss & Giroux, 1953.

Reissman, F., and Miller, S. M. "Social Change Versus the Psychiatric World View." *American Journal of Orthopsychiatry,* 1964, *34* (1), 29-38.

Rivera, G. *Willowbrook: A Report on How It Is and Why It Doesn't Have to Be That Way.* New York: Random House, 1972.

Rose, A. M. (Ed.). *Human Behavior and Social Processes: An Interactionist Approach.* Boston: Houghton Mifflin, 1962.

Rosenblatt, D. "Physical Plant, Staff Morale and Informal Ideologies in Mental Hospitals." In L. A. Pastalan and D. H. Carson (Eds.), *Spatial Behavior of Older People.* Ann Arbor: Institute of Gerontology, University of Michigan–Wayne State University, 1970.

Rotenberg, M. *Damnation and Deviance: The Protestant Ethic and the Spirit of Failure.* New York: Free Press, 1978.

Rothman, D. J. *The Discovery of the Asylum: Social Order and Disorder in the New Republic.* Boston: Little, Brown, 1971.

Rothman, D. J. *Conscience and Convenience: The Asylum and Its Alternatives in Progressive America.* Boston: Little, Brown, 1980.

Rush, B. *Medical Inquiries and Observations upon the Diseases of the Mind.* New York: Hafner, 1962. (Originally published 1812.)

Sanders, R., Smith, R., and Weinman, B. *Chronic Psychoses and Recovery: An Experiment in Socio-Environmental Treatment.* San Francisco: Jossey-Bass, 1967.

Sandman, P. G. "The Juvenile's Right to Treatment." In *Proceedings of the Second Annual Management Seminar, National Association of State Juvenile Delinquency Program Administrators.* Denver: National Association of State Juvenile Delinquency Program Administrators, 1974.

Santiestevan, H. *Deinstitutionalization: Out of Their Beds and into the Streets.* Washington, D.C.: American Federation of State, County, and Municipal Employees, 1975.

Schaff, A. *Language and Cognition.* (O. Wojtasiewicz, Trans.) New York: McGraw-Hill, 1973.

Schein, E. H. *Organizational Psychology.* Englewood Cliffs, N.J.: Prentice-Hall, 1965.

Schrag, C. "Leadership Among Prison Inmates." *American Sociological Review,* 1954, *19,* 37-42.

Schrag, C. "Foundation for a Theory of Correction." In D. R. Cressey (Ed.), *The Prison: Studies in Institutional Organization and Change.* New York: Holt, Rinehart and Winston, 1961.

Schweitzer, A. *On the Edge of the Primeval Forest: Experiences and Observations of a Doctor in Equatorial Africa.* (C. T. Campion, Trans.) New York: Macmillan, 1931.

Scull, A. T. *Decarceration: Community Treatment of the Deviant—A Radical View.* Englewood Cliffs, N.J.: Prentice-Hall, 1977.

Secretaria Status Rationarium Generale Ecclesiae [Secretary of the State of the Accounts of the Church as a Whole]. *Statistical Yearbook of the Church, 1977.* N.p., n.d.

Segal, J. "Correlates of Collaboration and Resistance Behavior Among U.S. Army POW's in Korea." *Journal of Social Issues,* 1957, *8* (3), 31-40.

Segal, S. P., and Aviram, U. *The Mentally Ill in Community-Based Sheltered Care: A Study of Community Care and Social Interaction.* New York: Wiley, 1978.

Segal, S. P., and Moyles, E. W. "Management Style and Institutional Dependency in Sheltered Care." *Social Psychiatry,* 1979, *14,* 159-165.

Sellin, T. "Correction in Historical Perspective." In R. M. Carter, D. Glaser, and L. T. Wilkins (Eds.), *Correctional Institutions.* Philadelphia: Lippincott, 1972.

Shye, S. *A Systemic Facet-Theoretical Approach to the Study of Quality of Life.* Jerusalem: Israel Institute of Applied Social Research, 1979.

Shye, S., and Wozner, Y. *Organizational Quality: A Conceptual Framework and Empirical Study.* Jerusalem: Israel Institute of Applied Social Research, 1978. (Mimeograph.)

Siegel, M. H. "A Halfway House Fights Loneliness." *New York Times,* December 9, 1972, p. 39.

Simon, H. A. "Some Strategic Considerations in the Construction of Social Science Models." In P. F. Lazarsfeld (Ed.), *Mathematical Thinking in the Social Sciences.* New York: Free Press, 1954.

Skeels, H. M. "Adult Status of Children with Contrasting Early Life Experiences." *Monographs of the Society for Research in Child Development,* 1966, *31* (3), 1-65.

Snow, G. *The Public School in the New Age.* London: Geoffrey Bles, 1959.

Sokoloff, H. D. *Desert Developmental Center.* Las Vegas: Nevada State Division of Mental Hygiene and Mental Retardation, 1975.

Sokoloff, H. D. "Architectural Implications." In R. B. Kugel and A. Shearer (Eds.), *Changing Patterns in Residential Services for the Mentally Retarded.* (Rev. ed.) Washington, D.C.: President's Committee on Mental Retardation, 1976.

Solzhenitsyn, A. *One Day in the Life of Ivan Denisovich.* (M. Hayward and R. Hingley, Trans.) New York: Praeger, 1963.

Solzhenitsyn, A. *The Gulag Archipelago: 1918-1956.* (3 vols.) (T. P. Whitney, Trans., vols. 1 and 2; H. Willets, Trans., vol. 3) New York: Harper & Row, 1974-1978.

Sommer, R. *Personal Space: The Behavioral Basis of Design.* Englewood Cliffs, N.J.: Prentice-Hall, 1969.

Sommer, R. *Design Awareness.* San Francisco: Rinehart, 1972.

Sparrow, G. *The Great Forgers.* London: J. Long, 1963.

Spiro, M. E. *Kibbutz: Venture in Utopia.* Cambridge, Mass.: Harvard University Press, 1956.

Spitz, R. A. "Hospitalism: An Inquiry into the Genesis of Psychiatric Conditions in Early Childhood." *Psychoanalytic Study of the Child,* 1945, *1,* 53-74; 1946, *2,* 113-117.

Spitz, R. A., and Wolf, C. M. "Anaclitic Depression: An Inquiry into the Genesis of Psychotic Conditions in Early Childhood." *Psychoanalytic Study of the Child,* 1946, *2,* 313-341.

Spivack, M. "Archetypal Place." In T. O. Byerts (Ed.), *Housing and Environment for the Elderly: Proceedings from a Conference on Behavioral Research Utilization and Environmental Policy.* Washington, D.C.: Gerontological Society, 1973.

Stanton, A. H., and Schwartz, M. S. *The Mental Hospital.* New York: Basic Books, 1954.

Stotland, E., and Kobler, A. L. *Life and Death of a Mental Hospital.* Seattle: University of Washington Press, 1965.

Street, D., Vinter, R. D., and Perrow, C. H. *Organization for Treatment.* New York: Free Press, 1966.

Strumilin, S. G. "Rabochii Byt i Kommunism." ["Working Life and Communism."] *Novyi Mir (New World),* 1960, *36* (7), 203-220.

Stürup, G. K. *Treating the "Untreatable": Chronic Criminals at Herstedvester.* Baltimore: Johns Hopkins University Press, 1968.

Sykes, G. M. *The Society of Captives: A Study of Maximum Security Prisons.* Princeton, N.J.: Princeton University Press, 1958.

Sykes, G. M., and Messinger, S. L. "Inmate Social Systems." In R. A. Cloward and others (Eds.), *Theoretical Studies in the Social Organization of the Prison.* New York: Social Science Research Council, 1960.

Szasz, T. S. *The Manufacture of Madness.* New York: Harper & Row, 1970.

Szurek, S. A. "Dynamics of Staff Interaction in Hospital Psychiatric Treatment of Children." *American Journal of Orthopsychiatry,* 1947, *17,* 652-664.

Taylor, D. A., and Alpert, S. W. *Continuity and Support Following Residential Treatment.* New York: Child Welfare League of America, 1973.

Taylor, F. W. *On the Art of Cutting Metals.* New York: American Society of Mechanical Engineers, 1907.

Thomas, G. *Is Statewide Deinstitutionalization of Children's Services a Forward or Backward Social Movement?* Urbana: School of Social Work, University of Illinois, 1975.

Thomas, L. *The Lives of a Cell: Notes of a Biology Watcher.* New York: Viking Press, 1974.

Thomas, W. I. "The Configurations of Personality." In C. M. Child and others (Eds.), *The Unconscious: A Symposium.* New York: Knopf, 1928.

Thompson, J. D. *Organizations in Action.* New York: McGraw-Hill, 1967.

Thompson, J. D., and Goldin, G. *The Hospital: A Social and Architectural History.* New Haven, Conn.: Yale University Press, 1975.

Thoresen, C. E., and Mahoney, M. J. *Behavioral Self-Control.* New York: Holt, Rinehart and Winston, 1974.

Thornberry, T. P. "Race, Socioeconomic Status, and Sentencing in the Juvenile Justice System." *Journal of Criminal Law and Criminology,* 1973, *64* (1), 90-98.

Tillion, G. *Ravensbruck.* New York: Doubleday, 1975.

Tobin, S. S., and Lieberman, M. A. *Last Home for the Aged: Critical Implications of Institutionalization.* San Francisco: Jossey-Bass, 1976.

Tönnies, F. *Community and Society.* (C. P. Loomis, Trans.) East Lansing: Michigan State University Press, 1957.

Townsend, C. *Old Age: The Last Segregation.* New York: Grossman, 1971.

Trieschman, A. E., Whittaker, J., and Brendfro, L. K. *The Other 23 Hours: Child-Care with Emotionally Disturbed Children in a Therapeutic Milieu.* Chicago: Aldine, 1969.

Trigg, R. *Reason and Commitment.* Cambridge, England: Cambridge University Press, 1973.

Ullmann, L. P., and Krasner, L. *A Psychological Approach to Abnormal Behavior.* Englewood Cliffs, N.J.: Prentice-Hall, 1969.

U.S. Commission to Examine the Organization of Discipline and Course of Instruction of the United States Military Academy at West Point. Washington, D.C.: U.S. Goverment Printing Office, 1881.

U.S. Congress, Senate Committee on Veterans' Affairs. *Study of Health Care for American Veterans.* Washington, D.C.: U.S. Government Printing Office, 1977.

U.S. Congress, Subcommittee No. 2. of the Committee on Armed Services, House of Representatives. *Hearings on H.R. 9832: To Eliminate Discrimination Based on Sex with Re-*

spect to the Appointment and Admission of Persons to the Service Academies. Washington, D.C.: U.S. Government Printing Office, 1975.

U.S. Department of Commerce, Bureau of the Census. *Marital Status and Living Arrangements: March, 1974.* Current Population Reports, Series P-20, No. 271. Washington, D.C.: U.S. Government Printing Office, 1974.

U.S. Department of Commerce, Bureau of the Census. *Statistical Abstracts of the United States, 1977: 98th Annual Edition.* Washington, D.C.: U.S. Government Printing Office, 1977.

U.S. Department of Health, Education and Welfare, National Center for Health Statistics. *Utilization of Short-Stay Hospitals: Annual Summary for the United States, 1974.* DHEW Pub. No. (HRA) 76-1777. Rockville, Md.: National Center for Health Statistics, 1976.

U.S. Department of Health, Education and Welfare, National Institute of Mental Health. *Statistical Notes*: 104 (April 1974); 106 (May 1974); 107 (July 1974); 114, 115 (April 1975); 116 (June 1975); 126 (March 1976); 138 (August 1977). Various titles. Rockville, Md.: National Institute of Mental Health.

U.S. Department of the Interior, Bureau of Indian Affairs. *Statistics Concerning Indian Education, Fiscal Year 1975.* Lawrence, Kans.: Haskell Indian Junior College, 1976.

U.S. Department of Justice. *Prisoners in State and Federal Institutions on December 31, 1975.* Washington, D.C.: National Criminal Justice Information and Statistics Service, 1977.

U.S. Department of Justice, Law Enforcement Assistance Administration, National Criminal Justice Information and Statistics Service. *Children in Custody: A Report of the Juvenile Detention and Correctional Facility Census of 1971.* Washington, D.C.: U.S. Department of Justice, 1971.

U.S. Department of Justice, Law Enforcement Assistance Administration. *Sourcebook of Criminal Justice Statistics, 1976.* Washington, D.C.: U.S. Department of Justice, 1977.

U.S. Naval Academy, Annapolis. *Catalog of Course of Instruction.* Washington, D.C.: U.S. Government Printing Office, 1978-1979.

"Village's War with West Point." *San Francisco Sunday Examiner and Chronicle,* November 4, 1979, p. 7.

Vinter, R. D., with Newcomb, T. M., and Kish, R. (Eds.). *Time Out: A National Study of Juvenile Correctional Programs.* Ann Arbor: National Assessment of Juvenile Corrections, University of Michigan, 1976.

Vladeck, B. C. *Unloving Care: The Nursing Home Tragedy.* New York: Basic Books, 1980.

von Bertalanffy, L. *General Systems Theory: Foundations, Development, Applications.* New York: Braziller, 1968.

Watzlawick, P., Weakland, J. H., and Fisch, R. *Change: Principles of Problem Formation and Problem Resolution.* New York: Norton, 1974.

Weber, G. H. "Conflicts Between Professional and Nonprofessional Personnel in Institutional Delinquency Treatment." In L. E. Hazelrigg (Ed.), *Prison Within Society.* New York: Doubleday, 1969.

Weber, M. *The Theory of Social and Economic Organization.* (A. M. Henderson and T. Parsons, Trans.) New York: Oxford University Press, 1947. (Originally published 1925.)

"Weekend with the Moonies in Boonville." *San Francisco Chronicle,* December 11, 1975, pp. 10-11.

Weeks, A. L. "Boarding Schools in the USSR." In M. Wolins (Ed.), *Successful Group Care: Explorations in the Powerful Environment.* Chicago: Aldine, 1974.

Weinberg, I. *The English Public Schools: The Sociology of Elite Education.* New York: Atherton Press, 1967.

Weiss, J. D. *Better Buildings for the Aged.* New York: Hopkinson and Blake, 1969.

Wheeler, S. "Role Conflict in Correctional Communities." In D. R. Cressey (Ed.), *The Prison.* New York: Holt, Rinehart and Winston, 1961.

Wheeler, S. "The Structure of Formally Organized Socialization Settings." In O. G. Brim, Jr., and S. Wheeler, *Socialization After Childhood: Two Essays.* New York: Wiley, 1966.

Wheeler, S. "Socialization in Correctional Institutions." In D. A. Goslin (Ed.), *Handbook of Socialization Theory and Research.* Chicago: Rand McNally, 1969.

Wicker, T. *A Time to Die.* New York: Quadrangle Books, 1975.

Wilson, M. *Good Company: A Study of Nyakusa Age-Villages.* Boston: Beacon Press, 1951.

Witkin, H. A., and others. *Psychological Differentiation.* New York: Wiley, 1962.

Wolins, M. "Cost of Care in a Children's Institution." In *Cost Analysis in Child Welfare Services.* Washington, D.C.: U.S. Government Printing Office, 1958.

Wolins, M. "Developmental Research and Public Policy: A Commentary." In J. M. Romanyshyn (Ed.), *Social Science and Social Welfare.* New York: Council on Social Work Education, 1974a.

Wolins, M. (Ed.). *Successful Group Care: Explorations in the Powerful Environment.* Chicago: Aldine, 1974b.

Wolins, M. "One Kibbutz as Foster Mother: Maimonides Applied." In M. Wolins (Ed.), *Successful Group Care: Explorations in the Powerful Environment.* Chicago: Aldine, 1974c.

Wolins, M. "Political Orientation, Social Reality, and Child Welfare." In M. Wolins (Ed.), *Successful Group Care: Explorations in the Powerful Environment.* Chicago: Aldine, 1974d.

Wolins, M. "Observations on the Future of Institutional Care of Children in the United States." In *Child Welfare Strategy in the Coming Years.* Washington, D.C.: U.S. Department of Health, Education and Welfare, Office of Human Development Services, 1978.

Wolins, M. "Work and the Internat." *Residential and Community Child Care Administration,* 1979, *1* (1), 21-40.

Wolins, M., and Piliavin, I. *Institution or Foster Family: A Century of Debate.* New York: Child Welfare League of America, 1964.

Wolpe, J. *Psychotherapy by Reciprocal Inhibition.* Stanford, Calif.: Stanford University Press, 1958.

Wooden, K. *Weeping in the Playtime of Others: America's Incarcerated Children.* New York: McGraw-Hill, 1976.

Wozner, Y. "Diary of a Madrich." Unpublished paper, 1955.

Wozner, Y. "Meoni: An Experiment in the Rehabilitation of Youth." *Saad 2,* March 1965, pp. 18-25. (In Hebrew.)

Wozner, Y., and Lev, I. "Token Economy in an Institution for

Disturbed Youth." *Delinquency and Social Deviation,* 1975, *5,* 19-30. (In Hebrew.)

Yablonsky, L. *The Tunnel Back: Synanon.* New York: Macmillan, 1965.

Zald, M. N. "Power Balance and Staff Conflict in Correctional Institutions." *Administrative Science Quarterly,* 1962, *7,* 22-49.

Zborowski, M., and Herzog, E. *Life Is with People: The Culture of the Shtetl.* New York: Schocken Books, 1962.

Zubek, J. P. (Ed.). *Sensory Deprivation: Fifteen Years of Research.* New York: Appleton-Century-Crofts, 1969.

Name Index

Subject Index

professionals and goal divergence in, 51-52; role structures in, 143, 145-147; as teaching institutions, 42-43; as total institutions, 28

Identity, self- and institutional, 159-165
Ideological internats, authority in, 196, 233. *See also* Hospitals; Leadership; Religious internats
Ideology: and Activity patterns, 34; and decision making, 243-244; and goal convergence, 46-47; and organizational integration, 152-156; as unifying force, 194-198, 256-257; 271. *See also* Values
Indian boarding schools, 6, 8, 21, 113
Infants, in internats, 7, 11
Initiation rites, 123-124, 127-128, 160-161, 263
Inmate culture, 120, 123, 129-130, 147
Inmates: decision making by, 234-236, 251-252; environmental needs of, 134-136; identity of, 160-165; integration and segregation of, 137-141; long term, 191-192; passivity or revolt choices of, 148; personal space needs of, 136, 184-185; qualitative and quantitative Mastery of, 243; rights of, 109-112, 268-269; role conflicts of, 141, 145-148. *See also* Populations
Inspirational decisions, 69-72
Institutional neuroses, 104, 110
Internats: abolitionist demands for, 62-65, 73-74 (*see also* Deinstitutionalization); benefit dimensions in, 67-69; change patterns in, 95; commonalities among, 1-2; competitors of, 89-92; criticisms of, 3, 224-227; defined, 25-28; deterrent functions of, 66, 99; as differential totalities, 230-234; discrimination patterns of, 13-15, 99-100; informal structures of, 220; instrumental recommendations for, 260-271; in-

ternal time sense in, 169-171 (*see also* Time concepts); intra- and intersystemic attributes of, 208-218; location of, 182-184 (*see also* Community; Isolation); long-term residence in, 191-192; permeability of, 100-101; prestige and goals of, 40-41 (*see also* Elite institutions; Goals); primary and secondary customers of, 77-84; problems attending release from, 81-84; regulators of, 92-96; resources of, 30-31 (*see also* Resources; Work); as social disposal mechanisms, 63-64; social standing of, 37-38; standard specifying for, 95-96; systems models of, 200-222; theoretical model of, 36-38; as totality, 25-30, 227-230; as vessels or instruments, 237-239. *See also* Inmates; Populations
Isolation: adaptation problems of, 78-84; and community goals, 45, 182-184, 203; in differentiated and undifferentiated systems, 208-211; in internat settings, 33-34, 137-141; and power issues, 65-66; and Reclaiming goals, 42; and social values, 115-116; and time sense, 167-168. *See also* Time concepts
Israel: internat populations in, 12; kibbutz systems in, 35, 114, 207, 214; Youth village facilities in, 58

Janizaries, Turkish, 113, 188
Johns Hopkins Institute, 177
Joint Commission on Accreditation of Hospitals, 61, 93
Jonestown, 65, 208, 228
Judgmental decisions, 69-72
Juvenile homes: location of, 183-184; staff needs for, 86

Kibbutz, 35, 114; goal directed behaviors in, 207, 214

Labor camps, 206
Leadership: charismatic, 32, 163-164, 217, 226, 239-241; in ideo-

AP